That men do not learn very much from the lessons of history is the most important of all the lessons of history.

— Aldous Huxley

PRAISE FOR *THE PRINCE AND THE ASSASSIN*

It illuminates a fascinating but forgotten milepost in Australian history.
— Professor Geoffrey Blainey, AC

A compelling account of one of the most controversial political crimes in Australian history, it shows how religious zealotry, bigotry and political over-reaction can bring a community to the brink of disorder.

It reveals disturbingly that when the criminal law is rushed and under political pressures, it can go awry.

Mr Harris is not only a sound researcher, but a very readable narrator.

His story brings lessons from the nineteenth century of Queen Victoria to the twenty-first century of Al Quaeda.

All contemporary politicians and community leaders dealing with the continuing fallout from 9/11 should read it.
— Professor Greg Woods QC, legal historian.

Marvellous...A truly gripping tale, wonderfully researched.
— Jane Ridley, Author, Broadcaster and Professor of Modern History, University of Buckingham, United Kingdom

A gripping tale of royal debauchery, abandoned priesthood, mental infirmity and Irish rebellion, leading to the attempted assassination of Queen Victoria's favourite son...This book has the excitement of a racy political crime thriller, backed by the most sound historical research. It gives the impression of an account written by an eyewitness. There are lessons for us today from the politicians' overreaction to what was mistakenly viewed as an existential threat to Australian society.
— Mark Tedeschi, AM, QC Senior Crown Prosecutor, NSW

...One and half centuries later, in an era of fresh anxiety about terrorism, Australia is again facing a test of character. This time it is Muslim Australians who bear the brunt of prejudice, suspicion and guilt by association. Harris's book, a fascinating read at multiple levels, helps frame current anxieties in a deeper context.
— Professor Greg Barton, Research Professor in Global Islamic Politics, Alfred Deakin Institute (ADI), Co-Editor, *Islam Christian Muslim Relations*, Senior Fellow, Hedayah, Abu Dhabi

PRAISE FOR *SOLOMON'S NOOSE*

Impressive research and a story that challenges the imagination — except that it's true.
— Les Carlyon, award-winning author of *Gallipoli* and *The Great War*

The haunting story of the convict who became the British Empire's youngest executioner. Beware the shock of the true.
— Andrew Rule, award-winning author/journalist.

Intriguing story…captivating tale…a fascinating read.
— *The Australian.*

A vivid picture.
— *Sydney Morning Herald.*

Quite gripping.
— *The Age.*

A ripping yarn.
— *The Sunday Age.*

Fascinating. A remarkable footnote to the penal era (which) reveals many tantalising facts, each one a potential starting point for another book.
— *Herald Sun.*

Research is superb.
— *The Examiner.*

An illuminating look at the difficult birth of a nation through its darkest period.
— *SmithJournal.*

A chillingly real account…a vivid picture of Van Diemen's Land in Australia's formative years.
— *New Idea.*

Absorbing….a fascinating story…of what convict life was like and its implications across a broader society striving to take advantage of the opportunities of this fledgling country.
— *Limelight Reviews.*

The reader (will be) indisputably captivated…a moving and often poignant description of crime, life and death in colonial Tasmania.
— Tasmanian Historical Research Association.

Published by Melbourne Books
Level 9, 100 Collins Street,
Melbourne, VIC 3000
Australia
www.melbournebooks.com.au
info@melbournebooks.com.au

National Library of Australia
Cataloguing-in-Publication entry (pbk)
Title: The Prince and The Assassin: Australia's First Royal Tour and Portent of World Terror
Author: Steve Harris
ISBN: 9781925556131 (paperback)
Subjects: Saxe-Coburg and Gotha, Alfred, Duke of, 1844-1900--Assassination attempt, 1868.
Royal visitors--New South Wales--Sydney.
Attempted assassination--New South Wales--Sydney.
Judicial error--New South Wales--Sydney.
Offenses against heads of state--New South Wales--Sydney.
New South Wales--Politics and government--1851-1891.
Cover Design: Sean Hogan--Trampoline

Also by Steve Harris *Solomon's Noose: The True Story of Her Majesty's Hangman of Hobart*

Printed in Singapore

THE PRINCE AND THE ASSASSIN

Australia's First Royal Tour and Portent of World Terror

STEVE HARRIS

M

MELBOURNE BOOKS

CONTENTS

INTRODUCTION

The two guns sat comfortably in the palm of each hand. Alfred Albert's eyes took in every small detail of their blue nickel finishes, triggers and barrels. He instinctively felt the weight of the Colt 'navy' pistol and the Smith and Wesson 'old army' revolver, perhaps surprised by their relative lightness.

Through his service in the British Navy he was not unfamiliar with weaponry, but this was personal. He was a central figure in the story they represented, one with threads running through the reach and rule of the British Empire, the reign and influence of Queen Victoria, the future of Empire and Royalty in the face of republican pressures in places like Ireland and Australia, and man's eternal conflicts over matters of national security, law, religion and politics.

As he fingered the old American Civil War weapons, Alfred

might have appreciated they, like him, had come together at Sydney Harbour from the other side of the world, each in the name of security, but then come to be front and centre of the biggest crime in Australia's young history and a 'reign of terror' in the world's most remote land.

The guns were two of the thousands, favoured by Colonel Samuel Colt, Indian fighter General George Custer and frontiersman James Butler ('Wild Bill') Hickok, which had been abandoned after the Civil War, and imported into the frontier of an emerging Australia for use by gold-diggers, farmers and constables.

Two of them, sold as 'righteous' rather than cheap copies, were procured by a young man who had crossed the world as an immigrant with a family pursuing religious and political freedom, and been knocking on the door of becoming an ordained priest. Henry O'Farrell had a crucifix in his pocket, but procured the guns because he had another calling in his mind, an Englishman called Alfred.

It was almost 100 years since another English naval officer, Captain James Cook first planted a flag in the sandy shoreline of *Terra Nullius* to claim the newest and most distant addition to the British Empire. Queen Victoria had despatched her favourite son, Prince Alfred Ernest Albert, to undertake a Royal journey unequalled, before or since, in distance and duration, with a threefold agenda: to reinforce the Britishness and loyalty of those who had been transported, freely as migrants or compulsorily as convicts; to shore up a devotion to the Crown and Empire in the face of any republican ambitions; and to try to ensure Alfred remained trouble-free and thus a bona fide spare and acceptable heir should his elder brother Edward continue to demonstrate an unsuitability to be King.

Alfred was barely interested in the political machinations of Windsor Castle and the Admiralty, barely tolerant of the pomp and protocols of being a Royal, and hardly fussed about matters of State and Empire. His appetite was for the joy of hunting and gambling during the day, and the carousing pleasures of the night, away from the repressive eye of his mother.

And as far away as anyone could be from his mother's eye, Alfred cared little for whatever anyone in London thought of the political success of his historic Royal tour, or what the colonial administrators and citizenry of Australia thought of his behaviour.

But now, the visit over, standing in his wood-panelled cabin on *HMS Galatea* inspecting the Civil War guns, Prince Alfred knew that the story behind the guns would be the talk of the Empire, ensure his voyage was seen as one of triumph, and he would be able to dine out on the tale for many a soirée.

A minute of madness at Clontarf on Sydney Harbour had instantly transformed Australia from unprecedented joy to unprecedented anger and moral panic, rocked to its foundations by the shame of the most serious assassination attempt on a member of the Royal family.

The shooting ignited the first experience of the fear of international political terror, of being at the front-line of a new global criminal conspiracy to overthrow colonial rule. It unleashed treason against security, justice against vengeance, self-interest against public interest, martyrdom against madness, religion against law, colonial masters against local administrators, truth against deceit.

This is the story of Alfred Albert and Henry O'Farrell, and how their worlds and lives collided in that moment of madness, and the story of the reverberating passions and forces which followed, some of which are still being felt.

1
ALFRED, THE WOULD-BE KING

Alfred is really such a dear, gifted and handsome child that it makes one doubly anxious that he should have as few failings as mortal man can have.
— Queen Victoria

As a young boy, Alfred Ernest Albert had no real sense his life was different from every other boy in the British Empire.

His 'mama' was Queen Victoria, head of nation, Empire and Church. His 'papa' was Albert Francis Charles Augustus Emmanuel of Saxe-Coburg-Gotha, her first cousin. After an arranged introduction, Victoria quickly abandoned her reluctance to entertain the 'odious' idea of marriage so early in her reign. The stoutish and diminutive Victoria, not even 5 feet tall, was instantly besotted by the handsome Bavarian, 'excessively handsome…such a pretty mouth…a beautiful figure…quite a pleasure to look at Albert'.[1]

She sent for Albert four days later to tell him she would be 'too happy' if he consent to her wish that they marry. Ignoring the advice of her Prime Minister and mentor, Lord Melbourne, that 'cousins are not a very good thing', the 20-year-olds married four months later. Victoria bluntly forewarned Albert she was too busy as Sovereign to agree to his proposed two-week honeymoon, but she might have regretted this after their first night together. She wrote she had:

> never never spent such an evening…his excessive love and affection gave me feelings of heavenly love and happiness I never could have hoped to have felt before. He clasped me in his arms, and we kissed each other again and again! His beauty, his sweetness and gentleness, – really how can I ever be thankful enough to have such a Husband! Oh! This was the happiest day of my life!…I feel a purer more unearthly feel than I ever did. Oh! was ever woman so blessed as I am![2]

Such love and feeling was not reflected on the outcome of their sexual pleasure, despite having no shortage of opportunity. Victoria had her first seven children in 10 years but she and Albert were decidedly Queen and His Royal Highness first and foremost, Mama and Papa second. Affairs of Empire trumped anything emerging in the nursery, as Alfred would learn.

Parental warmth was not a compensation to life inside the ancient fortress walls of Windsor Castle, overlooking the Thames River. The resolute nature of the castle stone was reflected in a household run on strict teutonic lines, as decreed by Albert, with high expectations and ready punishment such as a whipping or solitary confinement for shortcomings.

There had been jubilation across the Empire when in November 1841 Victoria gave birth to the first male heir in 80 years. But Edward's destiny quickly became one of parental doubt. Victoria was not enamoured with babies, who if ugly were 'a very nasty object, and (even) the prettiest is frightful when undressed' and she abhorred their 'terrible frog-like action'[3] and described them as 'mere little plants.'[4]

And in Victoria's mind her first-born son, was indeed ugly. 'Too frightful', she declared and for at least 18 months she took the view he was unworthy of even being called Edward, calling him 'the boy' while others came to know him as Bertie. More seriously than his looks, Victoria and Albert saw him as perhaps mentally retarded. They commissioned a phrenology assessment which described the boy's brain as 'feeble and abnormal', underscoring parental judgments about 'our poor strange boy', 'a stupid boy',[5] and 'totally unfit for becoming a King'.[6]

Intellectually he suffered by comparison with their first-born daughter, Vicky, known as Pussy. She was their exemplar, precocious and intelligent, able to read and write before turning five, with governesses and instructors at Buckingham Palace imparting French, German, Latin, literature, and history, and Albert politics and philosophy. Seven-year-old Edward struggled to endure and absorb six hours of solid instruction every day, especially in German, the household language of Albert's Duchy of Saxe-Coburg and Gotha (Later reborn as Windsor at the behest of King George V after German Gotha bombers struck England in 1917, killing more than 800 and causing anti-German riots).

Alfred Ernest Albert created a better first impression than his 'ugly' brother on his birth at Windsor Castle on the morning of 6 August 1844. The Queen thought he most resembled her beloved and handsome Albert, and that could only mean good things, while Albert described him as 'unusually big and strong.'[7]

The parental denunciation of Edward as a disappointing and possibly retarded heir was reinforced by his understandable diffidence to royal expectations and strictures, creating a cycle of negativity. Edward was convinced he would not sit on the throne—

while 'Mama is now the Queen...Vicky will have her Crown and you see Vicky will be Victoria the second'[8]—and so began a life-long pursuit of personal escapism and pleasure.

Victoria and Albert could see the seeds of debauchery more than duty, a particular anathema. Victoria and Albert were each familiar with family members who were not moral exemplars. They abhorred such behaviour, both personally and because they took it as their mission to inspire a higher morality for all Englishmen in the hope it would arrest any decline which risked a French-like revolution.

Victoria and Albert endeavoured to keep Edward on a righteous path as best they could, while also working to keep Alfred as isolated as possible from Edward's influence, and ensure the spare and preferred heir was well placed should Edward never make the throne, or perhaps in the future could not produce his own male heir. While Albert promised Alfred, or Affie as he was known, would be taught 'to love the dear small country to which he belongs',[9] the Queen had to stave off efforts to make him a King in Germany when he was just five-years-old. He had to be raised as a possible King of England.

But the boys were not rivals. They initially shared a bedroom—'I think that Affie likes being with me, and I like having him too, because it as a much better match for me than older persons',[10] Edward said, and each endured the same arduous education six days a week, chafed under the royal regime, and yearned for more fun. Occasionally boys were brought in from Eton College for them to play with, but Alfred and Edward shared a special bond as they each paid the dues of destiny, and tried to look out for each other to avoid punishment. Albert occasionally meted out a whipping and when 11-year-old Alfred was caught smoking he was separated from Edward and ordered to endure three days solitary confinement at Royal Lodge, south of the castle in Windsor Park. He did occasionally play with the boys but Victoria, herself brought up in an exclusively adult environment, was not a frequent visitor to the nursery, and the young princes were known to careen down palace corridors screaming out 'The Queen! The Queen!' if they sensed her approach.

Albert chastised Victoria over the lack of joy she gained from her children. 'The trouble lies in the mistaken notion the function of a mother is to be always correcting, scolding and ordering them about', he wrote. Edward later said that for he and Alfred 'there was no boyhood'. They both evidenced irritability. Edward complained 'other children are not always good…why should I always be good?…nobody is always good'[11] and when Alfred did not want to do something he petulantly declared, 'boys never!'[12]

Their upbringing was regimented and repressive. Alfred's formal education began alongside Edward with Henry Birch, a young Eton graduate who focused on English, geography and mathematics, while others came in to teach religion, writing, French, German, drawing and music. But after Edward's negative phrenology assessment Albert lost faith in Birch and replaced him with Frederick Gibbs, a dour barrister and fellow of Trinity College. He was told by Albert's long-time friend and advisor from Coburg, Baron Christian Frederick Stockmar: 'If you cannot make anything of the eldest, you must try with the younger one.'[13]

Beyond the heavy education agenda, for eight-year-old Alfred there was aristocratic instruction on 'manners of conduct towards others in appearance, deportment and dress' and 'acquitting oneself credibly in conversation, on whatever maybe the occupation of Society', and riding, military drill and gymnastics. His day was royally filled from 8am to 7pm six days a week.

Alfred's escape was to spend as much time as he could playing with toy ships in imaginary naval voyages and battles. His imagination matured into a desire to be free to steer his own life course, not one strictly directed by his parents. He could sense his brother struggling with the parental judgment of being unworthy of a mandated role he did not savour but had to spend his life in waiting. They could be forgiven for a shared feeling they were on an unwinnable quest. The Queen bluntly told her children: 'None of you can ever be proud enough of being the child of such a Father who has not his equal in this world—so great, so good, so faultless.'[14]

Alfred pleaded with his father. 'Please papa', let me join the Navy, he repeatedly asked. Albert was disappointed he had failed to persuade his son to follow his own interests to become an engineer, but warmed to the boy's persistent pleas to join the Blue Jackets. He was also concerned that Alfred's teenage years would come under the corrupting influence of his brother.

Albert allowed him to be coached in mathematics and geometry by a retired Naval chaplain, William Jolley, and seamanship on a training ship at Portsmouth, under Captain Robert Harris.

Albert came to think it a good idea for his son to gain life experience and competencies away from the influence of his 'idle' brother, and he rationalised it as something parents could not prevent.

> As regards his wish to enter the Navy, this is a passion which we, as his parents, believe not to have a right to subdue…it is certainly not right to break the spontaneous wish of a young spirit…we gave him an engineering officer as instructor, hoping to interest him in this branch, but his love for the Blue Jackets always turned up again, and always with greater force…with the remarkable perseverance which this child possesses, it is not to be expected that he will give up the idea easily.[15]

Queen Victoria was not amused. She felt Affie was 'a good, dear promising child', and daughter Victoria had just left to marry Prince Frederick William of Prussia (to whom she had become engaged three years before when she was only 14 and he was 24). It was 'too wretched… horrible!' for her two favourite children to leave 'tame, dull, formal England' and what even she called 'the prison life of Windsor.'[16]

She felt 'papa is most cruel' but Albert was convinced the distance and discipline afforded by the Navy, and some modest exposure to Royal life in European ports, would stand Alfred in good stead, whether he would only ever inherit his German Duchy of Saxe-Coburg and Gotha, or circumstances meant he had to take the English throne. Alfred would 'become more generally competent' and be more ready to be a King than by staying at home under his brother's influence, or moving to Bavaria and becoming more 'German' which would make any English prospects more problematic.

The Queen acknowledged the 'sad contrast'[17] between the heir and spare heir, and reluctantly agreed. It was necessary because 'he is really such a dear, gifted and handsome child that it makes one doubly anxious that he should have as few failings as mortal man can have.'[18]

Her hope for Alfred was in proportion to the trepidation she felt about Edward succeeding her. When he turned 17 Victoria wrote:

> I tremble at the thought of only three years and a half before…he will be of age and we can't hold him except by moral power! I try to shut my eyes at that terrible moment!… oh! dear, what would happen if I were to die next winter. It is too awful a contemplation.[19]

A year later she and Albert sent him a stern 18th birthday message full of exhortations about moral duties and how only through punctual and cheerful performance of those duties 'the true Christian and the true Gentleman is recognised'.[20] Edward burst into tears.

While Edward would be denied any escape into military service, Alfred's wish was granted just two weeks after his 14th birthday. After passing entrance exams at the Britannia Royal Naval College in Dartmouth he could enter Her Majesty's service in August 1858 as a naval cadet on *HMS Euralyu*s.

Alfred was excited, but leaving all that was familiar was still a big step and he sobbed when farewelling his parents.

Two years later, in a novel but strategic move, Victoria sent both the teenage princes abroad as part of their Royal training and separation. Alfred was sent to South Africa, where he laid the foundation stone of the breakwater at Table Bay, opened a library and enjoyed a hunting party which shot between 600 and 1000 animals. Edward went to Ireland, Canada and the United States—a land still seen as one full of revolutionary republicans and democrats—where he was seen to have acquitted himself well, although it was felt he looked with too much pleasure on the 'vast array of beauties lined up for him' at a dance in Cincinnati, and the *New York Herald* reported he 'whispered sweet nothings' to his dance partners.[21]

The following year saw a more negative episode, a life-changing affair which would come to shape the whole family forever.

Edward, who had been attending Cambridge University, was despatched to a 10-week military training camp at Curragh, 30 miles from Dublin in County Kildare, accompanied by his governor, Robert Bruce, whose task was to fulfil Albert's wish that his son become 'a good man and a thorough gentleman'.

The Queen wasn't confident. Her instincts told her Edward was more his mother's son when it came to sexual appetite, and not his father's son when it came to strict propriety. She told her uncle, Prince Leopold Franz Julius of Saxe-Coburg and Gotha: 'Alas! Sons are like their mothers—at least the eldest are supposed to be...and so I think Bertie has avoided all likeness to his beloved father.' That was to become all too clear at Curragh. Edward had dutifully promised to 'do my best now to make the best use of the short time I now have before me for acquiring knowledge and instruction'. But he hadn't said anything about acquiring carnal knowledge and instruction.

Notwithstanding Governor Bruce's supervision, two Grenadier Guards ventured to the outskirts of the 12,000-strong military camp, where some 50 or 60 women, known as 'wrens', lived in nest-like abodes of mashed bog earth and gorse branches as victims of the Great Famine, engaging in prostitution or pursuing matrimony.

The red-tunic Grenadiers recruited and briefed Nellie Clifden, a vivacious and promiscuous 17-year-old known for sharing her affections around London's hot spots of the day such as Cremorne Gardens and Mott's Dancing Rooms. In a bedroom in the officer's quarters she faced a young soldier, 20-years-old, tall, bearded and a little unsteady on his feet. Nellie unbuttoned his uniform, which featured the Royal cypher and Grenadier motto, *Honi soit qui mal y pense* (Evil be to him who evil thinks) embossed on each button.

Edward didn't think Nellie was in any way evil. He happily and proudly wrote in his engagement diary of 6 September 'Curragh, NC, 1st time'. Three nights later he summoned Nellie back for a follow-up appointment, 'Curragh, NC, 2nd time' and again the next night 'Curragh, NC, 3rd time'.[22]

Word of the triple treat spread from the soldiers, delighted with their stewardship of the future King, to the gentlemen's clubs of Ireland and then England, and gossips like Lord Torrington. Edward and Alfred were likely to have shared and relished the intimate details of the first 'Princess of Wales', although Alfred later thought one of their friends was out of line in naming a racing mare 'Miss Clifden'.

But it was no relish for their Royal parents. Prince Albert was seriously ill, but when his most trusted friend, Baron Stockmar, heard the gossip he felt compelled to tell him his son had been initiated in what he called 'the sacred mysteries of creation'.[23] Albert was mortified. He had an intense revulsion of all things sexually improper. His libidinous father Duke of Saxe-Coburg had an embarrassing affair with a courtesan, his mother Luise was flirtatious, prompting rumours of Albert's legitimacy, and his brother had a scandalous affair with a servant girl in Dresden. When Albert was only a boy of seven, his father divorced his mother on a charge of adultery, banishing her to Switzerland with a pension and a ban on ever seeing her children again. Victoria, whose own father had only married her mother after dismissing Thérèse-Bernadine

Mongenet, known as Madame de Saint-Laurent, his faithful mistress of 28 years, also feared one or both the Princes would turn out like the 'mad' George III or the 'wicked' Carlton House set of George IV and his fascination with erotica, or William IV with 10 illegitimate children.

Royals were known to exercise what they saw as an aristocratic prerogative for pleasure, but Victoria and Albert kept their sexual pleasures and shared love of nude paintings to themselves. Alfred and Edward were on their moral frontline, and now their heir to the throne might have undone all their good work and put his own future at risk: what if the girl had given him a disease, or became pregnant and filed a paternity suit, or ruined their chances of securing him the matrimonial advantages of a wealthy European aristocratic family?

Albert wrote to Edward that his behaviour caused 'the deepest pain I have yet felt in this life'.[24] He knew he was 'thoughtless and weak...but I could not think you depraved!' The sacred mysteries of creation, he said, 'ought to remain shrouded in holy awe until touched by pure and undefiled hands', and as a young man responding to 'sexual passions' he could not understand 'why did you not open yourself to your father', who would have reminded him of the 'special mode in which these desires are to be gratified... by...the holy ties of Matrimony'.[25]

'If you were to try and deny it', Albert added despairingly, 'she can drag you into a Court of Law to force you to own it and there with you (the Prince of Wales) in the witness box, she will be able to give before a greedy Multitude disgusting details of your profligacy for the sake of convincing the Jury; yourself cross-examined by a railing indecent attorney and hooted and yelled at by a Lawless Mob!! Oh, horrible prospect, which this person has in her power, any day to realise! And to break your poor parents heart.'[26]

'You must not, you dare not be lost', he said.[27] The pressure was on to secure a suitable marriage before the Prince was 'lost'. He was despatched to Germany, officially to observe Prussian manoeuvres, but in reality to meet the woman who his parents, with the help of daughter Vicky, secretly determined should be his future wife.

Their desire was another dynastic link with Germany and more 'strong blood' as the Queen called it, but they had to be sensitive to what England would accept. After reviewing seven young princesses it was arranged for Edward to meet 16-year-old Princess Alexandra of Denmark.

Albert was impressed enough to say frankly that 'from that photograph I would marry her at once.'[28] And he and Victoria also could not help but notice Alfred's keen interest in 'Alix'. On the strength of photos alone, Alfred made no secret of his wish to marry her himself if Edward remained hesitant. If Edward became 'obstinate', Victoria said, 'I will withdraw myself altogether and wash my hands of him, for I cannot educate him, and the country must make him feel what they think…Affie would be ready to take her at once, and really if B. refused I would recommend Affie's engaging to marry her in three years.'[29]

While Alfred wondered who might win Alix he returned to single life on the sea, occasionally visiting his sister Victoria who was told by the Queen that his behaviour was 'much improved but he must be looked after and is never allowed to go about alone'.[30]

Prince Albert, meanwhile, wasn't done with Edward's Curragh affair. Despite feeling ill with crippling insomnia and neuralgia—'*Bin recht elend* (I feel miserable)' he complained in his diary—he met his son in a tense encounter in pouring rain at Cambridge University. Albert forgave his son but warned that forgiveness could not restore the state of innocence and purity which he had lost forever.

Three weeks later Albert was on his death bed. His demise in December 1861 was put down to typhoid fever, although later it was thought more likely to be stomach cancer. But for the grief-stricken Queen Victoria, there was no doubt: her beloved husband had died at the age of 42 from the shock of his son's degrading nights with an Irish harlot. 'What killed him was that dreadful business at the

Curragh…Oh! that boy…I never can or shall look at him without a shudder', she wrote of Edward.[31] And she meant it, making her contempt known for the next 40 years.

Alfred, at sea off Mexico, was the last child to hear the relayed news of his father's death. Heart-broken at being the only child not at the funeral, it became his custom for the rest of his life to spend the anniversary of his papa's death alone in private remembrance.

His brother, blamed and shunned by the Queen, was now even more determined to pursue matters of pleasure, and enjoined Alfred in that pursuit between his Naval excursions. Even while waiting to be engaged and finally married to Princess Alix in 1863, Edward embraced the freedom and privacy of his Marlborough House in The Mall. The princely pair were the stars in the 'fast set' of Marlborough, enjoying numerous house parties, dinners, balls, races and theatre. And the company of women, be they wives of their friends or ladies of the theatre in London and Paris, in the company of rich and fast friends like Charles Wynn-Carrington—who later had his own affair with Nellie Clifden and went on to become a future Governor of New South Wales. And in sojourns across the Channel they conquered Paris one bottle, one boulevard, one brothel at a time.

The Queen detested such hedonistic behaviour, fretting over a French-style revolution if the upper classes did not cease to be 'frivolous, pleasure seeking and immoral'[32] but it did not slow the princes down. Victoria feared that under Edward's influence Alfred would continue to 'fall into sin from weakness'[33] and was relieved he was at sea more than at Marlborough.

But Alfred was enjoying the life of a sailor prince. He joked to his aunt Princess Alexandrine in Saxe-Coburg 'I have now got the two letters RN fixed to the end of my name…as the old maids say that it is alright because I have come back to the Royal Nursery'[34] but he firmly told others that RN definitely did not stand for Royal Nursery.

He endured some early criticism, unusual for the times. After he had progressed to midshipman on the *St George*, he was christened

'Midshipman Easy' by *Punch* magazine, referencing the spoiled son of foolish parents in an 1836 novel. Others ran headlines 'The Boy Sailor' and 'Alfred the Great Roughing it'. Victoria was particularly upset by the *Times*, with what she felt was an 'imprudent' reference to the cost of Alfred, as 'Mr Midshipman Easy', and 'the Princely Hero of a Court', with all the 'royal receptions, and royal salutes, and royal fiddle-faddles of every description' when he reached Fleet ports around the Mediterranean. 'We want him to learn his profession, not in a vapid half-and-half, Royal Highness kind of way,' the *Times* said. 'He was sent out to be trained to salt water, and it is upon rose water that his first lesson in navigation is taking place.'[35]

Queen Victoria requested there not be public receptions when Alfred's ship visited Malta, Gibraltar, Morocco, Tunis, Egypt, Syria, Turkey, Palestine and Corfu. But there was never a shortage of military men and officials, and their wives and society ladies, keen to demonstrate royal and loyal affection.

An article in *Household Word,* edited by Charles Dickens, said Alfred was as popular with his messmates 'as any other sensible, good humoured and high spirited English boy might be', but lampooned the way local officials and military bowed 'almost to prostration to a little boy in a cadets uniform'. This was a sycophancy that Alfred ought to be removed from, and if an illustration in the *London Illustrated News* had portrayed them 'creeping on their bellies to lick the dust off the Prince's shoes the effect of abjectness could hardly have been stronger'.[36]

Alfred's fellow 'middies' seemingly agreed, and adopted their own little ceremony: whenever a Royal salute was fired they would bump him, or put him over a table in the gunroom and ceremoniously deliver a mock beating with a dirk scabbard to ensure he did not 'give himself airs'.[37]

Notwithstanding Albert's earlier efforts to ensure that while it was Her Majesty's Navy, Her Majesty's sailor son ought to be afforded no special favours, within five years Alfred was promoted to Lieutenant on the *Raccoon*, although that was delayed at one point 'on account of him having allowed some slight indiscipline among the crew of his boat'[38] Another 'slight indiscipline' included efforts to source some additional income by selling some of the Queen's correspondence.

But that was the least of it. As the Queen was to learn, what happened in ports like Malta did not always stay in Malta.

During Fleet visits to La Valetta, locals declared 'viva Alfredo' and in the ensuing receptions, operas and balls, Alfred enjoyed the warm embrace of various contessas wanting to dance with a Prince who perhaps stood a heartbeat away from the throne. Life for the British establishment in Malta was high spirited: '...if you don't want to be made love to you should not be so pretty' was a sentiment recalled by a prominent society lady.[39]

Alfred danced until the early hours 'exhibiting high pleasure and delight', as the *Malta Observer* reported. And did more than dance. Gossip reached London in 1862 that a 'dashing young naval officer had got into a scrape with a lady. The Queen was onto it.'[40] Alfred, in the grand Hanoverian family tradition, had an affair in Malta with 'a lady of rank', the start of a life-long affection for the pleasures to be had while in port in Malta. (Alfred would later name his third child, born in Malta, Victoria Melita, in honour of the island, the name thought to come from Greek word for 'honey').

The Queen, who had not forgotten or forgiven Edward's behaviour in Ireland, and always worried about him taking Alfred down the low moral road, lamented Alfred's 'thoughtless and dishonourable behaviour' without 'a particle of excuse'. She told Princess Victoria, 'The conduct of Affie has dealt a heavy blow to my weak and shattered frame and I feel quite bowed down with it'. Vicky empathised, wondering 'how could Affie be such a goose, to play such a silly trick and stand in his own light...I feel so pained to think that he could be so thoughtless as to add to your grief by misbehaviour. It is so disheartening, as he had been going on so well in every respect and is such a darling'[41] although she too was annoyed Alfred could indulge 'amusing ladies plenty of his time'.[42]

Victoria felt the misbehaviour even more than Edward's Curragh escape—'the bitter anguish that followed Affie's conduct is far worse than Berties'—and she was reluctant to even see him. 'I had wished not to see him and thought for himself it would have been better. But for the world it was necessary so I saw him. It was very trying.'[43]

In what would have been an excruciating maternal confrontation for any son, let alone with the Queen, Alfred exhibited sufficient anxiety and subdued tone to at least 'show me he feels enough'. But Victoria lamented having to handle such matters without the help of Albert or a male of sufficient age and experience she asked General Jonathan Peel who could 'help her with her sons' and 'keep them in the path of duty'[44] and away from their 'wickedness' with women, which sometimes forced payments to keep irate husbands quiet, or the risk- of prostitutes, who Albert had warned 'will consider you good sport'.[45]

To Victoria, even the illness of Alfred's younger brother Prince Leopold, a haemophiliac, was, she told Vicky, ' less trying than the sinfulness of one's sons—like your two elder brothers...one feels that death in purity is so far preferable to life in sin and degradation.'[46]

And she was also dealing with government ministers over another plan for Alfred to become a king. When King Otto abdicated the Greek throne in 1862 Athens chose Alfred as his successor, a Greek plebiscite backed the move with 'the Alfred fever...raging all over the country' and *The Times* declared the appointment 'certain' because 'the Greeks have no other candidate'.

The Queen was aghast. Alfred was much too needed in England as the spare heir, she protested. Edward might not have children or might die, and typhoid could quickly decimate a court. So 'we could not spare one heir'. Besides which Alfred was too young, had other 'duties' in line at Coburg, and his children couldn't possibly be brought up as Greeks.[47]

Victoria enjoined the British Government to vehemently oppose the move and her Greek tragedy was averted. Alfred was instead formally designated Duke of Saxe-Coburg and Gotha, the small kingdom of his father's family. The ruling Ernest II had salaciously lived up to the title of 'father of his people' but was officially childless, and while the title would normally fall to his brother Albert's eldest son, Edward was Queen Victoria's heir apparent so he renounced in favour of his brother.

Despite the reinforced Germanic link, Alfred continued to cause Victoria anguish. She saw men in the image of her husband, or after his death as a 'John Brown', evidencing what she saw as Albert and her close servant's sense of nobility, selflessness, dignity, devotion and humility. Or a 'John Bull', living life hard, displaying raciness, arrogance and a devotion to the pleasures of table, turf, and bed.

To her disgust, Alfred was, like his brother, more John Bull. She complained to her daughter 'he gives me cause for sorrow and anxiety (I mean morally)'. She was particularly determined to prevent him from 'getting into mischief' with Alix, his future sister-in-law and Princess of Wales, who Alfred had been ready to take her 'at once'. While she was now engaged to Edward, Victoria confided to Vicky:

> we do all we can do keep him from Marlborough House as he is far too much épris of Alix to be allowed too much there without possibly ruining the happiness of all three and Affie has not have the strength of mind or rather of principle and character to resist the temptation, and it is like playing with fire.[48]

He caused his mother a different anguish when he fell seriously ill in Malta, and her heart sank 'as I realized my darling Boy had the same fever as his Father!...But God's will be done! I can only hope and trust.' Receiving telegram updates every two hours, she could not 'contemplate the possibility of his also being taken from me', but some newspapers reported 'unpleasant rumours' Alfred had passed away.[49]

He did recover, but suggestions his health might force him to leave the Navy were not well received. Lord George Clarendon, former Secretary of State or Foreign Affairs, warned he was 'a baddish fellow and will give great trouble at home' if he left the Navy.[50]

He stayed in the Navy, and as a 'baddish fellow' bounced back into his life around the Mediterranean, Marlborough and Paris. There was an abundance of wine, cigars and women. Some of the women were actresses and singers chosen for the stages of London and Paris as much for their physical attributes as any artistic talent, attributes to be enjoyed on and off the stage.

Victoria was determined to 'save' Alfred, and had long been plotting a marital solution. She did not imagine the task to be too difficult because 'there is a greater choice and his wife need not unite so many qualities as Bertie's must, for many reasons public and private'[51] but she wanted Alfred to 'fix his affections'[52] securely, even if he could not marry until he came of age. She plotted with other Queens in Europe to introduce Alfred to a parade of princesses. Her preference was one 'thoroughly and truly German, which is a necessity' and the parade of prospects included Princesses Catherine of Wurttemberg, Catherine of Oldenburg, Elizabeth of Weid, Marie of Saxe-Altenburg, and Frederica of Hanover, daughter of Victoria's first cousin, George V, the blind and last king of Hanover.

Victoria and Vicky exchanged notes dissecting the looks, character, health and ages of candidates from Wurttemberg, Oldenburg and Saxe-Altenburg, seeking to guide Alfred to their preference of a Germanic princess who was not 'ugly', 'sympathetique' to his personality, and from a family without too many health issues due to in-breeding. They frowned on princesses who were 'sickly looking', or had bad teeth, large hands and feet, and unhealthy family members. Alfred assured his mother that Princess Marie of Altenburg evidenced 'only one tooth (which) is not good, and she has not got large feet and hands', and she had made 'a very favourable impression' on him. He described her as being 'very pretty, very tall, slight, with beautiful large thoughtful grey eyes, fine marked features and very dark hair!'

Victoria was pleased Alfred was interested in someone thoroughly German, and so preferable to others who were 'really objectionable on the score of health and blood' telling him firmly 'it cannot be' for him to marry anyone with 'generations of blindness and double relationships But she was concerned Alfred would not be hastened toward any marital conclusion with a Princess who was 19 'and cannot be left in uncertainty to be snatched away by others… if he doesn't in the end…like Princess Marie of A…he must look for somebody else,' she told Vicky.

But Alfred was not taking his mother's wishes on board, continuing to assess other princesses. The King of Prussia conferred an Order of the Black Eagle on him, which the *Times* called 'a very questionable honour'. This was 'monstrous' criticism, the Queen said, 'it is the pure vulgarity of the Press. I took it…as a valuable token of the King's wish to be on good terms with England. Oh! What I suffer, no one knows.' Vicky advised Alfred that 'now he knew the princesses he must seriously reflect in his own mind and balance all the advantages and disadvantages before he settled anything and at any rate should look for an opportunity to make better acquaintance with the one that pleases him most before he fixes his choice'.[53]

But Alfred was not rushing to settle on one female in his life. He remained determinedly without a 'fix on his affections', enjoying the freedom that came with being a sailor prince in the Mediterranean, and there would also be talk of his love for a 'commoner' and affections for various duchesses and ladies in London.

Victoria said he was vague and wilful, and now distrusted him completely. There was no doubt in her mind what was needed. In the absence of marriage, some 'responsibility and the separation from his London flatterers will do him good',[54] and also keep him from causing 'mischief' with Princess Alix.

So in early 1866 she devised a plan for him to assume a more royal and respectable profile. She had him invested as Duke of Edinburgh,

Earl of Ulster and Kent, appointed master of Trinity House, awarded the freedom of the City of London and granted Parliamentary approval of a £15,000 Royal coming-of-age stipend—a significant rise on his £1 a day naval lieutenant remuneration. But more significantly, she sought a fast-track for Alfred to the command of a ship. And a ship on which he could undertake a long voyage.

With the help of a special order allowing him to be promoted to Captain without first being a Commander, Alfred was given command of the *Galatea,* one of the fastest and best equipped ships of its day, at the age of 21. Named after the goddess nymph of calm seas, the 26-gun steam-powered, 280-foot long frigate had served in the Channel squadron and North America, with a top speed of 13 knots.

Mindful of previous criticism of her son doing it easy in the Navy, the Queen wrote to the Prime Minister, Lord Derby, to ensure Alfred was 'in command of his ship, the *Galatea*, as a captain in her Navy and not as a Prince', and urged that 'the Admiralty must make no difference' to his treatment, and he should 'conform to what every other captain on duty must do'[55]

After Alfred talked to Edward about the appeal of a voyage that would take him away from the scrutiny of London and Victoria's marital machinations, the heir encouraged the Queen, saying the brothers had often spoken of a voyage, and cleverly tapping her concerns about 'fast' behaviour said both the Fleet Admiral and the Naval chaplain instructing Alfred both felt it would be 'a good thing'.[56]

The Queen had what she wanted. And the voyage she had in mind was as far as the Empire extended, all the way to Australia. She presented it as completely Alfred's idea. 'He of his own accord proposed a voyage to Australia and I encouraged him very much in this plan, as it is a Colony of such importance, one in which beloved Papa took such interest and to which none of our Princes have yet been.'[57]

But Alfred evidenced some 'reluctance and suspicion' about just how long a voyage she had in mind. Some newspapers suggested it could be as long as two years, but Alfred did not want to miss the next society season, which ran from Christmas to about June. As he later told friends, picking up on life and old friends in London after any voyage was difficult, 'to say nothing of the fairer sex whom one may have left disconsolate.'[58]

By mid-May word began to spread that Alfred had left his Clarence House in the Mall, accompanied by friend Elliott Yorke as equerry, and would board the *Galatea* in Gibraltar and then depart from Marseille for a tour of the most distant and remote colonies.

But before Alfred began his official assignment, he wanted to pursue some unofficial assignations in Paris with his brother. As soon as he arrived in Marseille he handed over command of *Galatea* and took a train to the French capital. Like his brother, he had come to love the city, and all its delights. Alfred wasn't quite as outgoing as Edward but he was still a young man with royal privileges but without the same scrutiny as his brother, and still without 'fixed affections'.

What Alfred did that Parisian summer would be fondly remembered, but also mark the start of a year that could never be forgotten.

2

ALFRED, THE UNPRINCELY

That frivolous and immoral court did frightful harm...and was very bad for...Affie...the utter want of seriousness and principle.
— Queen Victoria.

The Continent's biggest city was abuzz as tens of thousands of visitors flocked to the *Exposition Universelle de 1867*, a world fair to demonstrate all the brilliant éclat that was France, and surpass Paris' first exposition in 1855 and the underwhelming 1862 exposition put on by rival Britain.

Exposition Universelle des produits de l'Agriculture, de l'Industrie et des Beaux-Arts de Paris was Emperor Louis Napoleon III's proclamation of Paris as the heart of a new world order, the mother of an emerging global civilisation of peace and prosperity under the cultural and spiritual leadership of France.

Seven million people descended onto the grand new boulevards of Baron Georges-Eugène Haussman to absorb 50,000 exhibits of human activity and excellence from 42 nations, a Napoleonic demonstration that the bounty of man and nature could be transformed into a universal harmony for all. As Victor Hugo effused in a preface to the exposition guide: '…O France, adieu!… thou shalt no longer be France: thou shalt be Humanity! No longer a nation, thou shalt be Ubiquity…as Athens became Greece, as Rome became Christianity, thou, France, become the world.'[1]

Notwithstanding the French challenge to her Empire's pre-eminence, Queen Victoria would not be in attendance. She had visited the first Paris exhibition, taking her family at a pivotal moment in the rapprochement between the two countries in the Crimean War. Napoleon visited Windsor and then went on a full charm offensive with Victoria's family as his guests in Paris, refitting the Palais de Saint-Cloud for their stay, and purchasing anything which was seen to please the Queen at the exposition.

Edward, the Prince of Wales, had also been seduced, as Victoria presciently noted. 'The beauty of the French capital, the liveliness of the French people, the bonhomie of the French Emperor (Napoleon III), the elegance of the French empress (Empress Eugénie) made an indelible impression on his pleasure-hungry nature.'[2]

Now in 1867 both sons had a pleasure-hungry nature, but the Queen was, six years after her 'day turned into night' when her beloved Albert died, still in isolated mourning. Alfred and Edward were tired of the permanent black dress, and what would be her insistence that Albert's rooms and routines remain exactly as when he was alive, such as servants daily delivering hot water for his shave, keeping his nightdress in her bed, and even visiting his cows.

Some had expected Victoria to abdicate soon after Albert's passing, and whatever the concerns about Edward, her isolation worried the British Government which well understood that

Royalty's public standing and influence, even its existence, depended on public connectedness. It was difficult enough to justify royalty by divine right and absolute authority, so loyalty and esteem was essential and this required visibility. But Victoria refused invitations to commemorate the opening of public buildings, ensured the weddings of her children were drab and private affairs, and only rarely appeared to unveil a statue of her husband or reluctantly open Parliament.

Anti-monarchical sentiment, if not outright republicanism, mounted. Victoria was hissed and booed on a rare trip to Parliament, such that even she wondered if 'something unpleasant' might happen. Newspapers and MPs questioned the cost of royalty and suggested Victoria was teaching people to think little of her office and that 'the monarchy is practically dead.'[3] A notice appeared on the railings of Buckingham Palace declaring 'these commanding premises to be let or sold in consequence of the late occupant's declining business.'[4]

There was 'a great crisis of Royalty', as Prime Minister William Gladstone observed. The Queen had an 'immense fund of loyalty but she is now living on the capital', he said, because Royalty was stuck in 'a deep and nasty rut'[5] as 'the Queen is invisible.'[6] And her heir was not seen as the answer. 'The Prince of Wales is not respected',[7] some Freemasons writing letters hoping the Prince of Wales would 'never dishonour his country by becoming its King'[8] and one MP opining that even the staunchest supporters of Royalty 'shake their heads and express anxiety as to whether the Queen's successor will have the tact and talent to keep royalty upon its legs and out of the gutter.'[9]

Nevertheless the Widow of Windsor could not be persuaded from her black isolation, but diplomatic and political reality meant she could not prevent Edward and Alfred providing a royal presence in Paris.

The princes were ready for Paris, and she for them. Edward was married, but his slender attractive wife Princess Alix and a growing family was no restraint on his appetite for a good time and female company. Carrying their third baby, Alix at one point was almost near death, a bout of rheumatic fever forcing her to lay in bed with a frame to keep the bedding off a troubled leg. But as soon as three-month old Louise was christened in May, Edward left behind his ailing wife—and gossip that he might have contributed to her increasing deafness by passing on syphilis—to await Alfred's arrival in Paris. 'She don't mind at all,' he told the Queen, dismissing her concerns.[10]

The Queen was worried. She and Prince Albert thought the requirement of royalty was discipline, and that ostentatious courts, frivolous pleasures, immoral leadership and flattery of the monarch could only ever led to societal trouble. Now their two sons, well known for their 'frivolous pleasures' were heading for the 'immoral court' of Paris she despised.

And while 'Dirty Bertie' drew the most attention in free-spirited, boozy private men's clubs like the Jockey Club and the new Yacht Club de France, Alfred had also learned much from the tutelage of his brother and fellow sailors. And since the arrival of Edward's first son, Prince Albert Victor, he no longer had to endure the strictures of being the spare heir.

Courtesans would cheerfully say that 'every girl is sitting on her fortune if only she knew it', and now the exposition city was opening its bosom, and more, to its visitors. Alfred arrived in Paris early on 13 May to join his brother in a full feast of the high life before setting off for a long journey to faraway Australia.

By the time they left six days later, correspondents in Paris pointedly wrote that the future King and his 'sailor brother' had been 'feted to their hearts content' and must have 'taken home a very lively remembrance of their visit'.[11]

On the surface, they were dutifully engaged in the exposition on the great military ground of Champ de Mars, especially the armaments and naval displays, and fulfilled a full card of official banquets, balls and receptions. Even official events raised some eyebrows. At the British Embassy, supper was just getting underway at 2am when guests were taken aback by Alfred's surprise party offering: his Scottish piper, in full highland uniform, marched in, lustily playing his bagpipes. The *Illustrated London News* said highland music might be acceptable in the mountains, 'but is certainly out of place in the salons of Paris'.[12]

After supper the princes 'danced on, with unflagging spirit, until half past five' and at a ball at Tuileries Palace, the two 'indefatigable dancers' made them 'general favourites with high and low'.[13]

The 'high' were the aristocracy of Europe and Asia, where Alfred rubbed shoulders proudly wearing the sash and Grande-Croix badge of the Légion d'honneur, Honour, presented to he and Edward by the Emperor.

The 'low' were *les amoureux,* with whom the princes rubbed more than shoulders. This was their private mission, to have a right royal time immersed in the gastronomic, theatrical and sexual fare of the *demi-monde* (half-world) a term originally coined by playwright Alexandre Dumas to describe the world of women who lived and thrived in the freedom and ambiguity on the edge of respectable society.

Paris was the epicentre of decadence in the court of Napoleon III and the Empress Eugénie, constructed around the Emperor's own voracious sexual appetite. Nubile ladies-in-waiting with low-cut dresses and nicknames such as Salopette or Cochonette, meaning slut or sex-mad, were maintained by Eugénie, and courtesans, dancers and actresses gave the theatrical quarter of the capital a reputation as the clitoris of Paris.

In close to 200 brothels—endorsed by Napoleon as a necessity to minimise sexual disease—enterprising madames in their *maison de tolerance* offered themed rooms providing all manner of outlets for aristocracy wanting to unleashing inner perversions and tastes. As Alexandre Dumas the younger wrote, 'Women were luxuries for public consumption like hounds, horses and carriages'.[14]

With the right beauty and cunning a *cocotte* could graduate from entertaining favoured guests in private rooms to become a *grande horizontale* to rich patrons, including emperors and aristocrats from throughout England, Europe and Russia, archbishops and the bourgeois. Such women with lavish apartments, servants, personal carriage, fabulous gowns, extravagant jewels, prominent clients and outrageous exploits were known as *mangeuses* (eaters-of men and fortunes).

Their luxurious mansions featured boudoirs with featured tableaux painted by Toulouse Lautrec, erotic imagery on everything, including radiators, and individually themed rooms. One at Le Chabanais, where Edward would come to have a coat of arms on his preferred bed, was in the style of an Orient Express carriage, complete with railway soundtrack. Special guests bathed with prostitutes in a giant copper bath filled with champagne, and when his gastronomic girth later threatened to restrict his sexual appetite, Edward would come to enjoy threesomes in a handcrafted 'love seat'.

One *mangeuse*, Giulia Benini Barucci, marketed herself as La Barucci, 'the number one whore in Paris'. She had a mansion on Champs Elysee, complete with liveried footmen and a grand white-carpeted staircase with velvet covered banisters. It was rumoured that when she first met Edward she begged forgiveness for being 45 minutes late and promptly lifted her crinoline skirt to reveal nothing but 'the white rotundities of her callipygian charms', telling others 'I showed him the best I have, and it was free!'[15] La Barucci kept letters and photos of her aristocratic clients, with her brother Piro not averse to demanding additional payments from some. Along with letters 'of a delicate nature' from Edward, she also kept a large photograph of Alfred in full Highland costume inside a crimson velvet frame signed 'Alfred', and an album of the Royal Family inscribed 'Alfred to Giulia 1868.'[16]

Another royally favoured *mangeuse* was Coral Pearl, formerly Emma Crouch. Although not conventionally beautiful, Cora was sexy, with a tiny waist and fine breasts. She delighted men with her spontaneous and outrageous spirit. When a dinner party guest broke an expensive glass, she impulsively broke the rest of the set to make him feel more comfortable. She became famous for attending a masquerade ball as 'Eve', with 'little deviation from the original', dancing naked on a bed of orchids, bathing in champagne in front of male guests, and urging a group of clients around the dinner table to be ready to 'cut into the next dish': herself, carried in by four men on a huge silver platter, naked except for a sprinkling of parsley.

By the time the princes arrived Pearl had 'already munched up a brochette (skewer) of five or six historical fortunes with her pretty white teeth',[17] a fortune that would include three Parisian houses, including a small palace, courtesy of Prince Napoleon, the Emperor's wealthy cousin, and jewellery worth more than a million francs and a stable of 60 horses.

This was the world which Alfred and Edward had come to know and love. Now, while tensions emerged in the affairs of Europe as Chancellor Bismarck sought German unification under Prussian leadership, pressure which would ultimately lead to the Franco-Prussian War and Napoleon's defeat, capture and exile in England, the princes pursued their favourite haunts.

Fashionable cafés like Café Anglais provided gastronomic satisfaction, and so much more. During the exposition it held the famous *Dîner des Trois Empereurs* or Three Emperors Dinner, in honour of Tsar Alexander II, Kaiser Wilhelm I and Otto von Bismarck. Sixteen courses with eight wines were served over eight hours at a cost of 400 francs per person (about AUD$13,000 in today's prices).

From the respectable salon maintained downstairs, where married women could be safely seen amid rich wallpaper, walnut, mahogany, and gold leaf patina mirrors, gentlemen could quietly make their exit via a hidden staircase to where a courtesan of choice would entertain them in *cabinets prive*. Café Anglais' 22 private rooms featured what food historian Nathanial Newnham-Davis would describe as 'scene of some of the wildest and most interesting parties given by the great men of the Second Empire.'[18]

For the princes, a seemingly respectable night at the 'ballet' or 'opera' might be much more about the star performers, those 'vivacious blondes (who) display their unconcealed attractions', as one Irish journalist wrote. It was hard to resist the 'unconcealed attractions' of performers like Coral Pearl and Hortense Schneider, a voluptuous 34-year-old singer who a police file indicated could 'have driven an archbishop to damnation'.[19] She was famous as a diva soprano on stage, and for her off-stage provision for visiting Royals as *le Passage des Princes* — en passage, or just passing through.

Pearl and Schneider co-starred in Jacques Offenbach's operetta *La Grande Duchesse de Gerolstein*, a biting satire of royal misbehaviour at the *theatre des varieties*. The leading men of the Jockey Club and English and French nobility attended, one observer noting that only women of the *demi-monde* could be seen in the boxes.

Jockey Club members generally did not turn up to the theatre until they had finished dining, forcing most theatres and Opera Paris not to schedule any prime items until after interval, during which time patrons visited the *Foyer de la Danse*, an exclusive salon where performers were selected for a personal après-show performance.

In the exclusive Offenbach performance, Alfred watched Schneider play a coquettish monarch with a dangerous weakness for men in uniform while Pearl, in the sensation of the season, played Cupid, appearing 'half naked' in diamond-encrusted bikini and boots. A critic in *The Examiner* said she was the most notorious and 'fastest' member of the *demi-monde* who evinced 'not one artistic quality in a part which demands many'.[20]

Artistic quality was not a princely priority. In *Nana*, Emile Zola's later researched novel about the *demi-monde*, a 'Prince of Scots' visited Hortense Schneider in her dressing room, where she received him still scantily dressed in her Duchess costume. Zola described the prince, bearded and of pink complexion, as having 'the sort of distinction peculiar to a man of pleasure', and 'his eyes half-closed, followed the swelling lines of her bosom with the eyes of a connoisseur'.[21]

Princess Victoria was also in Paris. She had not seen much of her brothers, but had seen and heard enough to tell her mother there was 'much that shocks and disgusts me here', including theatre which made her 'very hot and uncomfortable.'[22] She lamented: 'What mischief that very court and still more that very attractive Paris has done to English society…what harm to our two eldest brothers.'

Queen Victoria did not need to be reminded of the evil of Paris. She told her daughter: 'Your two elder brothers unfortunately were carried away by that horrid Paris…that frivolous and immoral court did frightful harm to English Society…and was very bad for Bertie and Affie.'[23] She was well aware of the excesses of the city, where she could see a 'fearful extravagance and luxury, the utter want of seriousness and principle in everything…all showed a rottenness which was sure to crumble and fall'.[24] High-ranking officials were also lamenting the princes' behaviour. General Sir William Thomas Knollys, comptroller of Edward's household, noted in his diary that reports of their visit were 'very unsatisfactory', including suppers 'after the Opera with some of the female Paris notorieties' and he later opposed Edward returning to Paris after the exposition given 'the scenes I had led to believe had taken place'. Lord Stanley noted in his diary: 'Much talk in society about the P of Wales and his disreputable ways of going on. He is seen at theatres paying attention to the lowest class of women, visits them at their houses etc.'[25]

Already concerned by what she sensed went on at Marlborough House, the Queen was appalled by what she heard of her sons' latest behaviour in 'horrid' Paris. Edward was concern enough, but now Alfred was becoming just as 'decadent' and 'a source of no satisfaction or comfort'[26] as he too 'succumbed to Venus'.[27]

It was a real relief he was leaving for a long sea journey to the far reaches of the Empire. Her hope was that safely away from immoral company, he might learn to become more disciplined and royal. His hope was for a break from maternal and royal expectations on an unprecedented sea voyage and the savouring of Antipodean pleasures and liberties.

Neither could have any idea that this was a voyage that would culminate in unimaginable events which would shake a country and Empire to its foundations.

3
HENRY, THE WOULD-BE PRIEST

The display of Master O'Farrell…surprised me…the educated class of Australia Felix will therefore borrow an example from the St Patrick's Society of that day…and try if they can conduct themselves as…consistently.
— John Pascoe Fawkner, founder of Melbourne.

Henry O'Farrell was born on a level of Empire very different to Prince Alfred, but he too would voyage to the other side of the world and struggle with his destiny and moral compass.

He was only a baby when he left his Irish homeland, too young to understand the passion and pain of his countrymen striving to overcome poverty and British subjection. And too young to know he was leaving Ireland, but Ireland would not be leaving him.

In 1836 his father William, a butcher, and mother Maria took their family from Arran Quay on the Liffey River in Dublin, to sail across the Irish Sea, another ordinary family among tens of thousands seeking something better in Liverpool, Glasgow, London or Manchester.

Capitalising on cheap fares—as low as 10d in steerage and 3d on deck—William O'Farrell chose Liverpool, the Merseyside city which by 1841 had the highest percentage of Irish-born, about one in six, of any English city. Here he renewed his butchery trade in Edge Hill, not far from the thriving docks where some 40 percent of world trade was now passing and where the world's first inter-city passenger railway station had opened just six years before.

Irish migrants did much of the construction and labouring work of the rail revolution, including the Liverpool–Manchester Railway and Grand Junction Railway workshops, where William O'Farrell met their appetites with sausages and steaks. He did well, a 'butcher boy of Arran Quay' who became 'tolerably successful' as a butcher and 'saved a considerable sum of money'.[1] But all was not tolerable. Local English Protestants feared for their jobs, with political and religious leading to physical clashes with Catholic workers. Preachers castigated 'the evil of Popery' and a 'conspiracy' to overthrow the Church of England. Hugh McNeile, an Irish-born Anglican cleric, declared:

> The time has come when everybody must choose between God's side and the devil's. We must fight unto death. We must lay down our lives rather than submit. The struggle has to end only in the subjection of either Catholics or Protestants.[2]

Protestants like McNeile saw Roman Catholicism as threatening 'Britain's providential mission to defend and propagate reformed Christianity', a mission based on a strong notion of national supremacy reinforced by biblicality and royalty. Queen Victoria herself said her duty was to:

> maintain the *true* and *real principles* and spirit of the *Protestant* religion; for her family was brought over and placed on the throne of these realms *solely* to maintain it; and the Queen will not stand the attempts [that are being] made to...bring the Church of England as near the Church of Rome as they possibly can.[3]

Young Henry O'Farrell was not to know the choice between God and Devil would become his own, and that leaving Ireland was not the family's escape from the British–Irish struggle. But William O'Farrell had felt the tumult and bloodshed of the United Irishmen Rebellion of 1798, when republican-minded Irishmen, influenced by the American and French revolutions, engineered an uprising against British rule, which under Elizabeth I, Charles I, Cromwell and William III had seen the best land confiscated by English and Scottish Protestants, and Irish society divided into the ascendant Protestants and the Celtic Catholic minority.

And while the '98 Rebellion resulted in an 1801 union whereby King George III ceased being King of Great Britain and King of Ireland to become the King of the United Kingdom of Great Britain and Ireland, there was little unity. The Protestant and Catholic tension and violence of Dublin had travelled to English soil.

William O'Farrell had lived his whole life hearing and seeing Irish Catholics painted as an evil threat to an empire and its religion, the enemy of its moral well-being. The *Liverpool Mail* even slated O'Farrell family heroes like Daniel O'Connell: 'One of the many obnoxious vices of popery is that where it prevails, it generates hosts of filthy and importunate mendicants, the vermin of the human race.'[4]

In 1841, hopeful he and his family could do better in a new land far away, William O'Farrell sailed with his wife, two sons, Henry and older brother Peter, and nine daughters to the Empire's newest outpost on the other side of the world.

This was as far away from the troubles of Ireland and England as could be, but the O'Farrells would soon discover great oceans were no barrier to old troubles.

The colony of Port Phillip had been founded only six years before they arrived, not from an official colonial expedition but the opportunistic John Batman and John Pascoe Fawkner venturing across Bass Strait from Van Diemen's Land in search of pastoral land, which they purchased from eight Aboriginal chiefs. They declared Birrarung, as the ancient Wurundjeri people called it, 'the place for a village.' The village became 'the settlement' and 'the township' under various names before becoming Melbourne in 1837 when Queen Victoria, who had just acceded to the throne as an 18-year-old, honoured the 2nd Viscount Melbourne, her Prime Minister and political mentor.

In 1839 the first immigrants from Britain sailed direct to Port Phillip. It was an arduous and sometimes perilous journey, lasting up to 17 weeks, but by the time the O'Farrells arrived a British ship was berthing every week, and they were now among nearly 17,000 people in the province of Port Phillip.

The collection of small clusters of houses, sheds and tents beside the Yarra Yarra River, surrounded by a few low-lying hillocks known as Batman's Hill, Flagstaff Hill, Eastern Hill and Emerald Hill, was nothing like Dublin or Liverpool, as eight-year-old Henry O'Farrell could readily see.

Most buildings were of 'wattle and daub', roofed with coarse shingles or sheets of bark. Bullock-drawn drays and horses battled mud or dust and tree stumps in the so-called streets, with laundry strung up between trees, mostly tea-tree and gums, as strange birds and wildlife screeched and hopped. The summer heat, flies and grasshopper plagues, and the silence of the surrounding bush, was a new experience. And amid the new settlers were about 700 members of three clans of the Aboriginal people who had been there for more than 50,000 years.

There was some English familiarity in a handful of more

substantial buildings, the uniformed presence of 10 constables and 25 soldiers, clothes of the fashionable, musical entertainment, and cricket games and horse-racing on the Maribyrnong River flats, where a few bullock drays were lashed together to form a grandstand and the seeds of the first Melbourne Cup to come.

Pubs were also numerous, sometimes rudimentary structures with names reflecting their owner's origins and clientele, like the Victoria and the Shamrock. But the alcoholic constitution was something else: public houses opened from 4am to 9pm, fuelling rampant drunkenness among men and women, such that in the O'Farrell family's first summer the *Port Phillip Patriot* headlined 'Something remarkable': there had not been a single charge of drunkenness at the police office the previous day and 'such a fact is worthy of record for its singularity.'

And what was a young lad like Henry to make of the sight of several hundred men, women and children 'dressed for the occasion' to follow two Aboriginals, the condemned Tunnerminnerwait and Maulboyheenner, as they were driven through the township on a cart to Tyburn Hill, named after London's execution place, for the colony's first public hanging? Hundreds 'most disgusting (in) spirit…(were) scrambling for places; several jumped upon the coffins'[5] while 'about 20 of the Aborigines were observed witnessing the execution from the branches of neighbouring trees.'[6] Or then seeing the men convulse for 30 minutes as they slowly strangled to death due to a botching by the volunteer hangman? Or the sights and tales of Aborigines carrying and throwing spears, escaped convicts, bushrangers, treadmills, stocks, duels, whippings, prostitutes, drunks and dandies.

For young Henry, this new world was a mind-spinning alchemy of the familiar and unfamiliar, freedom and violence. Georgine McCrae, wife of a solicitor, said Melbourne was a place which 'requires a constitution of Indian rubber elasticity to sustain it'.[7] She was talking of the climate, but her point was more universal. In the emerging society the 'gentlemen' of English birth and title found themselves competing with the 'gentlemen' of a transported polite society—Church of England clergy, barristers, university graduates, army and navy officers, and former civil and military officers of the East India Company—and in turn with the new riche of colonial merchants, squatters, bankers, and land agents.

New arrivals like the O'Farrells could never completely forget the 1690 Battle of Boyne, when William of Orange's crushing victory secured the Protestant ascendancy in Ireland for generations, but they could sense this was a new frontier of potential for those wanting improvement and independence, or escape financial loss, debt or disgrace.

A woman wrote to Caroline Chisholm in 1846: 'Oh what a difference there is between this country and home…Old England is a fine place for the rich, but the Lord help the poor'[8] and another told her children, 'we have brought our manners, our education and our individuality with us, but left conventionality behind.' Some optimistically declared 'this place is perhaps the most rising settlement in the world'[9] and a land dealer declared 'there is no doubt Melbourne will yet surpass London'[10] but there was a broad optimism that one's birth, background or religion might not matter so much in a new world where men cherished freedom and adventure, and could forge new definitions of merit, character, respectability and wealth.

The clash of English gentility and high-spirited men in pursuit of commercial and personal opportunity meant society was quarrelsome, especially over money, honour, politics and religion. The *Port Phillip Gazette* observed the settlement 'boils over like a bush cauldron with the scum of fierce disputes.'[11] 'Gentlemen' fought the 'respectable'. Overlanders from Sydney and Adelaide fought over-straiters from Van Diemen's Land. Port Phillip fought Sydney. Townsmen fought squatters. Convicts fought settlers. Aborigines fought pastoralists. English fought Irish. Orange fought Green. Protestants fought Catholics.

William O'Farrell and his family were among more than 2000 Catholics: freed convicts, pioneering settlers, and a rising number on the back of bounty and assisted passage schemes. But even 10,000 miles from home, Port Phillip was an English settlement with English/Protestant rule set against what was seen as inferior, ignorant, violent or seditious Irish Catholics.

Catholics and Protestants favoured their own when it came to doing business with butchers, bakers, pubs, clubs and drapers. Many immigrant Irish moved to the western side of Melbourne, amid emerging livestock sale yards, horse bazaar, slaughter-houses and nearby Flemington racecourse. Butchers wanted to be close to stock, which they slaughtered on their shop premises, rather than public slaughterhouses because, they argued, shops needed to be supplied quickly with fresh meat because of the warmer Australian climate.

It was here O'Farrell resumed his butcher's trade in Elizabeth Street, near the corner of Victoria Street. One of the 'wretched apologies for streets', it was more a gully in summer and a creek in winter, when so much water gathered at the intersection with Collins Street it was known as Lake Cashmore.[12]

He also resumed his interest in Irish affairs, one of the emigrants to advertise a meeting at which 'all true sons of the Emerald Isle are expected to be in attendance' to form an association to 'promote the education of Irish children and the cherishing of Irish patriotism'.[13] Five hundred Irishmen formed the St Patrick's Society of Australia Felix, the Latin name for 'fortunate Australia' or 'happy Australia' coined by New South Wales surveyor Thomas Mitchell after an exploration of Port Phillip pastoral lands.

O'Farrell spoke at the meeting, whose principal resolution was 'for the encouragement of national feeling, the relief of the destitute, the promotion of education and generally whatever may be considered by its members best calculated to promote the happiness, the honour and the prosperity of their native and adopted lands'.[14]

Rule 1 of the new society was designed to curb the sectarianism and feuds they wanted to leave behind, declaring membership to be open to any person 'of whatever political creed or religious denomination, being a native of Ireland or descended from Irish parents.'

William O'Farrell joined the committee, along with Belfast-born schoolmaster David Boyd, who was now teaching his young son Henry. Rev. Dr Boyd had distinguished himself in classics and mathematics at Trinity College, Dublin, before deciding in 1838 to pursue the adventure and opportunities of colonial Australia. Aged just 27 he began an 'academy' in Queen Street, impressing his young charges with his manly and intellectual qualities. One student recalled:

> He was an accomplished person. A first-rate classical scholar, with a fair knowledge of French, German and Italian, possibly Hebrew, for he knew pretty well everything, from astronomy to single-stick, fencing to comparative philosophy. He rode, drove, shot, fished, painted, was musical, mathematical, a mesmerist doubtless.[15]

O'Farrell was determined his sons Henry and older brother Peter would never be dismissed as 'mere Irish', seeking to give them the best possible introductions to education, church and society, or as the *Ballarat Star* later reported, 'educated in a manner to fit them for positions higher than the trade followed by their father.'[16]

But just as Henry was finding his feet in his first year in the new world of Melbourne he lost his mother. Just 46, the cause of her death was not recorded, but emigrant ships carried numerous diseases. In the streets of Melbourne, stagnant water and human and animal waste also fuelled dysentery, cholera, scarlet fever and 'colonial fever', later known as typhoid. An epidemic of 'colonial fever' in the 1841/42 summer killed 20 people each week.

The year 1842 also saw Port Phillip fall into several years of depression after the free-spirited pursuit of fame and fortune led to excessive and unsustainable land speculation, sharp deals and bank loans on questionable security. The problems were accelerated by a government decision to sell outlying land for only £1 an acre, collapsing livestock prices and causing widespread insolvency.

Without his wife and facing economic challenges, William O'Farrell wrapped himself and his sons in the arms of the Catholic Church and the new St Patrick's Society, the heartland of Irish Australian consciousness.

William's plans for his sons were based on faith, family and finance, a trinity that would change the lives of the whole family.

The O'Farrells were among the first to attend a rudimentary small Catholic chapel, built of old floorboards and salvaged building materials on what had been a treed site at the corner of Elizabeth and Lonsdale Streets. Called to St Francis by a bell hanging from a large gum tree, Henry listened to the preaching of the settlement's first priest, Father Patrick Bonaventure Geoghegan, and attend the first christenings, including Mary MacKillop, a future saint.

The Dublin-born Fr. Geoghegan, a chubby little man known for his liberal mind and tolerance, had been an orphan, spending five years in a Protestant 'proselytising institute' before he was 'rescued' by a Catholic priest and admitted into a new St Bonaventure's Charitable Institution in Dublin for a Catholic education before becoming a priest.[17]

He had been appointed by the colony's Sydney-based Archbishop, John Bede Polding, an English Benedictine monk with a vision for a Catholic Church founded on monastic ideals. He believed scholarship and sublime liturgy, accompanied by Gregorian chant, would, as in earlier centuries in Europe, civilise and convert this new country.

But most of Polding's priests, the first of whom came out as convicts, and their congregations, were, like Fr. Geoghegan, more Irish than English, and did not embrace his vision. Irish Catholics wanted the Church to take a more aggressive stand against inequalities, which Fr. Geoghegan experienced when he first went to pay his respects to Melbourne's first Anglican Bishop, Charles Perry. When presented with the priest's calling card he 'recoiled from it as if it were a snake (and) returned it with a caustic note, a freezing intimation that he could not recognise the Rev. P.B. Geoghegan in any shape or form, officially or otherwise, in fact conveying the idea that he wished to shun the card-sender as though he were an emissary from the Evil One'.[18]

Protestant–Catholic tensions also surfaced within the new St Patrick's Society. This came to the fore at the society's inaugural St Patrick's Day procession in 1843, when young Henry would have trotted happily behind a throng of men and women, dressed in green and wearing green and white rosettes and scarves. With a band playing cherished tunes such as *St Patrick's Day* and *Faugh-a-Ballagh* and behind a banner featuring a gilt emblem of an Irish harp, they proudly marched, some twirling a fighting shillelagh, and most 'liquoring up at frequent short intervals'.

At the rebuilt St Francis, Fr. Geoghegan delivered the first High Mass in Port Phillip, angering Protestant Irishmen who felt it undermined the society's non-sectarian principle. And more substantial tension was simmering. The St Patrick's Society met at the Builders Arms Hotel, a 'groggery' owned by an O'Farrell family friend, Timothy Lane. William Kerr, editor of the *Port Phillip Patriot* derisively nicknamed the hotel as 'the Greek and Co stables'. Influenced by anti-Catholic rhetoric of clergymen like the Scot, John Dunmore Lang, Kerr fuelled the Catholic–Protestant feud as journalist and as provincial grand master of the Orange Association, which asserted St Patrick's was 'a religious and political brotherhood, which under a pretence of nationality was fomenting sectarian strife and animosity.'

Irish interests were promoted by the rival *Port Phillip Herald*. Under the masthead motto 'impartial not neutral', owner-editor George Cavenagh allowed an Irishman, Edmund Finn, to write freely to balance the 'foul-penned ribaldry, unprecedented in the annals of decent or undecent journalism'.[19] Finn had arrived from Tipperary the same year as the O'Farrells. He was destined to be a priest but at 22 he migrated to Australia where he initially taught the classics but then achieved writing fame as the writer 'Garryowen', the name of a Limerick neighbourhood and popular Irish drinking tune. He became secretary of the St Patrick's Society when John O'Shanassy, a former squatter and founding spirit of the society became president.

Notwithstanding colonial challenges and tensions, it was an improvement on the sectarian violence of Liverpool and misery of Dublin. William O'Farrell would have felt both sadness and vindication when newspapers reported the Irish Famine as making his birthplace like a city of the plague, burying 'poor creatures in a large pit' and 'women children and infants of the tenderest age—all huddled together, like so many pigs or dogs, on the ground, without any other covering but the rags on their person'[20] and described an estimated 300,000 starving and destitute Irish men, women and children descending on the docks of Liverpool in just five months in 1847.

His butchery was surviving well enough, helping sustain the colonial boast of 'meat three times a day', and his sons, especially young Henry, were being embraced by a rising Catholic Church. After his wife's death he placed Henry as a boarder at the Melbourne Analytical Seminary for General Education run by an elocutionist, Mr James McLaughlin, to learn the classics, theology and elocution.

Henry was impressing influential men within the Catholic fraternity and beyond. A few days after the 1846 St Patrick's Day parade and patriotic banquet, the *Port Phillip Herald* received a letter from 'Pascoeville', the home of pioneer John Pascoe Fawkner, in which he said 'the display of Master O'Farrell, though a youth of sixteen (sic) years, actually surprised me...the educated class of Australia Felix will therefore borrow an example from the St Patrick's Society of that day.' Applauding what he had seen and heard at the dinner, he forwarded £1 for the St Patrick's Society school, and £1 for the society.

He had never been so pleasantly excited 'since I founded this Town of Melbourne in August 1835' as when he looked around the banquet and saw 'clearly manifest the true spirit of freedom, as displayed by the yeomen of Australia Felix...so many well-dressed, well-informed men united in the bonds of good fellowship'.[21]

In a banner-festooned marquee erected alongside the Builders Arms Hotel, president O'Shanassy said his first duty to the 300 guests was to pay 'undivided homage to her most gracious Queen Victoria', Prince Albert and their family, including princes Alfred and Edward, the latter 'destined, we fervently hope to be our future Sovereign.'[22]

Henry O'Farrell heard O'Shanassy, who would later become Premier of Victoria, declare that those who attacked the 'mere Irish' wanted to deprive them of religious and civil liberty, notwithstanding that Irishmen had long supported a monarchical form of government 'as the best safeguard for the happiness and liberties of people', and had 'left their bones to whiten on many a hard fought field, unwept, unhonoured and unsung...proving to the world their devoted adherence to the King.'

Irishmen would rally, he said, to any threat to the throne from a foreign foe, 'or a more insidious enemy, a domestic faction...likely to subvert the ancient equipoise of Queen, Lords and Commons'.

Fr. Geoghegan also proposed a toast to the clergy of all denominations and the inalienable right of free worship. But in the hearts of Irish Catholics like the O'Farrells, loyalty to the monarchy ought not be at the expense of loyalty to their homeland, and free worship ought to come with other freedoms and fairness.

'When an Irishman forgets his country he forgets himself',[23] Edmund Finn told the dinner, saying love of country increased in proportion to its impoverishment and trials. Irishmen might seek exile but this love 'hovers round him like a guardian angel...whispers to him...a gentle monitor warning him through his future career in life'.[24]

This 'guardian angel' hovered around Henry O'Farrell. He had left too young to have an Ireland to forget, but his mind had been shaped by continuous whispers, the stories of how oppression had forced his family and people to the other side of the world, where the battle continued.

Now he heard speakers, including his teacher, James McLaughlin, talk of a 'revolution' in the colony, a time in history when the colonist would 'not be respected by the weight of his purse, or by the number of his sheep and cattle stations...but by the good he confers on mankind by example and precept...there is a great revolution at hand—not of the sword for that has been too much already—but a revolution of the mind.'

William O'Farrell delivered a toast to the banquet stewards, but it was his son's address on behalf of the 'juveniles' which warmed John Fawkner and the St Patrick's audience.

'I have never before addressed a public assembly, and therefore it is probable that I shall require your indulgence,' the teenage O'Farrell said, 'and I know that you will grant it because you are of the generous and brave sons of the beautiful Green Isle'.

He spoke of the value of sound education, which could bring 'civilisation to the uncivilised, industry to the indolent, unity and peace to the fierce and intractable, and a knowledge of divine truth to all'.

Those who were educated and did not use it for a good purpose were worse than the most ignorant, 'for he abuses the gift of Providence, and sets a bad example to his less favoured brethren'.

He could not understand those parents and guardians iron-hearted to misery and degradation. 'Are they not warned almost every day of their existence by fresh proofs of the lamentable consequences of ignorance and early mismanagement?' He hoped the 'supreme dispenser of all events' would 'abolish this pernicious apathy' and inspire all minds with a desire for improvement and happiness, the path for 'peace, order and elegance' in the Australia Felix.

The passionate speech demonstrated an intelligence and confidence to hold the attention of others, although it also hinted at patriotic intensity and distaste for those in power and influence seen to be part of the Irish problem, not the solution. A mind that was perhaps capable of bringing anything but peace, order and elegance in the Australia Felix.

To his newspaper's report, the editor of the *Port Phillip Herald* appended: 'This speech, from the youth of the speaker, excited much admiration—ED.' It called him 'Master Daniel O'Connell O'Farrell' while the *Ballarat Star* referred to him as 'Master Henry James Daniel O'Connell O'Farrell' and Edmund Finn as 'D.O.C.' referencing Daniel 'The Liberator' O'Connell for his battle for Irish Catholic emancipation.

Three months later at a St Patrick's Society theatrical benefit, the first item was a verse recital by 'a show scholar',[25] the young O'Farrell 'of the Melbourne seminary, the youth who so creditably acquitted himself at the Hibernian Festival.'

The *Herald* reported that O'Farrell demonstrated a 'manifestly considerable presence of mind', the crowd so impressed that 'feelings of acclamation…accompanied him through its different stages.'[26] But the reality of Irish–Protestant tension was driven home to the O'Farrells the following month on the anniversary of the Battle of Boyne. The Orange Society of Melbourne celebrated by unfurling orange flags from the windows of the Pastoral Hotel, which excited 'all the prejudices, and all the animosities which have…been in existence for so many years between the Orangemen and those professing the Catholic Faith.'[27]

In what Edmund Finn described as 'a day of terror…the town looked as if in a state of siege',[28] an angry mob of Catholics demanded the removal of the banners and hurled stones. Despite the efforts of the mayor, 'the report of a piece (gun) was heard inside', and some of the mob rushed the Pastoral while 'the parties outside who were armed fired at the windows of the house, and were quickly replied to from within'.

Despite 'the continual fire kept up from the windows', Fr. Geoghegan tried to persuade his Church members to leave, while John O'Shanassy, who the anti-Catholic press described as a 'notorious ring-leader of the Irish rabble in civic matters',[29] tried to move the priest away from danger.

Several men were shot before the police eventually managed to disperse everyone, but tensions simmered. Superintendent Charles La Trobe and Town Magistrate William Mair ordered all pubs to be closed for the day, and went to the rival gatherings with mounted police. They found the Orangemen at a pub in Flinders Lane 'armed to the teeth' with 200 pistols and 70 muskets, and the Irishmen on the green facing Lonsdale Street prepared for 'war to the knife' with their own arsenal of guns, pistols and blunderbusses. The Mayor 'read the Riot Act' to each party and 'in the Queen's name' commanded them to disperse.[30]

The *Argus* gave full vent to anti-Irish Catholic sentiment, publishing a special report on the 'Popish riot' to be sent to the mother country on the next mail ship. It denounced the 'Popish rabble' and 'Popish murderers' for reducing Melbourne to the most unsettled districts of Ireland, 'the nest from which these birds of ill-omen were set loose on the province'.

An accompanying verse by 'Cromwell's Ghost' said those Melbourne Orangemen who dreamed the law in Australia would be 'strong enough at least to clip the Papist rabble's claws' had to realise they must emulate what their fathers had done in the 1798 Rebellion lest 'A Romish mob, uncheck'd, work out their Church's vile decrees'.[31]

While Orangemen and Protestants evoked Cromwell's maxim of 'put your faith in God, my boys, but mind to keep your powder dry', an undaunted Fr. Geoghegan convened a public meeting in the St Francis school-room to 'raise a fund for the relief of the poor Irish now suffering under the visitation of an almost unparalleled famine'. The ever critical *Argus* said it could not provide details because it 'could not reasonably be expected to adventure our own life, or ask a reporter to peril his, by attending such a meeting'.[32] Its editor claimed some society members had intimated their intention 'to assassinate him whenever opportunity offers.'[33]

Following the 'Popish riots', NSW Governor Charles FitzRoy prohibited party processions in Port Phillip, still run as an extension of New South Wales, with an exemption for English fraternities, the Freemasons and Odd Fellows. The St Patrick's Society suspended its annual march for several years, although 500 gathered on St Patricks Day in 1847 to lay a foundation stone for one of Melbourne's first halls, St Patrick's Hall, 'dedicated to the memory of Ireland', and attend a banquet at Queen's Theatre, where William O'Farrell was one of many speakers.

It was an auspicious day for the O'Farrells the following year when they welcomed the first Catholic Bishop of Melbourne, James Alipius Goold. The son of a prosperous family in Cork and Augustinian missionary, Goold was consecrated in 1848 in St Mary's Cathedral, Sydney, at the age of 35, before leaving immediately on a ground-breaking 600 mile coach journey to Port Phillip, arriving in 19 days despite heavy rain.

Escorted into Melbourne by more than 100 horsemen and 50 carriages, Goold enthused Irish Catholics as he quickly set out to make the church a more recognised influence. He fought with the Anglican Bishop about the use of the title 'Bishop of Melbourne', opposed Anglican claims of precedence at government functions, and defended Irish immigrant orphans being attacked by administrators because of their difficulties assimilating into a township environment.

The ambitious Bishop Goold, who inherited just two buildings and four priests, saw the need for an enhanced physical and fiscal Catholic presence. He created a new seminary attached to St Francis, which became the de facto cathedral church before determinedly beginning what became an 80-year project, the grand and gothic St Patrick's Cathedral on Eastern Hill in East Melbourne.

In addition to the cathedral project and securing 64 church buildings in his first 13 years, Goold also sought more clergy to meet the rapidly growing population. He particularly wanted some home-grown priests, especially as he found some of the colony's imported priests were 'bad and faithless', their example and scandal nearly destroying the 'faith of the people, as they had ruined their morals.'[34]

For William O'Farrell this was all a heaven-sent opportunity: his eldest son Peter had become a solicitor and was handling the growing legal issues and property profits of Dr Goold and senior clergy, and institutions such as the Bank of Victoria. Henry had been confirmed into the church by Archbishop Polding and was now a candidate to make his mark in matters of prophet, having been educated and mentored within leading Catholic ranks. He had made an impression on Archbishop Goold who now admitted Henry into his new seminary for theological education.

A father's prayers looked like being answered, but while his sons were making progress, William O'Farrell was too easily branded a 'mick shin-boner' or 'bog-Irish butcher'. This wasn't going to optimise life for himself or aid his sons' potential, so he successfully applied in 1848 to become a council rate collector in the Gipps ward, the area around west Melbourne where he had worked as a butcher, and then took on the role of Town Auctioneer of seized property.

The following year, 1849 William O'Farrell and 'O'Farrell Junior' addressed 400 Irishmen at the new St Patricks Hall on the sensitive issue of emigration from Ireland, questioning why Irish numbers were disproportionately less than Englishmen and Scots, and whether eligible Irishmen were being refused bounty passages because English emigrants were preferred.

The *Argus* said 'Mr O'Farrell, junior' strongly pressed the St Patrick's Society role to cherish Irish patriotism, noting the Irish were known to demonstrate 'justifiable ardour' and be 'most tenacious of their rights when those rights have once been clearly established'.

As England 'cannot find food for her starving subjects, but more particularly those of Ireland', there should be no hesitation in advising people to 'leave that country which is no longer their own, which has ceased to be that happy land'.

'Tyranny had grown strong', he said, and it was, 'notorious that offences are committed by individuals impelled to do so by want, and (now) being sent out as prisoners here, have that wish afforded them as felons which was denied them as freemen! Irishmen endure much from poverty, before they are betrayed into a dishonourable action... the Irish behold their more favoured countrymen in opulence, they are called upon to starve in the sight of plenty...perpetually in view whom they consider were the originators of all their misfortunes'.[35]

Instead of spending millions of pounds to transport convicts to Australia, it would be cheaper and more beneficial for both England and Australia if some of those funds assisted more settler migration.

O'Farrell also said: 'With regard to Ireland we may exclaim: Bleed, bleed, poor country! Great tyranny, lay thou thy basis sure, For goodness dare not check thee!' and while other nations would gladly populate 'for such a prize as Australia. I shall not pursue the current of...free thoughts, they are too high and daring to be uttered by Irish lips in these times.'[36]

Around the time Henry O'Farrell was talking of tyranny and daring, the St Patrick's community was absorbing the news that a young unemployed Irishman, William Hamilton, had aimed an improperly loaded pistol at Queen Victoria during a carriage ride, the fourth attempt on her life. Hamilton was not represented at trial, and only had to wait a few minutes before the Chief Justice sentenced him: seven years exile for his bid for 'notoriety', to be transported to Melbourne.

While the assassination attempt was the talk of the town, the O' Farrells were all being embraced by the Catholic Church. William O'Farrell had become a property agent and dealer, while Peter advised and managed land deals for the Catholic hierarchy. After being tutored in the new seminary the Bishop conferred 'minor orders' on Henry in a three-hour ceremony at St Francis Church, one of the first ordinations in the colony.

In the ceremony, just before Christmas 1850, the crowded church was reminded of the custom of taking those 'who were fitting and had an inclination for spiritual calling in order to advance them to that holy state', and putting them on the path to priesthood.

A few months later, the Bishop, mitred and in pontifical robes, ordained Henry as sub-deacon,[37] and presented him with his own robe and empty chalice—'see what kind of ministry is given to you'—and blessed him. Then in 1852, having met the pre-requisites of church knowledge and age, Henry was ordained as deacon.[38]

A deacon's role included preparing and presenting bread and wine and sacred vessels for the Holy Sacrifice and Eucharist, solemnly chanting the Epistles, and helping minister Mass to prisoners in Melbourne's new Pentridge Stockade.

Henry was now also bound to celibacy, the renunciation of marriage 'for the more prefect observance of charity'. Bishop Goold would have given the traditional warning at the ceremony about the gravity of the obligation: You ought anxiously to consider again and again what sort of a burden this is which you are taking upon you of your own accord. Up to this you are free. You may still, if you choose, turn to the aims and desires of the world. But if you receive this order it will no longer be lawful to turn back from your purpose. You will be required to continue in the service of God, and with His assistance to observe chastity and to be bound for ever in the ministrations of the Altar, to serve who is to reign.

Following ordination, Henry's next step on his pathway to priesthood was to travel to the Continent to further his education with visits to centuries-old Irish colleges and seminaries in France, Italy and Belgium as well as visits to England and Ireland.

Just as Queen Victoria and her government hoped Prince Alfred's travels would 'complete' his development as a more bona fide royal, so William O'Farrell and his Catholic Church hoped Henry O'Farrell's travels would 'complete' his development as a bona fide priest.

4
HENRY, THE UNPRIESTLY

Celibacy and drunkenness cause the blackest of crimes all over the world among the Catholic priesthood.
— Peter O'Farrell

Henry O'Farrell was well on his way to becoming a priest. As he readied for a 'finishing' education in theology at the ancient Irish colleges of France, Italy, Belgium and Ireland, the Catholic hierarchy in Australia sent introductory letters to their European network, although some hinted at nervousness about his intense manner. His priest Fr. Patrick Geoghegan mentioned to Bishop Goold that he might 'mention to Shiel (privately of course) O'F's application', referring to Fr. Laurence Bonaventure Shiel, who had just arrived as president of the St Francis seminary, later St Patrick's College.[1] Perhaps O'Farrell's youthful intensity about Irish matters was on their minds. He would inevitably be exposed in Europe to discussion about the relationship of Dublin and Rome, and the role of the Catholic Church in the plight of Ireland and its emigrants in colonies like Australia. In the Melbourne he was leaving, Irish immigrants were still accused of being idle, ignorant and immoral and denied the same opportunities as the English and Scotch. And divisions within the Catholic Church were also becoming more evident. Local papers reprinted the open letter of Dublin's Father Thaddeus O'Malley to Irish Catholic clergy, 'What will the Priests do now for Ireland?' He challenged those who would do nothing while Ireland tottered to hopeless ruin due to pestilence and famine visited on them by 'the perverse will of an insolent dominant faction'.

Henry's words to the St Patrick's Society that educated men who did nothing were worse than the ignorant were amplified by Fr. O'Malley. In the death struggle of the Irish, he said, those who did nothing to save them were 'virtually the abettors of that proud and cruel domination that presses its armed heel upon their neck'.[2]

Priests ought not be instruments of repression, but seek a voice in national politics to help deliver equality and compatibility. The 'duties of patriotism require a sacrifice…for priest or layman…the priest is free from the enthralments of domestic ties, and has no family but his flock, for whom as a faithful shepherd he is ever ready to sacrifice even his own life'.

Rome had acquiesced to the argument of English Benedictine monks like Archbishop Polding that the Catholic Church in the new world of Australia had to be accommodated within an English administration, and his fear that increased Irish Catholicism risked sectarian troubles. But Henry's Irish mentors wanted their Church in Australia to move away from its English orientation, and in Ireland the Catholic Church was becoming more unified, nationalist and assertive under the leadership of Archbishop Paul Cullen at All Hallows College in Dublin, the single biggest source of Irish priests to Australia. Here O'Farrell could have expected to mix with 'graduates of a robustly nationalist, even Fenian, outlook'.[3]

Henry would have much time to reflect on how English power had much to answer for, and the need for those of education, power and influence to do more. There would also be time for the free-spirited nature of Paris to challenge his commitment to celibacy and the Church.

Whatever his mind was making of all this, in the winter of 1854 he received word his father had died, aged 62, at his brother's home *Maritemo* in South Melbourne.

Henry and his brother might have anticipated a financial windfall.

On 27 July, *The Argus* referenced 'the will of William O'Farrell, late of the City of Melbourne, in the Colony of Victoria, gentleman, deceased', naming Henry's brother Peter Andrew Charles O'Farrell, 'gentleman', and brother-in-law William Lane, 'merchant', as executors. They moved within days to dissolve the estate. On 1 August, the *Argus* advertised O'Farrell's properties at 'extremely low prices (with) liberal credit': 12 newly built two-bedroom brick cottages in Stuart Street, near Swanston Street North; 42 acres of land in Prahran near St Kilda racecourse; 945 acres on the Merri Creek at Plenty; 200 acres in East Brighton; and building allotments in Kyneton, Kilmore, Gisborne and Wangaratta.

The will provided several legacies for various Catholic charities and associations, and £300 for the 'sole and exclusive use and benefit' of Bishop Goold, along with £800 for a nuns convent, St Patrick's cathedral, St Francis Church, St Francis Seminary, Friendly Brothers and Catholic Association.[4] Goold had ministered to William O'Farrell in his declining health before departing for a trip to Rome to present some Victorian gold to Pope Pius IV, utilised Peter O'Farrell for legal and financial advice, and mentored Henry O'Farrell.

Peter O'Farrell did not delay sending the Bishop a cheque for the total £1100[5] on the basis, he said, it would be refunded if it was found the estate's assets were insufficient. Which is what they found.

'My father was thought to be rich and he would have died well off but for ruinous speculations', Peter O'Farrell would write, claiming he and his family were financially disadvantaged as a result of the speculative deals and debts.[6]

Back in Australia, Henry was without his father and a diminution of the financial support which had sustained his education, priestly training and travel. And somewhere in Europe, or immediately after his return to Melbourne, his priestly destiny was lost.

Some said he 'suddenly disappeared' from a college in France 'without making any communication to the superior' before re-appearing in Australia[7]. Others reported he had been ready to take holy orders 'but falling in love with a young lady prevented him from following this course, and he accordingly turned his attention to more practical pursuits'.[8]

A veteran Ballarat merchant and Catholic, James Tappin, said ill-health was not the issue, as the *Ballarat Star* had suggested. 'The fact was his educational superiors both here and abroad rejected his candidature, considering him from their knowledge of his proclivities as being totally unfit for holy orders.'[9]

Other reports cited a dispute with Bishop Goold. His brother Peter told colleagues 'he has had a dispute with the bishop on some religious points and has given up his intention of joining the priesthood'.[10]

Perhaps the dispute was over some misbehaviour in Europe, or the vow of celibacy had proved challenging. Peter was in no doubt that a bachelor priesthood flew in the face of the law of nature laid down by the Almighty for all his creatures, and that 'celibacy and drunkenness cause the blackest of crimes all over the world among the Catholic priesthood'.[11]

Or perhaps Henry's travels had reinforced his view that the Church leadership was not prosecuting Irish interests strongly enough and not evidencing the sacrifice required by duties of patriotism, as advocated by Fr. Thaddeus O'Malley.

Or it could have been a falling out over family money or morality. Peter accused the Bishop of trying to gain from his father's supposed wealth—the body was 'scarcely cold before Dr Goold insisted on hearing the will read'—and despite the estate being found 'worthless' had reneged on repayment of his father's legacies. He spent the rest of his life castigating the Bishop as a 'swindler' who 'hugged the golden calf to his heart', and did nothing to address the immorality of some priests. Some brothel landlords, he claimed, told him 'some of their best customers were priests' and the Bishop himself had mistresses and had paid 'hush money' to their husbands to avoid scandal.[12]

Whether it was from 'incompatibility or sentiment of others', as the *Ballarat Star* said, or personal conflict over his identity and purpose, Henry was not to be ordained as a priest. Despite the hours of study in Melbourne and Europe, the efforts of his father and family to support the Catholic Church, the encouragement and support of senior clergy and taking deacon orders, Henry, or someone else, had come to a judgment that it was not to be.

Henry's passion for Ireland now exceeded his passion for the Church. He was 'genial, warm-hearted and enthusiastic', one report said, 'but possessed of an undeniably national bias, and no amount of the *dulce et decorum est proclivity pro patria mori* as regards Ireland', a line of Latin poetry about sweetness, honour and preparedness 'to die for one's country'.[13]

Fr. Laurence Shiel, the new St Francis Church seminary head, was perhaps referring to Henry when he wrote to a colleague in early 1856 saying that he 'never corresponded with 'O'Farrell', who was now 'sufficiently removed from here: on the occasion of a Governor's soirée he had to be dissuaded from attending in his habit: *coelum non animant mutant, qui trans mare currunt* (those who cross the seas may change their horizons, but not their character.'[14]

Having lost his mother and father, been denied his destiny to be a priest and not received an inheritance he might have expected, and with Peter regaling against what he saw as a financially and morally corrupt Catholic hierarchy, Henry now heard more and more Irishmen agitating about English oppression.

The nature of what was going on in Henry O'Farrell's mind was not clear, even to his own family and St Patrick's Society friends, but they felt Henry needed time away from Melbourne and its gold-rush fever and to go west to a quieter life in country Victoria.

A businessman John Carfrae was introduced to Henry at his brother's office in 1855, just after his return from Europe where

> he had been educated for the priesthood and was to be ordained by the Roman Catholic Bishop of Melbourne. At the time he appeared a retiring but well-informed gentlemanly looking man of 20. About a week after, on inquiring of his brother, he (Peter) replied 'Henry is an extraordinary young man, he has…given up his intention of joining the priesthood. He has gone to Clunes to learn sheep farming.'[15]

Clunes was the first gold-rush town in Victoria, and here lawyer William Lane, Henry's brother-in-law and a brother of the treasurer of St Patrick's Society, co-owned a squatter pastoral and mining business. The isolated ovine environment did not sustain Henry, and he soon moved from Clunes to the gold-rush town of Ballarat to operate a hay and corn business with a cousin, Joseph Kennedy. This became such a 'flourishing and lucrative business' it allowed them to speculate in the share market and they became 'possessed of a good deal of landed and house property.'[16] Much of the property was on Soldier's Hill, named after the Colonial soldiers stationed there prior to the 1854 Eureka uprising when hundreds of gold miners, led by Peter Lalor, brother of a leader of the Young Ireland uprising in 1849, revolted against 'a tyrannical authority' resulting in the death or serious wounding of about 34 rebels.

Business success seemingly went to the cousins' heads, and

they began to acquire a reputation for 'habits of intemperance', as the *Ballarat Star* described. Henry was seen, when sober, as 'a steady, trustworthy person', although 'eccentric to be sure in some particulars', and their days combined business and drinking—one staying 'sober while the other was doing the convivial, and in his turn attending to business while his partner enjoyed a little relaxation'.[17]

They did well enough for Henry to take another trip to Europe, this time without any Catholic ambition or patronage, a former Ballarat priest even describing him as 'an indifferent and unobservant' Catholic who held an 'obscure and unknown place'.[18] The trip coincided with a new group of Irish freedom fighters gaining attention. Calling themselves Fenians, after an ancient Celtic tribe, they formed in 1858 in Ireland and America, with ambitions in Canada, England, New Zealand and Australia.

The first transcontinental insurgent group, the Fenians took advantage of an industrial age spawning a new mobility of people via steamers and rail, easier access to money as modern banking began dealing with funds across countries and oceans; increased voice through new telegraph technology and cheaper printing, and greater access to weapons, especially after the American Civil War.

When Henry returned around 1862, it was to a country which had still not shaken its colonial view that the Irish were a threat to national and empirical security, in an Empire increasingly hungry for the 'loyalty' of colonies like Australia, in a world in which the Irish fight for freedom was becoming more intense and more international.

And his Church was not doing enough for the Irish cause, as he saw it, and furthermore had abandoned his family. His brother suffered a major falling out with the Church after some blamed him for debts associated with building St Patrick's College in Ballarat and St Patrick's Cathedral. Then after losing a libel case which followed a fatal carriage accident, financial and professional pressures forced Peter to send his French-born wife and children to Paris in the hope of rejoining them later. He was expelled from the Law Institute, of which he was vice-president, and forced to resign from all community roles, including the Board of Visitors at Yarra Bend Lunatic Asylum.

Faced with insurmountable debts, the loss of his Catholic base and professional disgrace, the 'leading solicitor of Melbourne and prominent society man' as newspapers described him, asked Bishop Goold to at least help him with 'permission to conceal himself in St Francis Presbytery'. But this was denied, and colleagues said Peter became so 'intense' and 'bigoted' that in the heat of a religious argument 'he would bring the blood from his hands, through the pressing of the finger-nails into the palms of his hands.'[19]

He also carried a gun, which he slept with, and a bottle of poison, declaring he would never be taken alive. Henry, a police superintendent said, later claimed to have been 'principally instrumental' in aiding his brother's escape to the United States, where he reportedly spent time in a lunatic asylum for attempting to shoot the Archbishop of Quebec and wrote several pamphlets on what he saw as the injustices and immorality of Archbishop Goold. He sent copies to the Pope and other senior Catholic leaders in Rome, and presumably to Henry. On his eventual return to Melbourne, Peter would attempt to shoot the Archbishop.

While the Sheriff declared Peter '*non est inventus*', Henry sought a compulsory sequestration of Peter's estate and to secure some of his furniture being held under Sheriff's orders at the Port Phillip Club Hotel. Around this time Henry 'left the impression of being a very excitable man, very argumentative, rapid in utterance and cantankerous'.

The brothers, formerly shining lights in the Catholic Church, were now in a very different place, Peter in self-exile in the United States, Henry personally isolated and 'excitable' and dealing with another setback when his Ballarat business partner Kennedy, died, 'so confirmed a drunkard he…fell a victim to delirium tremens'.

Some saw O'Farrell as merely intense and erratic, others spoke presciently of him as 'one who having attached himself to an idea would pursue it at any cost to himself or to others'. He frequently alluded to his experiences on the Continent, saying he preferred its manners and customs to those of England, and fulsomely supported Chartism, an English working class campaign for increased democratic rights. And he 'exceeded the wildest radical in his hatred of aristocracy.'[20] One who met him at the Melbourne Cricket Ground went further, describing him as 'a very dangerous man'.

Without the financial and personal support of his father, brother and business partner, Henry began to spend more time among hundreds of gold speculators, dealers and agents who clustered in Ballarat at what was known simply as The Corner, where the vigorous trading in mining stocks and ventures ranked it as one of the world's busiest financial hubs. Henry lost heavily on failed mining companies, which led to the loss of some property assets. As he tried to speculate his way out of trouble he sank further and 'drank more heavily than he had done previously'. He avoided many former acquaintances, made frequent threats and expressed 'a determination to take the life of persons offending him'. The *Ballarat Star* said he was 'greatly embarrassed' by his plight, and while affable and gentlemanly when sober, drinking to excess was 'completely upsetting his mental equilibrium'.

He now lived by himself in his hay and corn store, often went for days without a meal, and walked alone far into the countryside for, he said, his health. A neighbour witnessing a bout of delirium tremens thought he was evidencing 'the worst species of insanity'[21] and another found him crawling on the floor. Local doctors, often called in, found him 'occasionally, extremely violent'.

Henry had also 'secreted' two pistols from a pawnbroker. At the same time, more reports of Irish patriotic uprisings and rebellious acts were appearing in the newspapers. The *Freeman's Journal* reported crowds of 30,000 Fenians in New York endorsing militant cries, such as Colonel William Roberts' declaration that 'Ireland must be free and we shall free her (long and enthusiastic cheers again and again)...the sword shall now be the arbiter of her destinies...blood must wash out what blood and crime have stained (loud cheers)'.[22]

Irish American arms and funds supported the Fenians and a secret Irish Revolutionary Brotherhood, later the Irish Republican Brotherhood, formed local cells swearing an oath to do whatever it took to make Ireland an independent republic, and Fenian-minded Irishmen, including some senior organisers, emigrated to colonies including Australia.

Irishmen around the world sensed an uprising in Ireland was imminent, but British authorities raided the IRB offices and arrested its leaders, including some Irish Americans, and seized revolutionary documents.

When news of Fenianism breaking out in America reached Ballarat, Henry 'pronounced himself a decided partisan of (Fenian) Head Centre (James) Stephens', one of the founders of the Irish Revolutionary Brotherhood.[23]

He would have been disappointed the uprising had failed, but also outraged by reading reprinted extracts from *The Times*:

> Nationalities fill the world with their complaints, but are never able to right themselves, and cannot even stand alone without aid...they are too distinct to assimilate or get on well with their neighbours...they can neither comprehend nor be comprehended and are eventually crushed and ground to powder rather than affiliated. Ireland has hitherto been too Irish to make her way with the rest of us. A time may come when the proportion of Irish to English there, or rather of all foreigners to the natives, will put the country into a better condition for the great race of nations. Ireland may then be no more distinct from us than Lancashire or the valley of the Clyde.[24]

Authorities in Australia did not need talk of uprisings to be nervous about Irish rebellion. This fear arrived with convicts exiled for riot and sedition. Governor John Hunter, who succeeded Arthur Phillip, frequently warned London that Irishmen, especially Catholics who outnumbered Protestants twenty-fold, were 'deluded' and 'turbulent' and put the colony's security at risk. Successive regimes brutally dealt with Irish plotting, proven or otherwise: suspects received up to 1000 lashes, priests were imprisoned, and at one major uprising at Castle Hill (later Vinegar Hill) about 15 shot dead and nine hanged.[25]

There were calls for a 'man of war' to be stationed in Sydney Harbour and two civilian para-military groups were organised and armed. The more recent presence of freedom fighters, such as the Young Ireland leaders exiled in 1849 and 1850, added to the nervousness of authorities.

While some said Irish and Fenian ambitions could never be 'more than a madman's dream', others, like David Buchanan, who narrowly escaped imprisonment for Chartist activity and fled to Australia to become a lawyer and politician, accepted that Irish advocates of physical force were driven by a sincere love of their country, and their spirit ought not die 'til it has consumed every vestige of wrong which has so ruinously fed upon their very vitals'.[26]

The fear of those determined to quash any such anti-Empire ambitions was illustrated when Buchanan gave a spirited address on 'The Wrongs of Ireland' to a packed audience in Sydney and was duly charged by the *Empire* with disloyalty, sedition and violation of his oath of allegiance to the Queen. In the subsequent libel case, Empire loyalists won a moral victory when the Chief Justice ruled in Buchanan's favour but awarded him no costs and damages of one farthing.

As argument raged over injustices, and whether fighting for Irish freedom was a madman's delusion or patriotic duty, Henry O'Farrell's mind regressed, forming a darker view of both his personal plight and Irish homeland, and a 'vindictive animosity' toward aristocracy and Catholic clergy, 'vilifying them in a most outrageous manner whenever they formed the topic of conversation'.

His sister Caroline Allan could see he was more restless, uneasy and excitable, deeply affected by financial losses flowing from his brother's troubles and his own speculative losses and rising debt. She could see he was drinking more and becoming more erratic. O'Farrell lived alone but also now sought female companionship 'he would otherwise have shunned'.

> O'Farrell…rigidly adhered through life to the vows of celibacy he had taken when admitted to deacon's orders. As illustrating his peculiar turn of mind and habit of living… he frequently made an arrangement with two neighbours… to spend an evening in his house, taking a sort of martyr pride in conquering whatever failings he might possess, though his visitors were allowed perhaps greater liberties than were either compatible with strict propriety…or with being mentioned in the columns of a newspaper.[27]

Perhaps he was testing his 'strength through resistance', the Catholic challenge of celibacy which his brother had warned would lead to a 'blackness'.

The blackness deepened. In September 1866 he suffered another attack of delirium tremens and threatened to kill a banking friend he had invited to his rooms to plead for a loan to overcome his ruined state. When told that a loan would have to be on the usual terms, 'he suddenly leapt from his bed, seized a sword cane, and would have killed or wounded the gentleman' if others had not intervened. The shaken bank official declared 'Oh, he's mad! he's mad!'[28] Police alerted O'Farrell's two sisters Caroline and Catherine, who travelled from Melbourne to attend to him and take him back to Melbourne. But they could not hold him or change his course.

Henry went back to Ballarat in 1867, of uncertain and fevered mind, as the colonies feverishly waited for updates on when His Royal Highness, Prince Alfred, would take the first step of Royal blood on Australia's shores.

5
ALFRED ON TOUR

May God protect him body and soul and bring him back safe and sound.
— Queen Victoria

After his right royal time in Paris, Alfred made a brief return to London to watch his mother lay the foundation stone to a statue of her beloved Prince Albert, and a quick visit to Coburg where in fluent German, he paid homage to his late father's home, further cementing ties between what newspapers described as 'the two great teutonic peoples'.[1] 'He was moved to tears when I wished him goodbye and gave him my earnest blessing', Queen Victoria wrote, 'May God protect him body and soul and bring him back safe and sound.'[2]

Her blessing was for the Admiralty's order for Alfred to take *Galatea* to 'the lands of South America, the Cape Colony, China,

India, Australia and New Zealand'. This would mark the first Royal visit to Australia.

Her prayer was for Alfred to safely complete the longest, most arduous and dangerous Royal voyage ever undertaken, a voyage which had claimed numerous convict and trading ships. And for him to return more 'sound' than 'fast'.

> May it be for his good and may he come back an altered being! His presence in my house during the last year was a source of no satisfaction or comfort. He only came for moments, and when he did, displeased high and low, and made mischief. In short he was quite a stranger to me, and I cannot deny that I feel very uneasy at his return – though I long to see him safe.[3]

She knew Alfred wanted to be back for the pleasures of the next 'season', but 'it did him so much harm last year...I and the Admiralty will be firm and do only what is for his good and the good of the Service'.[4]

The extensive voyage was unprecedented. Royals had toured Britain since Queen Elizabeth I made an annual summer escape from London to the countryside in a gold and silver carriage, looking a goddess to peasants in her dazzling dresses. But off-shore tours were unheard of until Victoria sent Edward and Albert to North America and South Africa, trips which would be easily surpassed by Alfred's voyage, which some newspapers likened to those of explorer James Cook.

Beyond trying to keep Alfred away from a personal path of decadence, the Queen and Admiralty understood the political, military and public relations value of visits to important colonial ports. The Queen knew the British public felt let down that her grandfather King George III had failed to protect British interests in the Americas, and after the Indian mutiny in 1857 and the recent devolution of Canada to self-rule, there was a need for the Empire to evidence more support of fellow 'Britons' in outposts such as Australia and New Zealand and reinforce empirical loyalty through royalty.

British newspapers acknowledged that 'the distance from England to Melbourne is too immense to leave room for hope that even in these days of rapid transit the monarch of Great Britain can ever personally visit so remote a corner of the Empire' so it was 'a good fortune' that one of her sons was a sailor.[5]

The empirical and parental collusion required Alfred to play what *The Times* described as his 'humble part' by visiting an Australia where in one generation 'under our feet a whole world of life and hope has sprung into existence…getting on towards two millions of British subjects, the greater part of whom have only heard of British Royalty' and where 'every soul is home-sick' and tired of colonial life which was 'sad at the best'. While the presence of princes in England was familiar and 'the novelty has passed', this was not the case in Australia, where the colonies, towns and classes fought over 'which should do the most honour.'[6] The *Times* would be amused and bemused by such 'excesses', but Alfred's ground-breaking voyage would become the template for royal visits reinforcing symbolic and sentimental ties, such as the 1901 visit of heir Prince George and wife Princess Mary to open the first Australian Parliament, and the visits of Queen Elizabeth and various princes and princesses every decade since, each evoking a sense of stability and security in a changing world.

But in the uncharted waters of 1867, there was little distinction between what was 'official' Royal or naval business, and what was 'private'. It wasn't even entirely clear how long Alfred would be on tour. The London correspondent of *The Age* wrote that the 'lucky sailor' may be on 'a three-years in and out pleasure cruise around the world'.[7]

Whatever the duration, the Queen saw the value of separating Alfred from Edward and the 'fast set'. 'I hope the responsibility and the separation from his London flatterers will do him good,' she told

Victoria.[8] She had no apparent concern about his safety at sea, or growing Irish resentment and restlessness, including an abortive Fenian attempt to seize Chester Castle in February and the imminent hanging of the 'Manchester martyrs' after an attempt to rescue two Irish Brotherhood members from imprisonment led to the death of a policeman.

So on a sunny June 11, 1867, *Galatea*, one of the finest vessels in the world, headed south-west from Gibraltar. Along with the crew of 540 men and boys, Alfred had some of his aristocratic equerries and friends: the Honourable Elliot Yorke, Lieutenant Arthur Haig of the Royal Engineers and Francis Charles Needham, Lord Newry. Twenty-five-year-old Newry was an Eton and Christ Church graduate whose middle-aged father scandalised Victorian society by his relationship with his 20-year-old ward, and building an underground tunnel between their two adjoining houses. The younger Newry was especially fond of sketched and photographic erotica.

Also in the Royal party was Oswald Brierley, the only one who had ever been to Australia, who would become marine painter to Queen Victoria after recording Alfred's historic voyage; Reverend John Milner as chaplain, and Dr James Young as staff surgeon. Alfred also had his own Scottish piper, and Jacko, a monkey who had his own formal naval papers with a rank of 'cook's chum' and duties as 'a general nuisance'.

From the familiarity and security of the Mediterranean, *Galatea* steamed into the uncertainty of the Atlantic, headed first for Rio de Janeiro and then Cape Town before steering east to Australia.

At Madeira Islands Alfred stocked up with sample vintages of the famous dessert wine popular with England's upper class, and in Rio he was knighted by the Emperor of Brazil with the insignia of the Southern Cross. In South Africa the Prince laid the foundation stone for the graving dock for the Royal Navy's ironclads, and laid low an old bull elephant nominated as a suitable royal trophy, hunted over several days with the aid of dogs.

The imprecision of the original plans for the voyage was underscored in Cape Town where Alfred received 'a most unwelcoming letter from the Admiralty telling me to remain away six months longer than was originally intended'. Alfred wrote to a close friend, the Duchess of Sutherland, saying he would seek a compromise to ensure he was home by August the next year, and that 'if you have a spare bedroom' he hoped to be invited to stay.[9]

It was only now that news of the Royal tour reached Australia by sea. On 10 July, four weeks after *Galatea* left Gibraltar, *The Age* reported, not entirely accurately, that 'the Duke of Edinburgh is about to proceed on a world cruise in *HMS Galatea*. After visiting the Cape, India, China and Japan, he will proceed to visit the Australian colonies'. The following day it said 'the date of his arrival cannot be fixed with anything like accuracy' but everyone should be ready to receive him by October, although the length of stay in various ports would depend on 'circumstances'.[10]

An earlier letter from the Admiralty, dated April 22, announced that the *Galatea* would 'proceed to the West Coast of Australia, and will visit Adelaide, Melbourne, Sydney, Brisbane, Hobart Town, Van Diemen's Land, and also Auckland and Wellington in New Zealand, and may probably proceed from thence to Tahiti, calling at Rio or St. Helena on his return to England via Cape Horn.'[11]

The vague detail, and apparently not appreciating Hobart Town was not a separate place to Van Diemen's Land, or that the name Tasmania had been formally in use for more than a decade, was a surprise to some, but most felt it 'not too early to prepare for giving the Queen's Son a right hearty welcome'.[12]

From Cape Town, *Galatea* set out on 2 October for Australia. The 6286 mile voyage of 29 days was marked by death: a sailor died from a fever contracted at Cape Town, a Maltese cook also died suddenly, and then Jacko, the monkey, fell overboard and drowned. Said the Prince: 'Poor little fellow. If I had been on deck I think I should have gone overboard after him: we shall never get another like him.'[13]

Perth made its preparations, including a welcome verse reassuring 'gallant' Alfred he was still in 'fatherland', but a stopover was abandoned, perhaps because of Naval nervousness about unrest from locals outraged that 62 Fenian political prisoners, including 17 alleged militants, were about to be despatched on a convict ship from Portsmouth to Western Australia.

Alfred's historic conquest of Australia began on 31 October at Glenelg, South Australia. From his earlier experiences in Mediterranean ports and Cape Town, the Prince would have fully expected some pomp and ceremony of local dignitaries and devoted citizens. And he knew some English newspapers, evoking Cook, Drake, Homer and Darwin, had admonished him to do something significant to benefit humanity by discovering an island or undertaking valuable research.

But Alfred would have anticipated that this farthest distance from the Mother Country was one where official fuss would be kept to a minimum, there was no grand challenge, and he could embrace an Antipodean good time of dining, drinking, gambling and shooting.

No one could anticipate, however, the desperation of the Empire's most far-flung people to demonstrate their loyalty and progress and ensure Britain continued to love and defend them, possibly under the leadership of Alfred if he became Lord High Admiral, or even the first King of Australia.

The prospect of a King of Australia had been raised as early as the 1850s. Victorian politician George Annand advocated a new kingdom with Melbourne as the capital, and Sir Charles Nicholson, a central player in the London circle of Australian colonists, said Prince Albert had told him 'direct' that Alfred would undertake a world cruise and visit Australia. When the prospect of a visit by Alfred was again mooted in the *Naval and Military Gazette* in London in the early 1860s, the *Melbourne Herald* argued the colonies could now afford royalty, with a million people and millions of pounds of revenue comparing favourably with European kingdoms like Belgium, Denmark, Holland and Greece. A Royal visit was seen as an opportunity to challenge the English view that Australians lived 'on the very outposts of civilisation with habits partaking as much of the Aborigines as those which belong to civilized life' and demonstrate that Australia was 'not one whit' behind anyone in England when it came to loyalty.[14]

Some did sense such a visit may have been primarily driven by Queen Victoria's dismay over some of Alfred's unroyal behaviour. Under the headline 'The Prince Alfred problem', the *Sydney Morning Herald* said jealousy of Edward's bride-elect Alix, 'whom he may have seen or admired as soon as, or even before the Prince of Wales', was a possible catalyst for the mooted trip, but it was 'far more within the bounds of probability that it was deemed advisable to get him out of the way, and draw off his mind from some little love affair of his own which was unsuitable to his rank and prospects. Her Majesty, being a lady of great good sense and prudence may have advised this course, just as for other reasons, also favoured the early marriage of the Prince of Wales'.

The *Herald* said the temptation for a Prince to become King with a Court of his own, with 'flatterers and fair ladies all in a row must be too much for the brain of any prince in his teens', and some in high quarters thought that becoming governor of Victoria would be 'a tolerably good bit of "holding ground" for Alfred for a season and try his hand at 'ruling', before taking on something more ambitious.[15]

John O'Shanassy, the St Patrick's Society president who had become Premier of Victoria and favoured monarchical institutions over 'petty ephemeral republics'[16] called for an 'invite (to) the sailor son of Her Majesty to become King of Australia',[17] residing in Melbourne as the capital of a new Australian kingdom.

'It is a fact', said the *Empire*, 'the project of creating a separate monarchy in Australia, and placing Prince Alfred on the throne, has been seriously discussed in very high quarters'.

He had been considered as King of Greece but 'how far more brilliant would be the prospects of an Australian kingdom!' with an alignment of youth in king and country. There was 'no great improbability in the supposition that if we asked for such a king to reign over us the request would be acceded to.' A new kingdom would unite the colonies, and the Imperial Government would furnish a fleet for Australia's defence. At some point, the *Empire* said, a decision had to be made 'between an Australian constitutional monarchy and an Australian republic. There is no blinking the question…is Australia to be a monarchy or a republic…we may rest assured that the people of the United Kingdom will have no desire to hold us in bondage whenever we want to set up in business for ourselves.'[18]

Now five years on, and Alfred's visit finally a reality, the desire to demonstrate loyalty to royalty, and showcase progress, was even more intense, and the prospect of Alfred on the throne of a new Australian kingdom was again seriously aired in London and Australia.

Adelaide wine pioneer and passionate advocate of free intercolonial trade, David Randall, argued the 'irritation, ill-will and jealousy' between the colonies was anomalous and costly to everyone. Citing the precedent of the confederation of the North American colonies, it was time to 'take advantage of the visit of HRH the Duke of Edinburgh and agitate for a confederation of the Australian colonies under Alfred as the Viceroy…of an Australian Empire.'[19]

A South Australian newspaper said if this occurred 'every member of that confederation would welcome the rule of our Sailor Prince'. He was a suitable and popular choice, and the people were 'monarchical to the backbone'. It was only a matter of time 'when the leading strings of Downing Street shall be cast aside', although colonial rivalries and jealousies had to be overcome, and 'separation from European Society is an immense drawback'.[20] In London an essay predicting Australia would follow Canada as an independent kingdom was reprinted in Australia. It was unnatural for thriving new colonies to be 'content to remain subject to a Government 15,000 miles away', but because of its dependence on the British Navy for defences, any separation of Australia from England had to be by negotiation not war.[21]

And *Echoes from the Clubs*, a journal for educated Englishmen, said England, 'questionless the greatest nation, not only of those now existing but of all that ever have existed' had a great opportunity to be magnanimous to its colonies: 'Nominally portions of the Empire, they really are quite independent. Were...Australia to desire severance from England tomorrow nobody would object. If a colony thinks it can govern by itself by all means let it try.'[22]

In Sydney, a 26-page pamphlet, 'A proposal for the confederation of the Australian colonies, with Prince Alfred, Duke of Edinburgh, as King of Australia', was produced. The pamphlet said 'sooner or later our severance from Imperial rule is inevitable' but in contrast to the recent American Civil War a monarchical solution to severance was available.[23] The timing of the severance argument was deemed by some officials as too 'seditious', however, and the pamphlet was suppressed.

But even among loyalists in England and Ireland there was acknowledgment that 'doubtless the time will come' when Australia, like Canada, would find itself 'strong enough to desire total independence...that independence would certainly not be sought unless an English Prince consented to wield the sceptre'.[24]

Now Alfred was on the doorstep. Some felt it time for Australian unity and Alfred to 'wield the sceptre', while others, lesser in number, felt the country could not be both republican and monarchical and should pursue the former. Republicanism was advocated by Reverend John Dunmore Lang and writers Charles Harpur and Daniel Deniehy. They distrusted a distant power and the colonial Tory class, or 'bunyip aristocracy'[25] as Deniehy termed it. After a tour of the United States in 1840 Lang warmed to Australia becoming 'a second America',[26] even contemplating an armed revolt in the wake of Eureka. He drafted a Declaration of Independence, saying the grievances of colonists in Australia were greater than those which American colonists had complained about before their declaration of independence.

But while republicans pressed for an independent government 'for the benefit of the people', Alfred would be under no illusion as to what the colonial establishment preferred. Among the welcoming transparencies and banners being prepared, one depicted the colony of Victoria, in female form, offering Alfred a crown with a verse 'welcome thou Royal Prince, Thy love to us to evince, Accept this Crown', another had soldiers and Aborigines hailing Alfred as King of Australia, another depicted allegorical figures of all the colonies under a 'federal union' crown atop Alfred's head.

Each colony and locality competed to show their loyalty to the Mother Country, which the majority still called 'home'. The *Times* declared that while many of the close to 'two millions of British subjects' had only heard of Royalty, 'the sentiment is in the blood, the bond cannot be broken.'[27] Colonists were deemed 'quite as British in taste, feeling and loyalty as the Britons who still live at home.'[28] Emotions swirled. There was gratitude for being so blessed as to have Queen Victoria send her Princely son to visit; a desire to demonstrate that distance did not diminish loyalty or Britishness; a fear of remoteness and losing British protection; nervousness about revolutionary unrest; a deep pride with progress but lingering embarrassment over criminal origins and social behaviour compared with the norms of London.

Some warned that royal fever risked colonists 'making arrant fools of themselves', as even those with little respect for colonial governors were intent on 'toadying and grovelling before the young sailor boy whose visit to Australia was expressly intended to be the means of instilling into his mind some little knowledge of the magnificent colonies over which at a future day it might be his fortune to rule'.

While Queen Victoria was 'much concerned about his welfare… should we kill him with kindness there will be no forgiveness'.[29]

But there would be no restraint. This was the proudest moment in the history of the country. Each city and town made plans for an endless number of triumphal arches, declarations of loyalty, parades, military salutes, foundation stones, balls, banquets, speeches, poems, songs, horse racing, regattas, cricket games, gold mining tours, pastoral visits, shooting parties, fireworks and Aboriginal corroborees.

No one having any idea of the itinerary or how long he might stay, each locality drew up a schedule which would keep a Prince fully occupied for weeks. All that was known apart from the Admiralty's advice about the ports of call was a circular-despatch from the Duke of Buckingham in Downing Street to the governors of the colonies, on 26 June.

> Sir—With reference to my despatch of the 1st of May, apprising you of the probability that H.M.S. Galatea, under the command of His Royal Highness the Duke of Edinburgh, would visit the colony under your government, I think it desirable that you should receive some instructions for your guidance as to His Royal Highness's reception. The Duke of Edinburgh, on his first arrival in a British colony or settlement, and on his final departure from it, but not upon other occasions, should have all the usual and proper honours paid to him by way of salutes, guards of honour, and other public marks of respect as a member of the Royal Family. His Royal Highness will receive addresses and make replies to them, and take part in public ceremonies in cases which are suggested or approved by the Governor or Lieutenant-Governor of the colony or settlement.[30]

Some had something much more than 'usual and proper honours' in mind. Rev. J.C. Symons told a Wesley College meeting he had heard that when the Duke of Edinburgh arrived 'it would be proposed to him that he should become the King of Australia, and if such a thing as that did happen and they obtained a monarch, much of the distinction between the different colonies would be forgotten—they would all be called Australia.'

Notwithstanding some high expectations, others recognised Alfred was a young Prince, and probably had his own personal agendas. 'He is but a youth, and as a paragraph in the last file of English papers plainly shows, he is still fond of enjoyment.' This alluded to reprinted reports hinting of the Royal pleasures at the Paris exposition, such as the ball where a spirited Alfred—'misguided youth!' did not leave until 4am.Others quoted foreign papers such as the *Cologne Gazette* describing Alfred as 'a magnet' for the ladies.

So with the varied hopes of his Queen and her colonies in train, the Sailor Prince prepared to take the first Royal step on Australian land in South Australia, the colony bursting with pride as the first to receive Royal blood. Alfred soon had a hint of the challenge of avoiding local fuss: the *Galate*a had barely arrived on a hot morning before local dignitaries unexpectedly began boarding the ship 'long before the visiting hours of polite society', including a delegation from Port Adelaide complaining it was not the landing site.

In the first official Australian welcome, the mayor of Glenelg, Edward Andrews, a newspaper proprietor, told Alfred: 'You will find a people free, enterprising, and self-reliant, who know how to combine independence of spirit with hearty, affectionate and unwavering loyalty to Her Majesty's person and Crown'. The first local newspaper report was favourable. 'The remark which has been so frequently applied to the royal family in general that their portraits never do them justice is specially true of the Duke of Edinburgh,' said the *South Australian Register*. It noted his well-formed face, a profile akin to the Greek type, his beautifully shaped eyebrows and 'the eyes are of the purest Teutonic blue.'

With unknowing prescience, it also noted that the 'Brunswick

Guelphs' were known for their strong nerve, and despite numerous and insane attempts at assassination 'they have never been known to lose their presence of mind...the same quality can be seen in (the) descendants'.

The *Register* correspondent said of the public's estimation: 'The impression...was obviously favourable. It could be read in the varied glances of admiration, concentrated upon him that his appearance far exceeded expectation...we might say that his face won every heart.'[31]

English newspaper correspondents filed less flattering reports. The welcoming decorations were criticised as 'sheer vulgarity', and the royal party would have 'some amusing stories to tell of life in the colonies when finally they return home.'[32]

But there was no doubt about the local sentiment. On a circuitous carriage journey into Adelaide Alfred passed through a village where settlers held a board stating in bold chalk letters, 'we love you for your mother'. Adelaide Mayor Henry Fuller said, in sentiments which Alfred would come to hear repeatedly:

> Though separated from Great Britain by many thousands of miles we have lost none of our attachment to the mother country, and have no doubt that the strong ties that unite so many dependencies to the British Crown will receive additional strength from this visit.

Alfred responded, as he would do countless times in the coming months:

> It will be my pleasing duty to communicate to the Queen the assurance of the strong attachment which exists towards your Sovereign and the mother country in this distant part of Her Majesty's dominions, where I feel certain that the affectionate ties which bind you to the 'Old Country' require no additional strength.[33]

Among the first 'levees', or royal walkabouts, even those who had reigned over the great southern land for centuries before European settlement were welcoming. At a trading station near the royal-sounding Lakes Albert and Alexandrina, 400 members of the Goolwa Aboriginal tribe greeted him under a red, white and blue banner with the inscription 'Goolwa blackfellow big one glad to see im Queen piccaninny'.[34]

As spokesman, teenager George Pantuni, described by the *Times* correspondent as a 'darkie', quietly told the Duke that while a corroboree demonstration was 'such as our fathers used to have before the white man came here', he did not wish him to think of them as wild blacks, because for seven years they had a Christian teacher and prayed every Sunday 'to the same God and hear of the same Jesus as your royal highness does'. They now prayed for God's blessing on the Queen and her children, and that He take care of Alfred 'until you see your mother's face in England again.'[35] The Prince watched Aboriginal men dancing with spears, boomerangs and waddies, before his highland piper responded with his bagpipes, much to the astonishment of the natives, who had never heard such music before.

But in a portent of some of the scandal to come, the *Sydney Empire* said it was regrettable that a proposition had been put to the Aboriginal women 'to strip and dance before the prince in a state of nudity'. The proposition was not taken up after the women made it clear they resented the proposal, one saying: 'what for me to do it more than white woman?'[36]

The Prince also enjoyed a torch-lit procession and German songs provided by the local German community, and in their language talked about being 'heir to a German throne'. Alfred was not enamoured of formal events, but colonial protocol provided some relief. After Alfred was invited at a state banquet to sip from a cup filled to the brim with local wine before it was passed on down the banquet table his friend Lord Newry sniffed: 'The colonials have a very hazy notion of protocol and precedence.'[37] And at least once Newry and Yorke were reported to be 'dissipated'. At the end of one dinner with a string of toasts and cheering for the Queen, the Prince of Wales, Princess of Wales, Duke of Edinburgh, the Mayor, Mayoress, Corporation of Adelaide, and the inhabitants of South Australia, some of the *Galatea* crew, now 'evidently beside themselves with joy and delight' threw their caps up towards the ceiling. Some of them obviously liked what they saw: police issued descriptions and reward of £1 for the apprehension of a dozen sailors who deserted.

More seriously, Edward Osbaldiston, a former Ballarat man who had previously worked for the South Australian governor and now worked as a footman, plundered Alfred's trunks containing about £7000 worth of jewellery. Police recovered a large amount at his house.

Fresh from shooting elephants in South Africa, Alfred was to do his own plundering around Australia. He began his hunting and shooting season with a moonlight excursion, killing 52 possums.

Whatever reception Adelaide had provided, or rival Sydney was planning, Melbourne, which had just overtaken Sydney as Australia's largest city, was determined to show its leadership in loyalty, civility and class. A determination which again irritated Alfred when over-eager dignitaries at Queenscliff, denied their own official reception, simply took matters into their own hands and sailed out to the *Galatea* in a pilot boat, whereupon the Prince ordered them off. On arriving at Port Melbourne he made the locals wait until the next day to welcome him, where he was reported to be still 'unsmiling'.

But Melbourne was smiling for him. Its population of 130,000 swelled to 230,000 for his arrival, the largest crowd ever seen in Australia. The colony 'has not known in her thirty years life a brighter day' and was quite beside itself as 'a Royal Prince, son of the greatest and noblest Queen that ever sat on the Throne of the British Empire, has landed on our shores'.[38]

This day, one newspaper declared, 'will forever be marked upon the Victorian calendar as one of the brightest red letter days…in the history of the colony…an epoch in the history of the times'.[39] And locals were reassured to see a friendly warship in their harbour. Four years before Melbourne was shocked when it woke to find *Bogatyr*, the flagship of the Russian Pacific squadron, in the bay as part of contingency plans to attack British naval ships should the American Union, which Russia backed, embark on war against Britain. And two years before an American Confederate ship, *Shenandoah*, docked for supplies and refitting in a break from capturing Union ships, and recruited some locals to help fight the 'Yankee' cause.

The Union Jack on a Royal Navy ship was a symbolic assurance of protection. Australia depended on England for security, but leaders also underscored the colonies' support of the Mother Country in its times of need. John Pascoe Fawkner reminded Alfred the colony had 'nobly' provided support in the Crimean War and Indian mutiny. 'The colonists have on several occasions shown their loyalty and affection for England, in addition to furnishing many millions of pounds worth of gold for aid in the war, they contributed largely to assist the sufferers, not only in their Indian rebellion but also in the cotton famine, by sending large sums of money to aid their suffering fellow countrymen.'[40] But the public mind was not military security. Melbourne was in a 'delirious state' with 'Duke fever a true epidemic', the *Times* correspondent said, something that would not be seen again unless Alfred 'shall come and be King of Australia.'[41]

Melbourne's illuminations, 'twenty times better than anything I ever saw in London' revived the notion of Alfred becoming ruler of Australia. Newspapers advertised tickets at up to £1 a seat for the best views to watch Alfred's arrival procession from newly erected grandstands, private rooms in Collins Street, hotels and even churches. Every window and balcony vantage point was full, every shopfront decorated. As church bells pealed and brass bands played, young girls threw flowers in his path, teary women waved handkerchiefs, and men waved their hats in scenes 'a man can only expect to see once in his life.'

> An immense stand was erected at the corner of the Town Hall, which was filled from top to bottom with ladies. The slope extending from Swanston St to Collins St to the Burke and Wills monument was reserved for the children of the public schools, who were assembled to the number of 11,000 for the purpose of singing the national anthem…the illumination of Fitzroy Gardens was splendid - there were 5000 lamps and 220 globes used…bonfires at Hawthorn, Kew, Woodend and Tarnagulla and on the principal hilltops around Melbourne…one of these bonfires contained 300 tons of wood and was visible for 30 miles.[42]

The Victorian Legislative Council's welcome, addressed to 'His Royal Highness Prince Alfred Ernest Albert, the Duke of Edinburgh, Knight of the Most Honourable Order of the Garter etc', congratulated him on his safe arrival in 'this most remote dependency of the British Empire, which has the honour of being named after Her Most Gracious Majesty the Queen', and assured him of 'our sincere loyalty, devotion and attachment to Her Majesty's throne and person'.

It was 'difficult to express the pleasure' of having one of Victoria's son's visit. For his part, Alfred said no response could adequately express the pleasure derived from 'the manifestations of loyalty and affection to the Queen (my mother).' He would never cease to rejoice that he had visited 'this distant portion of the Empire' and 'it will be most welcome to Her Majesty to hear that the country is so prosperous and happy; and I shall not fail to convey to Her Majesty the expressions of your loyalty and devotion'.[43]

But not all was affection and happiness. Irish tension and passion flared the next day after an Orange transparency bearing figures of William III crossing the Boyne with a figure of Britannia and motto 'these we will defend' appeared outside the Protestant Hall. Some protested at the provocation, throwing stones and threatening to destroy it. The next night a larger number abused the Orangemen and sang 'the wearing of the green'. One man called for the building to be burned, and more stones were hurled, whereupon shots were fired from the Hall, fatally wounding a 13-year-old boy, William Cross, and injuring two men.

Alfred was still at an official ball at 2am when news of the fatal incident came in 'with a report also that some Fenians were on the look-out to shoot the Prince. The authorities evidently entertained fears that something might happen, and took the precaution of providing an escort to attend the Prince from the ballroom to the Governor's house at Toorak.'

The *Galatea* diary was critical of the Protestant provocation, and said the shots were fired indiscriminately.

> Nobody can excuse the Orangemen for having...exhibited a party device which they knew would provoke retaliation... amongst the numerous causes which may have combined to produce Fenianism, it becomes a question of whether the constant irritation and annoyance inflicted on their enemies by Orangemen in the major celebrations of the "Battle of the Boyne" for the last 200 years have not had a much greater effect than all the other grievances – fancy or real – put together. It is scarcely possible to conceive that even less excitable people than the Roman Catholic population of Ireland would tamely submit to incessant taunts and most provokingly contrived devices and emblems to remind them of defeat and subjection.[44]

And while giving thanks to the Orange Institution in Victoria for its loyalty message, Alfred pointedly said:

> It must not be misunderstood as implying the belief that any one religious denomination is exclusively or pre-eminently imbued with that spirit of loyalty to her Majesty which I

> recognise with equal confidence and gratification in all her Majesty's subjects in this part of the empire.[45]

What Alfred and everyone else in Australia did not yet know of was an event which would be the genesis of untold consequences for all: the hanging of three Fenians in Manchester for their part in an ambush to free two Fenian leaders from a prison van which left a policeman dead. Known as the 'Manchester martyrs' their eloquent final speeches became the inspiration for *God Save Ireland*, which became Ireland's unofficial national anthem and inspiration for Irishmen wanting to make their mark against England.

While that news was still to reach Australia, the focus of Victoria turned to a plan, supported by the Governor's wife, Lady Georgiana Manners-Sutton, for a feast to ensure the poorer folk of Melbourne did not miss out on Royal festivities. *The Age* anticipated it would be surely 'the greatest event in the history of the colony' as the plan took on a life of its own with newspaper updates of the deliveries of copious amounts of bullocks, sheep, lambs, pigs, German sausage, bread, oysters, pies, puddings, tarts, cheese and cases of Bavarian beer, stout, ale, claret, port, champagne and colonial wine.

But by early morning it was clear the provisions of food and drink in the Zoological Reserve, and seating for 10,000 and space for another 10,000 spectators was clearly inadequate. By early morning what *The Age* described as 'the biggest assemblage of people there has ever been in Victoria' was evident, and by noon another 50,000 people, hungry and thirsty on a hot, dry, windy summer's day, were still making their way along the Yarra for a 'free guzzle' of wine and beer and a 'free feed'.

The banquet opening was delayed several times. People muttered about Royal punctuality, as officials vainly ordered the distribution of water and asked 100 concertinas and several bands to keep playing as tempers flared. Police Chief Frederick Standish galloped off to warn Alfred that he should stay away as the crowd 'upwards of 100,000, was so enormous, and the pressure so great, that there would be a great risk to life if the prince went into the grounds'.[46]

When it was confirmed Alfred would be a no-show, a 'bacchanalian picture of unbelievable horror' and 'a disgusting debauch' ensued. Barricades were toppled, tents for official guests levelled, food quickly consumed, and the pipes connecting a 500 gallon cask to the 'wine fountain' centrepiece were severed and the liquor liberally played over the crowd. Guards and mounted police were called in to send the remaining wine and beer away and persuade the crowd to go home.

Foundation ceremonies were more sober affairs as Alfred laid stones for various mechanics institutes, public and temperance halls, and the western stand at the Melbourne Cricket Ground, where the 'Natives of Australia' played 'The World' (another Royal no-show), but even these were not always incident free: after a foundation laying in Collingwood, a sudden and fierce storm erupted, killing a boy when a wall collapsed on him.

On his visits to regional centres, booming artillery often announced Alfred's arrival after carriage trips of up to 50 miles where trains were not available. In Ballarat he received a welcome address, and an inscribed plate of solid gold 9 inches wide and 7 inches deep. Forty thousand people seized every available rooftop, veranda, balcony and window to cheer and follow the official procession of various officials and grand orders of Odd Fellows, Foresters and Rechabites and a party of Chinese in fine ornamental gowns, who played whistle-pipes and tom-toms and waved fans; 'their almond eyes (opened) almost as if the son of the moon himself was making imperial progress through the flowery land'. Men raised their hats, women waved their white handkerchiefs and 'in the delicious ecstasy of their royal loyalty they threw flowers from balconies and galleries toward the Prince's carriage'.

Alfred and his companions Lord Newry and Elliot Yorke enjoyed the company of nearly 1000 women at the inauguration of a new Alfred Hall. While the *Ballarat Star* thought some of the women had a 'homeliness (which) highlighted the beauty of others', the colony could not supply a 'higher average of feminine good looks', while the 'general elegance of the toilets spread over all a republican equality of gaiety and grace'.

After an hour receiving dozens of guests and written addresses, Alfred bent his head to the ladies 'as if feeling that whole batteries were being discharged point-blank at short range upon him, as in sooth they were', and his demeanour 'no doubt won all the ladies hearts.'

Surely, the paper said, the whole spectacle of Ballarat's welcome would challenge the 'smart' writers of the *Saturday Review* in London who characterised Australia as a land of adventurers built on convictism.

Ballarat, built on the most celebrated gold mines in British possession, sourced the massive 150 pound 'Welcome Nugget' Alfred had seen at the Paris exposition. At the United Extended Band of Hope Mining Company, which had produced £620,000 pounds worth of gold in four years, Alfred was presented with some locally knitted socks and crafted fine patent leather boots, adorned with thistles, for the occasion.

After a 'slight refresher' of brandy and soda, Alfred entered a cage to be dropped by wire rope down a 400-foot shaft, lit by candles and gas, to where one of the horses permanently stabled underground dragged him in an iron wagon along an underground railway 1000 feet into the mine. After being quietly directed to look behind some boulders, the Prince picked away until, to no one's surprise, he found some gold-dirt. He enthusiastically kept digging alongside Lord Newry, and 'both amateur miners got rich dirt and pocketed every souvenir they could find'.[47]

The Royal party returned to the surface for more brandy and soda refreshers and for Alfred to receive a 22-ounce nugget, 'one of the finest specimens of gold ever found in the colony', one of many he would pocket on various gold mine visits. He later had a ring made from the Hope mine gold to add to his penchant for wearing as many as 11 rings, large massive gold affairs, 'so thick that he could not close his fingers, making his hands...like the fins of a turtle'.[48]

While miners, especially Irish, had agitated in the 1854 Eureka Stockade about colonial administrative tyranny, Mayor Emmanuel Steinfeld told Alfred at a banquet he was among 'people enjoying every political freedom, inhabiting a land flowing with milk and honey.'

But the mayor lamented the country was still seen as a last resort for migrants from Europe. This undoubtedly stemmed from 'deep rooted prejudices' in the mother country, but surely the royal visit would prove Australia to be prospering and progressing in every sphere, 'a true British and loyal community (cheers)...in the matter of loyalty, second to none in the world (immense cheering).'[49] After a rousing rendition of Rule Britannia, Alfred acknowledged the 'immense progress made in such a short time'.[50]

After staying at a ball until 1am, enjoying 24 sets of the quadrilles, polkas, reels and gallops with fashionable young ladies showcasing their fine silk gowns with low and off-the-shoulder necklines, Alfred boarded a special two-and-a-half-hour train to return to Melbourne, but not before telling Elliot Yorke to anoint a local firm as 'royal coachbuilders to His Royal Highness at Ballarat', and arrange to have the carriage shipped back to England.

He said he would like to return to enjoy himself privately at the races, and on Friday 20 December he arrived to attend the Ballarat Turf Club meeting at Dowling Forest. After 45 minutes of refreshments at Craig's Hotel Alfred was off to the races attired in morning costume and white hat, cigar in mouth, whipping four greys in a reminder of old Derby days.

A 'royal flush' in one race netted him £350, and after a dusty 10 mile ride back to the railway station, full of 'ladies, of all ages, sizes, and conditions, anxious, no doubt, to catch a 'last fond look' at the Sailor Prince', his train was delayed while 'bottles and other comfortable things were passed into the carriages'.

A visit to Bendigo did not end so well. During a torchlight parade, an exuberant crowd tossed fireworks onto a float featuring a wooden mock-up of *Galatea*. In the ensuing fire, several children, who had been manning the ship's deck, screamed as they tried to escape with their clothes alight, but one died on arrival at hospital and two others soon after.

And just as the royal party was about to enter a grand ball in a vast temporary hall of corrugated iron and timber, erected alongside the Town Hall, there was a cry of 'fire!' and in 15 minutes the richly decorated venue was 'a scene of charred rafters and pools of water'.[51]

As tragic as such events were, Alfred was not one to compensate by providing more royal presence. He found protocol tedious and often spurned welcoming officials. Dressed constantly in his shooting attire, he ordered his carriage to drive straight through Colac, ignored crowds at Mortlake who had waited four hours in the heat, paused at Camperdown only long enough to 'smirk' at the local greeting, and bypassed a welcoming group at Terang.

He was more enthusiastic and punctual when it came to the pleasures of gambling, dancing and shooting. Accompanied by his personal shooting aide, John Smith, formerly Queen Victoria's coachman, Alfred took every opportunity to take royal aim at Australia's wildlife and birdlife. Even a black swan was not safe.

At the estate of squatter Tom Austin at Barwon Park, near Winchelsea, south-west of Melbourne, the Royal party enjoyed 'excellent rabbit shooting' killing upwards of 1000 in less than four hours, 416 by Alfred himself. Austin had imported 24 rabbits in 1859 to breed as game for shooting parties, but the animal quickly bred its way into a national pest, such that in the year of Alfred's visit Austin recorded a kill tally of 14,000 of the 'underground mutton'. A few days later, at a squatter property at Mortlake surrounded by 500 miles of fencing, the Prince and 200 horsemen rode 12 miles to drive 35 kangaroos, both 'old boomers' and 'infantile joeys',[52] into a five acre enclosure surrounded by a high fence of bush timber and trees, where 'the Duke and his party took up a position inside with their rifles, whilst some horsemen, with stockwhips, and boys on foot, drove the animals backwards and forwards in front of the guns, where they were shot down.'[53]

Some of the royal culling found its way onto Alfred's plate. Accompanied by French and local wine, Alfred dined out on kangaroo tail soup, turtle soup, wallaby pie and emu egg omelettes.

But as much as the colony's fauna and culinary fare was pursued in regional Victoria, the feminine fare of Melbourne was also in royal sights.

Punch newspaper accurately foreshadowed what was to come in a spoof Royal letter to Australia:

> Mother wants me to see the world. She says I have been at home, dangling at her apron-strings long enough, and I don't say that she is wrong, mother rarely is...I am told there is plenty of fun to be got on your side. Lots of stunning girls, I hear. Well, you know, I am not fixed yet, so your squatters and gold-diggers' pretty daughters had better look out. You know the girls are always partial to a sailor chap, all the world over.[54]

6
ROYAL DEBAUCHERY

There will be rare food for scandal for many a day after his departure, I suspect.
— Curtis Candler

Alfred was not the first aristocrat to make his way to Australia. Many young sons were despatched by their parents, often to escape debts, debauchery or expensive mistresses. Lord Alfred Churchill, son of the Duke of Marlborough, arrived in a private yacht with a hold full of shoes and boots to sell. Lord Robert Cecil, the Marquis of Salisbury and future British Prime Minister, visited for 'health reasons'.

But a son of Queen Victoria was something else—if Alfred 'was not a king, or in prospect', the *Age* said, 'he was the next best thing to it, and so loyal people paid him due respect, flunkies thrust themselves upon him and ladies adored him.'[1]

Melbourne, and its ladies, did not suffer by comparison with London and Paris. The most prosperous city in Australia, well on its way to becoming the second biggest city in the British Empire, offered a full menu for any visiting 'gentleman' who enjoyed the good or fast life, and Alfred's reputation preceded him.

Painted transparencies were readied, showing buxom Antipodean maidens welcoming Alfred to Melbourne. Curtis Candler, the town coroner and Melbourne Club member, wrote in his diary that it was known Alfred had 'many of his family's tenderness as regards the sex' so his visit, caused 'a great flutter in the bosom of society' and in the *demi-monde*.

Society women were 'tremendous with expectation. Our duchesses are dying to yield', most 'eager' to evidence the Scriptural behest about 'shall love a stranger'.[2] And they were well prepared: the women of Melbourne 'fell to demanding at any price instruction in Scotch reels' after it was reported the Prince had danced a Scotch reel with a woman at Cape Town.

Locals went 'wild with delight…it was a season of unrestrained license – a perfect saturnalia' and while the Prince was but a youth he 'proved he could hold his own with the revellers' as balls and parties became the of order of day and night, and 'staid and hitherto decorous women neglected their households, and, it was said, forgot their wifely duties in their anxiety to bask in the sunshine of Royalty's favours'.

And the *demi-monde* of high-class brothels and 600 prostitutes was ready to sate Alfred's desires after a long period at sea. One, Annie McDonald, a handsome woman, responded to the call by Sir Redmond Barry, the colony's first Supreme Court judge and head of the Royal Reception Committee, for public bodies to send in applications to participate in the royal welcome procession. From her brothel in Stephen Street (now Exhibition Street), McDonald told Barry that:

> …as a public body of long standing, I shall be pleased to take part in the procession. Should enquiry as to

> my qualification be necessary, particulars can easily be ascertained. As your Honour is doubtless aware, I can also refer as to my capabilities as a public body to numerous well-known citizens, whose names, for obvious reasons, I cannot mention in this connection.

She offered to furnish any other information 'on personal application'.[3]

Candler, who also lived at the exclusive Melbourne Club, presciently diarised: 'There will be rare food for scandal for many a day after his departure, I suspect.'

It didn't take long before food was on the table. The day after *Galatea* arrived, Alfred's advance party of Lord Newry and Elliot Yorke dined with police commissioner Captain Frederick Standish at the Melbourne Club. The Collins Street club was founded in 1838, designed as 'a club on London principles amongst the gentlemen of Melbourne', a haven for wealthy squatters, judges, merchants and civil servants to engage in the gentlemanly pursuits of cards, drinking, dining and billiards. Over cigars in the smoking room they could openly discuss business, politics and the stage, any subject which 'came on the carpet' in Candler's words, including 'horizontal refreshment'.

Standish was a police chief and chief player, moving 'easily from the official world to that of the demi-monde.' The son of a Whig 'dandy' and chum of George IV, he enjoyed life around the clubs and theatres of London, dining, dancing and gambling before debts forced him to take an assumed name and escape to Australia.

He unsuccessfully tried gold prospecting, ginger beer making and sly grog trading before he was appointed Assistant Commissioner of the goldfields in Sandhurst (now Bendigo). Six years after his arrival he became the colony's police chief. He made his home at the Melbourne Club, where he served on the wine committee and shared the good life with lawyers like Butler Cole Aspinall and his patron, Judge Redmond Barry, who had prospered and become Victoria's first Solicitor-General despite being confined to his cabin on his voyage to Australia because the captain did not approve of his unconcealed love affair with a married woman passenger.

Overseeing the *demi-monde* 'in the Parisian manner', as a former Melbourne *Punch* editor described it, Captain Standish was 'furnished with a report every morning of the number and the names of those who have spent the night in the better class of brothels… calculated to lift the veil from the secret immoralities of many of the outwardly moral and respectable'.

Standish ensured gentlemen were suitably entertained and their reputations protected. That could be challenging, as when a naked solicitor-general had to be saved after he presented a cheque which was dishonoured and a brothel 'took away his clothes and he was a prisoner for 2 or 3 days until a brother barrister sent in a suit and released him'.[4]

Whenever a court appearance was unavoidable, Captain Standish called in fellow Melbourne Club member and player Butler Aspinall to secure a legal escape. Sometimes the police chief was host. At a later parliamentary committee inquiry, evidence was given that Standish gave a dinner 'at which the women present were naked and their chairs covered in black velvet, the better to show off the whiteness of their skin'.[5]

Standish was seen as the ideal 'bear leader' to the 'royal cub'. After an introductory briefing at the Melbourne Club, he took Alfred's colleagues to the nearby house of Mother Fraser. Like the finest Parisian madams, she provided comfortable carriages for her nymphs to shop for fashionable clothing in Collins Street so they stood out at the Theatre Royal, especially its popular Saddling Paddock bar, and the Casino de Venise in Bourke Street, seducing clients to her 40-room establishment of finely carved furniture, plush carpets, bronze and marble statues, silk hangings and gold mirrors.

Reclining on couches which 'embraced you with their seductive softness and elegant ease', clients' senses were roused by French wine, fresh flowers, fruit and oils so they were 'breathing…an aroma of luxury and love' while they considered the female menu. Mother

Fraser forewarned her regular clientele the establishment would be closed to them until the Prince and his party had departed.

To the despair of those knowing what Queen Victoria would have wished the Royal party quickly became the talk of the town, although mostly in whispers and in the politest of ways. Her Majesty's Governor in Victoria, Sir John Manners-Sutton, grandson of an Archbishop of Canterbury, and his wife, were especially anxious that Alfred keep early hours and good company. They made their Toorak house pleasant in the evenings and retired early, imagining, or hoping, the Prince and his party would do likewise.

But when what the Royal party irreverently called the 'old woman' and 'scruffy old bloke' were believed to be sound asleep, Alfred and company 'took flight to Melbourne where Captain Standish and some other choice spirits would point out the bye-ways of Melbourne by night', returning 'with the early milk and the morning papers'.

The Governor complained to Standish that 'His Royal Highness prefers your society' to which the police chief replied: 'Well Sir John, I really can't help his want of taste.' Lady Manners-Sutton thought Alfred 'a very thoughtless young man'[6] and the Bishop of Melbourne 'looked grave' at his language at one Royal dinner. Some of the 'staid old fogies' of the Melbourne Club also complained about the revelry as the night houses in Stephen Street 'had their share of patronage'. Annie McDonald did not succeed in her 'public body' bid to join Alfred's welcome procession, but had many 'interviews' before he left, and Candler referred to her as 'Lady Annie McDonald'.

On Alfred's first visit at the house of Mother Fraser he immediately went upstairs to join Sarah Saqui, 'a handsome Jewess in the prime of her life'. He spent an hour with her while his friends enjoyed generous amounts of 'fizz' with the other women and enthusiastically sang *God Save the Queen*. When the Prince came down, somebody asked Mother Fraser for the bill, and she replied 'Fifteen pounds'.

Saqui, sometimes referred to in the press as Pysche, was the daughter of an eminent London Jewish singer and musician, Isaac Saqui, and niece of Austin Saqui, a bookmaker and Melbourne Cup winning owner. She sometimes performed in music halls, known as 'the Divine Sarah' with 'a good voice and winning manners' but gained greater fame as the 'official wife' of the Duke of Edinburgh.

Alfred made himself quite at home at the house of Fraser, and enjoyed Saqui's company in private theatre boxes. The diaries of Captain Standish and Curtis Candler made frequent references to Ducal 'jolly' evenings ending 'at chez Sarah.' So much so that some men stole a coach builder's signboard proclaiming 'by appointment to his Royal Highness the Duke of Edinburgh' and nailed it over the door of the brothel.

What became famous as 'the Duke's Bed' became one of Mother Fraser's treasures. She adorned it with the Royal coat of arms and legend 'under the patronage of HRH the Duke of Edinburgh' and an inscribed motto, *honi soit qui mal ye pense* (Shame on him who thinks ill of it), the motto of the Noble Order of the Garter of the Queen and Princes Albert, Edward and Alfred. The bed, 'a relic of royal debauchery' in which 'the Duke of Edinburgh had dailies with Sarah Saqui' became the prime auction item in one of the best-advertised auctions ever held in Australia when Fraser died. The auctioneer sold the 'bedstead and bed, with the Royal coat of harms (sic), what the Dook and Sarah Saqui slept on'.

Respectable citizens were disgusted with Alfred's conduct and his public behaviour toward several women, including with the wife of a municipal magistrate, and 'left him in the hands of Captain Standish and his friends…When the royal lecher could not be found at other haunts those who wanted him could easily run him down at Mother Fraser's, or at another quiet cottage near the Carlton Gardens, where lodged an eminent London actress – of foreign extraction – who was said to keep in concealment for the Duke's especial gratification a certain little "dainty dish"'.[7]

The actress indignantly denied Royal company, and the Carlton cottage tenant, an alleged madam, also denied the Royal standard flew over her house. But when the actress left Melbourne Alfred was reported to have gone on board and remained until her steamer sailed. And in an 1875 court case a woman police described as a veteran brothel-keeper and prostitute said some of the Carlton cottage rooms had been hired by Alfred.

Under Standish's influence, Mrs Fraser's house and the Casino de Venise, co-owned by bookmaker Joe Thompson, whose 'Don Juan House' in East Melbourne had a dance room with mirrors from floor to ceiling, operated with virtual impunity. At the Casino, Candler saw what he said 'had a suspicious resemblance to pimping', saying someone, whose name he withheld, 'should be appointed by His Excellency Pimp in Ordinary to HRH.' Alfred could also safely spend 'many afternoons at the sergeant's cockpit', enjoying a punt at cock-fighting held at Richmond police depot.[8]

Newspapers openly described women such as Psyche, La Bella and Incognita as a 'member of the *demi-monde*' or as 'distinguished members of the *demi-monde*', when they joined the Royal party in private boxes at the theatre, masked balls and opera.

One opera evening featured Madame Celine Celeste, a French actress and dancer, who received Alfred's 'marked attention…and then his authorisation for her farewell performances in England to be under his special patronage.'[9] The Royal box included several guests in disguise, including Alfred's newly befriended bookmaker Joe Thompson. When Captain Standish was asked by Candler what had happened one Saturday night, 'or Sunday morning rather, after I went to bed…he disposed to draw a veil over proceedings. He was very mysterious from which I suggest the trio, the Duke, Yorke and himself had rather a fast night of it. It was whispered about that the Prince went on board the *Galatea* with the milk.'[10]

Alfred was the first notable victim of Marcus Clarke, who had just begun a newspaper stint as the 'Peripatetic Philosopher'.

In barely disguised terms, he referred to Alfred's relationship with bookmaker and Royal 'gamekeeper' Thompson: 'Joseph Thompson and a D-st-ng-h-d P-rs-n-ge…will represent Cupid and Pysche' at a ball. Cupid and Psyche was perhaps a knowing Clarke nod to a famous painting of nudes by Thomas Uwin, one of many which Queen Victoria presented to Albert.

Clarke wrote that it appeared 'the Sailor Prince follows the example of most sailors, and likes to have a fling on shore. Someone was telling me the other day that being tired of the conventionalities of Government House, he had suggested the propriety of a private residence for himself and suite nearer Melbourne. As Joe says to Pip, wot larks!' Yorke was also reported to have asked for a private key to the Bishop's residence at Bishopscourt in East Melbourne.

The following month Clarke wrote that 'scandal has been rife but it has been scandal of a kind that I should regret to be the means of propagating'.[11]

Alfred's preference for pleasure over propriety had been foreshadowed in London the previous year when American humourist Charles Farrar Browne, a favourite of Abraham Lincoln, asked him how he liked being a Prince. Using the nom de plume Artemus Ward, he wrote the response was:

> To speak plain, Mister ward, I don't much like it. I'm sick of all this bowin' and scrapin', and crawlin' and hurrain' over a boy like me…When the people cheer me I feel pleased for I know they mean it.

But if the

> one-horse offishuls could know I see threw all their moves, and knew how he larft at 'em in private, they'd stop kissing my hands and fawning over me as they do now…but I can't help bein' a prince. I would rather go through the country with the other boys and not be made a show of and be gaped at by everybody, and enjoy myself in my own way.[12]

Alfred could not help 'bein' a prince', and he was intent on enjoying himself in his own way, even at official events. At the Governor's Ball he enthusiastically engaged in the dancing, one saying he 'shouted just like any other wild Scotchman', and came on like a 'Bounding Brother.'[13]

One of the biggest society highlights was a fancy dress ball at the new Exhibition Building, which the previous year had staged the international exhibition of Australasia to promote colonial unity. Among the 3000 men and women who paid two guineas and one guinea respectively to raise funds to extend the Sailor's Home were 'wives and daughters and…young ladies who tell plainly enough by their eyes that they hope to see the Prince soon, and they are all arrayed with elegance, some of them with something more than elegance'.

Guests dressed queens, rajahs, dames, devils, shepherds, priests, priestesses, monks, Roman warriors, Maori chiefs, matadors, pirates, peasants, soldiers and even famous royal assassins. The disguises allowed a 'cardinal' to stalk a young lady 'whose femininity could not be hid by the gracefully disposed barrister's wig and gown', while Neptune 'flirted with flower girls' and Amphitrite made 'obtrusive demonstrations' towards a young middy.[14]

Alfred, dressed in royal blue Post Captain uniform, left about 1.30am but quietly returned in the disguise of a monk, one of 33 at the ball, to enjoy himself even more.

The prince so enjoyed his time in Melbourne that a scheduled 12-day stay in Victoria became six weeks, but it was time to leave. He did so, as in Paris, 'fully feted', and made clear his gratitude to Captain Standish, giving him a signed photograph and a horse shoe scarf ring of amethysts and emeralds. He was, said Standish, 'most kind and flattering in a final interview, and parting with him was painful'. Alfred, in addition to a ring on every finger, was also seen wearing a new gold bracelet, 'probably gage d'amour',[15] and had a keepsake collection of water-coloured photographs of beautiful Victorian women, taken by Melbourne's leading carte de visite portrait firm.

On board *Galatea,* Curtis Candler saw Yorke's cabin full of photographs, prints and paintings 'of a suggestive character', and Newry had a collection of photographs and sketches of 'some pretty girls, a few whores' from the Royal tour. One girl he had photographed and drawn several times, explaining she was 'his "muffin", a term I had never heard applied before.'

There were also 'drawings of women in naval uniform' and one sketch of 'how some of the Galateans 'man their yards', showing miniature women sitting atop pornographically outsized male organs. And Alfred was taking more than memories with him. 'Psyche', who had kept him close company, 'leaves Melbourne for Sydney when the Duke goes there, so I presume her fortune is made'.[16]

Alfred's behaviour would not have amused Queen Victoria, now again fretting over a French-style revolution if the upper classes of England did not cease to be 'frivolous, pleasure-seeking and immoral'.[17]

And it had not amused many in Melbourne. Just a day after his departure for a brief visit to Tasmania en route to Sydney, the *Age* was pointedly critical. 'We would ask the wise and experienced gentleman of the reception committee whether they would like their sons at the age of 23 to be exposed to dissipation and the temptation to which they have treated the Queen's son during his six weeks stay.' As for Lord Newry and Elliott Yorke, 'neither has elevated the youthful aristocracy of England in the estimation of colonists and the prince had been much better destitute of their company'.

It would be forever regretted that Alfred was not accompanied by 'a sage and mature mentor'. His Highness would henceforth have 'a peculiar interest' for Victorians, who might say 'put not your trust in princes' as his behaviour had 'helped considerably to unprince him'.[18]

Other papers said the 'royal wanderer and his followers enjoyed themselves immensely, if in many ways that Mrs Grundy would not consider quite consistent in the son of such a pattern monarch as Queen Victoria', referring to a well-known fictional character who epitomised propriety and moral behaviour.[19]

In London, blissfully unaware of what was transpiring, *Punch* published a letter from 'Britannia to Australia', in which the Mother Country asked for 'my young salt of a duke' to be sent home when he had had enough of boomerangs, whoops, waddies and corroborees, 'unless you determine to place him on a thrown of your own virgin gold as Australia's first king and be, perhaps, the second Alfred the Great'.[20]

But the prospects of King Alfred of Australia were diminished by his Melbourne visit. 'Our brief dream of royalty is ended', an *Australasian* editorial declared. Alfred, 'a hearty, sailor-like, good-humoured young man' was 'too young' to grasp the true ideal of his tour, and 'too careless' to observe the proprieties of the society he had left. If it was intended that Australia perhaps become a less antagonistic republic than North America, it was 'a grave mistake' in failing to send a suitable mentor. 'If it was intended by this visit to have a Royal Court established in their midst, the choice of courtiers was, to say the least of it, unfortunate.' Alfred had 'amused us' but not impressed with his capacity to rule, his determination to tolerate Royal duties and had 'failed lamentably' the kingly virtue of punctuality.

'Our colonial youth are not backward in what…is termed "fastness", but we believe they might take lessons…from these scions of British aristocracy. With these for our noblemen…who would be our noble women!'[21] A weekly journal later said Alfred's 'record of immorality has even put in the shade the achievements in the same direction of other members of the Royal Family.'[22]

The local *Punch* newspaper published a cartoon depicting a gushing visitor saying to a female friend: 'Oh! Fanny dear, I have come on purpose to hear you play that delightful *Galatea* waltz', to which the Lady of the House replies: 'Yes, certainly dear; but, but, you see, the, the fact is, my piano has gone to be repaired!' and under another headline 'Singular Omission', it reported that 'up to the time of going to press, there has not been the slightest mention of the appointment of a purveyor of muffins to HRH the Duke of Edinburgh'.[23]

Even some of those who had enjoyed Royal patronage complained they had been short-changed. Even Sarah Saqui and Mother Fraser: for a time eminently proud of the Duke's patronage, 'when the glamour had worn off Sarah said he was the meanest man she had ever encountered and Mrs Fraser was in accord: he used her house, he used her cellar, he used her people, but he never paid—he "bilked" her for everything'.[24]

After Alfred had hired one of Melbourne's three hansom cabs to transport him to and from the Melbourne Club, the frustrated carriage operator remained on the club front door until he was paid; prominent artist Nicholas Chevalier, whose work was the first Australian painting obtained for the new National Gallery of Victoria, was invited on the *Galatea* for its cruise to Tasmania and produced numerous water colour drawings for the Prince but received nothing more than 'a health invigorating trip', and the bill for sending to England the Ballarat carriage and other souvenirs was sent to the Colonial Government.

Reports of Alfred's behaviour eventually reached London. *Reynolds's Newspaper* said that despite the vast royal and naval expense, Alfred's mission to popularise royalty and cement ties to the mother country had 'entirely and signally failed', and his visit had 'precisely the opposite effect to that contemplated by his mother.' He had been capricious, discourteous, haughty, indifferent and insolent in Melbourne. He had 'grievously offended' people, welcomed with showers of bouquets but farewelled with brickbats. A Melbourne writer told the paper's London readers that if a poll had been taken on his arrival Prince Alfred 'would have been proclaimed King of the Australias', but the public mood had since changed considerably.

'Young men will be young men' he wrote, 'and I suppose princes have wild oats to sow as well as ordinary mortals.'[25]

Alfred's reputation had preceded him and was underscored in Melbourne where newspapers and journals slated his 'record of immorality' by 'casting a glamour over the most degrading forms of sexual excess'[26] a 'Royal rascal and roué' who 'showed himself to be a disgrace to the name and fame of England.'[27]

The Royal tour, at barely the halfway mark, was already memorable. But there was much more to come.

7

GODLY DELUSION

Tormented this nine months by various troubles…my earnest desire now is to find the peace the Church of God alone can give me.
— Henry O'Farrell

The start of 1867 did not bode well for Henry O'Farrell. He had lost his path to priesthood, his father, his brother to self-imposed exile and much of his money.

According to *the Ballarat Star*, he had become 'greatly embarrassed' by the way his life had turned out. Drinking and brooding, he was suffering bouts of delirium tremens, a nervous disorder resulting from the withdrawal of stimulants such as alcohol, known by some doctors as 'brain fever' and said by some to produce 'mania'.[1] In January, his sisters Caroline and Catherine were alerted after he had a severe attack of delirium tremens. They rushed to

Ballarat to see their brother being attended by two doctors and a chemist. Caroline said Henry was in bed and did not know her for several minutes and covered his head whenever Catherine neared.

One Ballarat correspondent said O'Farrell attacked or threatened his two sisters, but a friend's intervention saved them from injury. 'They told my informant that he had to their knowledge been in the habit of keeping a pistol secreted. While his friend stayed with him and his sisters, O'Farrell searched every drawer in the room, as if looking for this pistol.'[2] His sister said one day she saw him looking at some pistols saying he would shoot himself.

Caroline observed her brother 'cried very much...could not sit still...was very restless, very excitable', especially on the losses sustained on the departure of brother Peter. In his bouts of drunken delirium Henry talked of plots against him, and variously claimed he had been 'poisoned' by an old woman in the oyster saloon, a chemist and doctors.[3]

Dr William Whitcombe noted 'sundry eccentricities over several years in his conduct.'[4] One night he was found walking 'in a half nude state'[5] and was known for boasting of maintaining his vows of celibacy, spending days without eating, and travelling 24 miles to sit alone for hours on Mount Buninyong.

He began to suffer epileptic fits. One time Dr William Heisse gave him up, and he received the last sacraments of the church.

O'Farrell had always carried his 5 foot 10 inch frame quite upright, with dark brown hair and a clean-shaved face. But now he was showing signs of decline, gaunt and often florid with a wispy beard and thinning hair.

In early 1867 Dr Whitcombe attended him after a severe attack of delirium tremens, and two months later he had seen him several times in Ballarat Hospital 'suffering from dementia'. But Dr Whitcombe did not believe O'Farrell's issues were due to delirium tremens, 'nor, as far as I could learn, from the effects of drink in any of its forms.' He sensed something more sinister. 'I recommended that he should be placed under restraint, as not being a man who was safe to be at large.'[6]

Doctors and police were frequently called when he became agitated and threatened violence. A Ballarat police superintendent later wrote a memo, saying he knew O'Farrell drank heavily, was subject to bouts of delirium, and once asked for a pair of pistols 'to blow his brains out'.[7]

Unable to repay debts and issuing dishonoured cheques of as little as £8, Supreme Court action by the Colonial Bank of Australasia led the sheriff to hold a public auction on March 23 of O'Farrell's remaining assets of hay, oats, bran, pollard, potatoes, weighing machine, crushing machine, horse, cart, harness and furniture. The sale realised £60, about a tenth of his reported debt.

On the same day, O'Farrell was admitted to Ballarat Hospital, where he remained for two weeks. Despite being put 'under the restraint of a strait waistcoat' several times[8] the hospital discharged him: 'H. J. O'Farrell, merchant, aged 24 (this age was given by himself but it is thought he was much older), native of Dublin, admitted 23 March 1867, suffering from delirium, discharged 5 April 1867, cured.'[9]

It was not so much he had been 'cured'—resident surgeon Dr William Owen said in his opinion O'Farrell was 'a much fitter subject for a lunatic asylum than for a hospital'[10]—than the fact the hospital did not have the resources to care for mental patients , especially one who was agitated and frequently incoherent. One correspondent wrote of him being 'the terror of the neighbourhood' and said Dr George Butler had pronounced he was 'bordering on madness.'

When Henry turned up at Caroline's house in Melbourne at 4am he had no idea of the preceding weeks, or his previous visits. By now his sister would not allow Henry to go out with her children or go out with him alone: 'I considered him to be unsound in his intellect, that he was mad'.[11]

Several people later claimed they had told police of their concerns for O'Farrell, fearful of what he might do, but most didn't pay too much heed to a man described by some as evidencing 'excessive nervousness and timidity.' One explained:

> When in the least excited his hands would tremble violently, and he appeared to be a man so feeble of purpose and naturally so timid of character that the conclusion come to was that he had not hardihood enough to commit an act of violence – and that he was a mere talking windbag, whose words or threats were hardly worth serious notice.[12]

Feeble and timid to some, unsound and dangerous to others, O'Farrell's mind was clearly in ferment. He more openly declared support for the Irish cause and resentment of English oppression, and began to reconsider his distance from the Catholic Church.

His distress coincided with local reports of an imminent Fenian outbreak in Ireland. The *Times* said the prospect of an Irish rebellion had to be 'stamped out' just as if it were an agrarian plague, 'by slaughtering the cattle'; the *London News* said England had to put down with a 'relentless hand' any uprising or seditious movement; the *London Telegraph* said an 'iron heel' was required.[13] While the sentiments were readily amplified by the colonies' pro-English authorities and newspapers, local Irish support for the cause hardened with a more passionate voice at the *Freeman's Journal*. New editor Richard O'Sullivan was a younger brother of the O'Sullivans who owned and edited the aggressively nationalist Dublin newspaper *The Nation*. In his first editorial, O'Sullivan said:

> This is not the first time Ireland has arisen in rebellion and should she be defeated it most assuredly won't be the last... just and honourable men who will inquire why the Irish have flung down the gage to mighty England can learn their motive and learning them will not fail to respect and honour patriotism.[14]

O'Farrell, Irish-born and raised in the St Patrick's Hall fraternity, 'the cradle of liberty in Victoria,'[15] declared himself a partisan of Fenian leader James Stephens, founder of the Irish Revolutionary (later Republican) Brotherhood, who asked his supporters to swear an oath that

> …in the presence of Almighty God, that I will do my utmost, at every risk, while life lasts, to make Ireland an independent Democratic Republic; that I will yield implicit obedience, in all things not contrary to the law of God to the commands of my superior officers; and that I shall preserve inviolable secrecy regarding all the transactions of this secret society that may be confided in me. So help me God! Amen.

O'Farrell defended and advocated the Fenian cause, telling some anti-Fenians that 'monarchies were the curse of Ireland, and that the only proper form of government was a republic'.[16] Despite not becoming a priest, and being described by long-term Ballarat residents as a 'nominal Catholic'[17] he wrote in April to Dr Laurence Bonaventure Shiel, the Bishop of Adelaide, who he knew from his priest training at St Francis in Melbourne and when Shiel was Archdeacon in Ballarat.

He wrote: 'I have been vacillating a long time, so long that I almost despaired of ever summoning resolution enough to follow the good advice you gave me at our last interview.[18] He recalled that Dr Geoghegan, his former St Francis priest, had once 'reminded me of the orders I had received and kindly asked me to accompany him to Adelaide' when he became Bishop of Adelaide in 1858, but at the time he had refused due to as 'personal antipathy'.

'Now I am in a very different state of mind,' he told Dr Shiel.

> Tormented this nine months by various troubles – losses in business, in mining speculations, then my partner's awful death, and above all troubled by thoughts of my anomalous position – my earnest desire now is to find the peace the Church of God alone can give me…Excitement and partial

> dissipation reduced me twice to the very brink of the grave, and it was while an invalid that I had serious thoughts of changing my way of life.

O'Farrell proposed spending a year or so at the residence of a country clergyman to resume his ecclesiastical training, 'where I might learn the office, the ceremonials etc – so many things that I have forgotten – above all to control myself'. And a year or so without temptation. 'I want to expose myself to as few temptations as possible. I feel full of timidity, full of distrust of my strength to withstand temptation.'

But, he added, he would not want anyone in his family to know he was in Adelaide.

His reflective and articulate letter suggested Henry's health was occasionally having a better time of it, but his reaching out was doomed. The letter did not arrive before Bishop Shiel left for overseas and it was not until 30 July that he finally replied to 'My dear Henry' from a Franciscan convent in Wexford, Ireland.

Bishop Shiel explained his delayed response and told O'Farrell to 'go to Adelaide and present yourself to the Vicar-General…your best place will be with the Jesuits, who will treat you with every kindness and attention suitable to your position. I am delighted to find that you have yielded to the promptings of Divine grace. My God grant you perseverance'.

The Bishop said that by putting himself under the protection of the Blessed Virgin he would secure 'a renewal of the spirit of your vocation', and urged him to go to Adelaide 'at once', signing off 'May God bless you, my dear Henry'. He forwarded Henry's letter in the shipping mail to the Vicar-General of Adelaide, the Very Rev John Smyth, and told him 'The writer…will present himself to you; he is a deacon. You will deal with him according to my letter, which he will present to you'.[19]

But the Bishop's embracing letter did not reach O'Farrell. And in the perceived silence from his Church, or sensing outright rejection, he became more agitated.

A solicitor, George Godfrey, saw him often in his Melbourne office between June and August, and considered him 'a hard drinker, and very excitable, in fact dangerous man.'[20]

O'Farrell then abruptly left Melbourne. His sister Caroline was concerned about his mind and collection of pistols, daggers and swords, but remained supportive:

> When he went away he did not say where he was going... he said he would come back and say goodbye but he did not do so. I heard from him afterwards, when he was at Rockhampton and when he was at Sydney...I supplied him with money for his cost of living. I did so repeatedly.'[21]

O'Farrell arrived in a Sydney beside itself with excitement about the imminent arrival in Australia of the Queen's son. Newspapers also carried updates about Fenian and revolutionary anti-aristocratic activity abroad. One prominent story was of a young man, part of the Polish uprising of 1863, who endeavoured to assassinate the Czar of Russia, Alexander II at the Paris International Exposition 'because he has murdered my country'.[22]

The year had begun with Henry O'Farrell under pressure and in distress. Now he had been seemingly spurned by his Catholic Church, and Fenian resentment of the succession of Royals seen to have kept their Empire's foot on Ireland's neck was growing. And Orangemen continued to clash with Irish Catholics, with Sydney hearing the news of the fatal shooting of a boy outside Melbourne's Protestant Hall.

At Tierney's Currency Lass Hotel his strange behaviour led to him being asked to leave. When he heard a rumour that a Fenian cruiser was travelling to Perth to rescue some transported Fenians, and that *HMS Brisk* had been sent to destroy it, he excitedly expressed a hope that the Fenian vessel would sink the man-of-war. Another time he declared the Fenians were precisely right in blowing up Clerkenwell gaol in December in a Fenian escape attempt which killed 12.

The tyranny of distance from England meant there was no hope O'Farrell could make any patriotic mark in the Mother Country, and no hope of the reigning monarch ever visiting such a remote part of her Empire, so her visiting son was the closest anyone in Australia could get to Royalty. And one Irishman's mind turned to that realisation.

8

PRINCE, PROSTITUTE, PICNIC

I had a kind of presentiment that there was going to be something – an indescribable fear of some accident or bad news. The same feeling had depressed HRH's spirits for some time.
— Lord Newry

Having endured a frustrating wait, the first colony of New South Wales was preened and primed to trump South Australia, where he had been robbed, and Victoria, where people had been fatally shot and burnt, to 'avoid the gaucheries of the younger and less mature colonies' as the *Sydney Morning Herald* described.

It had been almost a century since Naval officer James Cook hoisted English colours and 'in the name of His Majesty King George III take possession of the whole Eastern coast' for the Empire. The 1023 First Fleeters of 1788, mostly convicts and their children, had grown to 100,000 Sydneysiders waiting for another Naval officer, Her Majesty's son, in command of *HMS Galatea*, the finest specimen of marine architecture that ever entered Australian waters.

On a rainy 21 January, after a brief side trip from Melbourne to Tasmania, where he met the Aboriginal 'royals', William 'King Bill' Lanne and Truganini, and rode his carriage past the cheers of Her Majesty's convicts, Alfred entered the Harbour which Governor Phillip had told Lord Sydney, Secretary of State for Home Affairs, was 'the finest harbour in the world'.[1]

Royal love was in the air. The Bishop of Sydney's wife, Jane Barker, noted in her diary: 'I cannot describe the sensation the very sight of the *Galatea* gave me...It seems a realisation of our union with England, that a son of the Queen should come out here.'[2] A week before his arrival, clergyman Zachary Barry penned a 27-verse Valentine's Day message from 'The Lady Australia to Her Prince', hailing the envoy of the Queen's love, 'the people's mother', and avowing the desire of Lady Australia to 'choose thee, Prince, my peerless knight'. More seriously, the *Sydney Morning Herald* said Alfred's was a voyage of 'national interest' designed for 'a national purpose.' The Prince 'came by special orders, in command of a ship representing the far-reaching and protective naval power of the mother country...with an express wish from the Queen that he should be received with the honours due to her son'.[3]

The national purpose was to unambiguously demonstrate loyalty to Royalty, and ensure continued Royal Naval protection against any sedition or foreign invasion. The Royalty play was unchanged since the earlier speculation of an Alfred visit in 1863, when the *Empire* said 'it is confessedly Imperial policy to create a veneration for monarchical institutions, as a balance to the rapid progress of democratic development.'[4]

There had been talk of the 'inevitability' of a break from Britain, perhaps as a republic, but, as John Lang lamented, it was universally admitted the time would come but it came with the perennial rider that 'nobody surely can be mad enough to suppose that the time has come yet!'[5]

And few were 'mad enough' to raise the idea during a Royal visit, for which Sydney presented nearly 50 steamers and smaller vessels and yachts from the Royal Sydney and Prince Alfred yacht clubs in the harbour to welcome the first Royal blood.

Aboard the steamer *Auckland*, Colonial Secretary Henry Parkes and Premier James Martin were resplendent in new blue uniforms with gold braid, cocked hats and swords on their hips. Around 10,000 people walked or rode their horses and carts to line the harbour shores. The next day Alfred ceremoniously landed ashore at a temporary stage, close to where the First Fleet had landed, to be formally greeted by Governor Lord Belmore, who had only been in the colony of 450,000 people for two months.

Behind the scarlet-covered stage, the official party was dwarfed by a welcome building featuring a 79 foot high dome and a series of smaller domes, decorated with flags and busts of Captain Cook and Lord Nelson, and adorned with banners, shields, lions and what resembled heads impaled on spears. The edifice was described by one correspondent as 'by Sir Henry Parkes out of the Taj Mahal.'[6]

Every building was festooned with arches and illuminated transparencies with messages such as 'Sydney Welcomes Victoria's Son' and 'England's Glory' , images of James Cook and Joseph Banks alongside Plato, Aristotle and Pheidias, and numerous floral decorations and illustrations of naval ships, emus and kangaroos. Both houses of parliament were lit and linked with thousands of coloured lamps, and the city marvelled at new electric lights beaming multi-coloured rays from the Observatory.

Massive crowds, many in newly acquired suits, waistcoats, hats and gloves, strained to see Alfred's carriage amid an endless parade of bands, fire engines, officials, mayors and councillors, the literary staff of the *Herald*, Lodges and Orders, naval and military, consular representatives, judges, university chancellors and professors.

Sydney Mayor Charles Moore told Alfred he was seeing 'but a faint indication of the sentiments of earnest loyalty and personal devotion to her Majesty the Queen which pervades all classes in New South Wales'. In reply, the Prince told the crowd he was convinced of 'the depth and sincerity of the loyalty which her Majesty's subjects in Sydney entertain for her throne and person'.[7]

This was, as Queen Victoria and the Secretary of State described it, another 'British community',[8] where the majority saw themselves as still British, and even the minority of native-born Australians referred to distant England as 'home'. Alfred could detect the loyal hand of one of Belmore's predecessors, Governor Lachlan Macquarie. He replaced William Bligh after he had been deposed by the mutinous NSW Corps in 1808 and sought to lift the colony beyond its penal origins and named the streets after the ducal titles of George III and his sons (York, Cumberland, Cambridge, Sussex, Clarence, Kent) or British officials (Bathurst, Liverpool, Castlereagh, Pitt).

The *Sydney Morning Herald* declared 'Australians are simply Englishmen in Australia...we are simply developing the old national life under new and somewhat less constrained conditions...(to) carry forward the national work of the mother country'.[9]

Sydney was certainly not constrained in having the social time of its life over a month of numerous events, official and otherwise. And neither was Alfred.

With a hand-crafted four-horse carriage and a richly furnished railway carriage at his disposal, his official events included a levee or walkabout, a military review in the Domain attended by nearly 50,000, a 'Duke's Day' at Randwick racecourse, a Citizen's Reception Ball for 3000 in Hyde Park, a massive fireworks display watched by more than 50,000 people, 10,000 school children singing *God Save the Queen* at the Domain, a horticultural exhibition at the Botanic Gardens, a Bible presentation by 12,000 children, and a harbour regatta to mark the 80th anniversary of British settlement.

Colonial Secretary Parkes also hosted Alfred on a visit to Parliament and to the Fort Street Model School, where about 1500 children were part of a pioneering effort to establish national education standards, and the Infirmary in Macquarie Street, where he was told five young women would soon arrive as Australia's first nurses, a fortuitous piece of timing as Alfred would soon discover.

Parkes also took Alfred to the Australian Museum, where among the exhibits was a case of live snakes, one of which was put on the floor. 'A mongoose, the property of Mr Parkes, was liberated... observed the snake and at once attacked it...in a few seconds (it) lay dead on the floor. Another smaller but not venomous snake was brought, and this shared the same fate...another mongoose... was set at liberty and he amused himself by catching and killing a number of small frogs.'[10] Alfred enjoyed another shooting expedition at Douglass Park, south-west of Sydney, where again 'rabbits fell in great numbers, his Royal Highness killing the most.'[11] He also dined on colonial delights such as alpaca and the plump Wonga Wonga pigeon.

His new actor friend Walter Montgomery had arrived from Melbourne for a 12-night performance of Hamlet at the Prince of Wales Opera House, the Great Australasian Circus in Elizabeth Street featured 'star equestrians of the world', and the Grand Hippodrome at the Albert Ground, Redfern, featured the Great World Circus Company's 'champion' acrobats, rope artists and Roman horse racing.

At a two-day cricket and athletic carnival at Redfern, 4000 people watched an Aboriginal Eleven on the eve of their historic first tour of England play an Army-Navy team, including men from the *Galatea*. Alfred's party considered the victorious Aboriginals, known by names such as Jim Crow, King Cole, Tiger and Red Cap, 'almost equal to the performance of the best professional players in England'. They also enjoyed a 'sham fight' with boomerangs and spears, and 'Dick-a-Dick' Jumgunjinanuke fending off a volley of cricket balls fired at him from 20 yards, using only a small native shield not more than three inches wide.[12]

Some English newspapers made fun of the unending displays of Australian loyalty. The *Times* offended many by not, as the 'leading paper of the world,' sending its own special emissary to cover the Royal tour, and after its local correspondent described the loyalty displays as 'more…vigorous even than our own,' sniffily commented that the colonies were not 'quite up to the ceremonials' and that Alfred 'will have some amusing stories to tell on his return.'[13] Others reported the reception afforded 'delight and amusement to the old country', but at least evidenced Australians had 'declared they are still Englishmen and that their loyalty is far from extinct.'

The *Argus* found it 'mortifying' that some English press portrayed locals as 'semi-savages dancing round a painted idol, in place of sensible, loyal Englishmen, expressing our joy after the manner of civilised nations at the first presence amongst us of a son of our SOVEREIGN,' just as Liverpool or Glasgow might receive the Prince of Wales if he paid them a long-promised visit.

'Shallow writers of the critical periodicals seem to find a satisfaction in sneering at our loyalty, ridiculing our receptions and even making light of our pretensions to the possession of the feelings, convictions and predilections of Englishmen.'

The *Pall Mall Gazette* and *Saturday Review* seemed to compete, it said, to treat Australia's reception with 'studied contempt…even our poor PRINCE…is almost plucked of his plumes as a member of the Royal Family.' The *Argus* asked:

> Are we the less Englishmen because we have ventured half round the world to gain more breathing room than we could find in the old country? Are our children likely to be disloyal towards the institutions of the land they are taught to call 'home'? We are proud to form part of the great British empire.[14]

The *Empire* applauded the sentiment of a Victorian politician, George Smith, who said:

> We are loyal to the real ties, the moral and mental ties, which bind us to England. We are loyal to England and Her Majesty as the impersonation of England, and to guard that grand old sea eagle's nest of Liberty from hostile hands… to keep it as the sanctuary of civilisation and progress… the nursery and the nursing mother of great men and great thoughts, we are as willing to spend the last penny of our money and the last drop of our blood, as are our brothers who remain upon her soil.[15]

From that sanctuary of civilisation came Her Majesty's own blood, but it was too early in Australia's history, said the *Empire*, to resolve the conflict between those 'rabid democrats' and 'rabid republicans' who saw the visit as one of 'frivolous notoriety' and 'flunkeyism', and those who saw the visit reinforcing 'the natural preference of mankind for monarchical government'. The *Empire* felt separation and the creation of an independent republic would one day become desirable, but there was 'no hurry' and 'gratitude and policy alike dictate to colonial democrats the propriety of remaining under the British flag for many years to come'.[16]

The Queen had frequently commented that Alfred had basically no interest in politics, and he gave no evidence to the contrary. As in Melbourne, Alfred dutifully did what he had to do and otherwise ran to his own beat. He barely tolerated officialdom and ceremony, prompting complaints to the newspapers about the 'weariness and disgust which HRH displays'[17] and speaking 'very imprudently' about his Victorian hosts.[18] Repeating his Melbourne ruse, Alfred again arrived at an all-night 'public fancy ball' for 1000 people at the Prince of Wales Theatre in his naval uniform, but slipped away to return as a monk with rosary beads and crosses, a flowing grey beard and pretending to have a feeble gait. One young man who had been amusing himself by tapping people on the shoulder and quickly scurrying away, tapped the 'antique monk' who turned and asked a nearby couple if they had tapped him: 'I thought you required me – do you know who I am?',[19] clearly delighted they had no idea.

And as in Melbourne, ladies of the colony were keen to link arms, and more, with the Prince and anyone else in the Royal party. Rev. William Creeny felt the Royal party had a tendency to 'fastness' and that Lord Newry looked 'the greatest scamp possible'.[20] Alfred had tongues wagging with his obvious like of a Miss Coveny. She had sailed from Sydney to Melbourne to attend Melbourne's fancy dress ball and returned to Sydney at the same time as Alfred arrived. She was 'the only unmarried lady he has danced with…He likes her and has honoured her everywhere they meet'.[21]

A 'Mrs Fraser…from Melbourne' paid him a visit and his Melbourne 'wife' Sarah Saqui was also said to have taken up residence in a cottage in Castlereagh Street. Here Detective Edward Broomfield, tasked with shadowing the Prince, diarised that Alfred spent a few hours 'on more than one occasion' at the property, owned by George Lamb. An 'old chum' later recalled in a six-part series on Broomfield's career, 'I think, however, that there was but one "lamb" In the fold – a ewe lamb – which the Duke visited.'[22]

Detective Broomfield also played a middle man role when a 'somewhat notorious' medical man, John Van Heekeren, who was well known to the police for abortion procedures for girls who loved 'not wisely but too well', asked him to take an envelope, addressed to Alfred, which he passed to police chief John McLerie and in turn to Lieutenant Haig. The Prince read the contents and quietly handed Haig a £10 note which came back to the doctor via the detective with a message from chief McLerie that the author was 'a damned scoundrel'.[23]

Those who could not see the Prince up close and personal flocked to the Sydney waxworks of 'Monsieur and Madame Sohier' to see his newly arrived wax form. Emulating Madame Tussaud's, wax modeller Ellen Williams and her phrenologist husband Philemon Sohier showcased Alfred among monarchs, military heroes and criminals.

Alfred broke his time in NSW with a brief side-trip to Queensland, where again the impression he left 'is not on the whole so favourable as the loyal subjects of his mother could have desired...he conducted himself throughout in a manner no way becoming a Prince'.[24]

Despite the picnic debacle in Melbourne, Alfred agreed to support a picnic in Sydney on 12 March to raise funds for improvements to the Sailors' Home, established to provide affordable accommodation for the 1000 sailors in port each year.

The chosen location was Clontarf, a popular harbour picnic spot long known as the Arcadia of New South Wales. It was the only option for a large-scale picnic with the harbour's oldest, largest and most shady pleasure grounds and the capacity for vessels to moor at a sandy beach. Clontarf was named after Irish High King Brian Boru's battle against the Vikings in 1014, and was synonymous with Irish events: a few months previously the St Patrick's society held its annual children's event at Clontarf, and the annual St Patrick's Day celebration was imminent.

For a fitting and triumphant finale before Alfred ended his historic visit, the grounds were readied for 'all the old sports of England' such as cricket, football, croquet and Aunt Sally skittles.

Guinness, stout, oysters and buttered brown bread were ordered for about 1500 guests before a noon lunch of chicken and lobster. More than 1000 magnums of champagne, 800 bottles of beer, and 'copious supplies of even more ardent spirits' were on hand.[25] A large marquee was provided for the luncheon, with additional tents for liquid refreshments, women and the bands of HM 50th Regiment, *Galatea* and German community. A private tent for the Prince, with carpet on the ground and a small table with a gold-embroidered red cloth, was topped by the Royal Standard and guarded by one policeman.

A 'gathering of the blacks' was underway. Some 300 Aboriginals—'the largest number…ever seen in the neighbourhood of Sydney' from Burrangong, Araluen, Clarence River and Moruya, were being collected to perform a corroboree at Clontarf. Led by the likes of Kings Tinboy, Lintot and Dickey, Queen Anne and Princess Charlotte, they were 'obviously unused to ways of civilised life, and stare about them with ludicrous astonishment as they go jabbering along.'[26] While organisers ensured there would be 'no opportunity of offending the delicacy of the white folk.'[27]

March 12 dawned a fine day. General business was suspended, all government and commercial offices closed. The Royal Standard was hoisted on the principal tower of Government House, designed by Edward Blore, the same man who designed Buckingham Palace. In the harbour *HMS* ships *Galatea*, *Challenger* and *Charybdis* and dozens of yachts were all decorated.

Five steamers were running every 30 minutes from Circular Quay and Woolloomooloo Bay, and shortly before one o'clock, Alfred, accompanied by the Earl and Countess Belmore, proceeded down the harbour in the steam yacht *Fairy*.

Alfred had been dismissive of the need for extra security, declaring: 'No! we do not want a guard. Sydney is not Melbourne.'[28]

But some sense of unease or foreboding was evident. Lord Newry wrote to his friend Dr Candler that 'I had a kind of presentiment that there was going to be something -- an indescribable fear of some accident or bad news. The same feeling had depressed HRH's spirits for some time and the evening before he was heard to say "I don't half like this picnic affair"'.[29]

The *Freeman's Journal* may have been the source of Lord Newry's presentiment. It had hinted at some nervousness, stating that 'so far at all events we may congratulate ourselves that the royal visit has been marked by no incident distressing to anybody' but Parkes considered the *Journal* had been 'treasonable' when it said the Manchester Fenians were hanged because it was 'politically expedient to make an example', and whether the execution would avert action by other 'republican conspirators…perhaps a month or two will tell whether we are right or wrong'.[30]

After the hangings and the Clerkenwell bombing, the *Journal* blamed the British Government, which

> deliberately chose to initiate this game of murder by hanging three men for the accidental shooting of one and now no human being can tell how the end of it will be. It is ridiculous to suppose that the hanging of three men, or of three hundred, will turn the Fenians from attempting the work they have taken in hand. Men who do the desperate deeds…generally care little about their own lives, and much less about the lives of other people.[31]

Journal Editor Richard O'Sullivan caused further outrage when he told a St Patrick's Day Regatta committee meeting it was 'quite true, he had refused to drink the Queen's health, and always declined in doing so'.[32]

Rumours of possible sectarian strife were in the air. Police later claimed they had 'intelligence' of plans by 'persons ill-disposed towards the English Government…for outrage of some kind'.[33] O'Sullivan and Catholics, including newly arrived Bishops from Ireland, had been upset by Henry Parkes, who long held a suspicion of Catholicism and had diminished state support and primacy of church schools, a move strongly supported by the Orange lodges, led by leading republican and anti-Catholic Rev. John Lang.

The colonies were reading constant reports of Fenian–English tension in England, Ireland, Scotland and Canada: alleged Fenian leaders being arrested, headquarters uncovered in Paris, gaols and Parliament House given extra military protection, reported plots to blow up cathedrals and railways, weapons and munitions being accumulated, and claims newspapers like the *Irishman* were openly preaching sedition and extermination of English landlords.

Rising concern about Fenian activity had been conveyed to the Queen in December. Closeted inside Windsor, she was not unduly worried, but some 240 extra constables were sworn in, Fenian prisoners were ordered to be photographed, and increased efforts made to infiltrate and find 'snitches', the genesis of counter-terrorism intelligence gathering. Colonial police were hearing troubling rumours of Fenian sentiment being aired at various social and political meetings. In Shoalhaven, amid alleged 'talk of politics and treason', one man was reportedly asked about the possible shooting of Alfred: 'Oh someone will be found that will do it…no sin to put anyone to death who stood in the way of the purposes of Fenianism' as 'the Royal family were in the way, and would soon be exterminated'. And in Penrith, a man heard his neighbour declare that while the Prince's tour was joyous at that point, 'the black flag will wave over his corpse before he leaves the country'.[34]

Police chief John McLerie, a prominent Freemason, was convinced there were many disaffected Fenian 'sympathisers and agents', openly corresponding and travelling between Ireland, Australia and America, but he could not find sufficient information about any 'seditious' activity to prosecute.

Police had been worried about the Prince's welcome procession. McLerie said 'Many persons (some of high standing) represented to me the danger of allowing Orangemen to walk in procession upon the occasion of the official landing as it would excite the Roman Catholics…hints and suggestions were not wanting that the life of His Royal Highness might be endangered.'

Archdeacon John McEnroe said any overt Orange activity could spark 'outrages' which were impossible to predict'. Anonymous letters claimed armed Catholics were prepared to confront Orangemen to 'revenge the wrongs of their countrymen in the affair at Protestant Hall' in Melbourne.

Parkes approved the swearing in of an additional 500 special constables for the procession, 'not with any reference to any anticipated peril to HRH', simply for the preservation of the public peace.' The recruitment did not eventuate because so few were willing to take the oath, but police persuaded both Orange and Catholic supporters to drop plans to march. McLerie did ensure police rode as escorts to Alfred's carriage, and he told the trooper in charge of the honour guard to ride abreast of the Prince because 'if the Royal personage were fired at, you would receive the shot', but said later this was 'a sort of jocular remark.' Whatever the quality of the 'intelligence', McLerie never informed Alfred that his life could be in danger, nor were any special directions given to those guarding the Prince.

Alfred's party was well familiar with Fenian agitation at home, and attacks by would-be assassins on Queen Victoria (although they could not know the co-incidence that one, Edward Oxford, had just arrived in Australia under an exile deal with the British Government). They had also seen local tension and violence in Orange–Green clashes in Melbourne, but while an escort of three or four mounted police was assigned to Alfred he often walked and rode around Sydney freely. When a senior constable suggested to his suite this was unwise, he was told the Prince's reply was 'he would do as he liked'.[35]

He pointedly refused a personal guard, notwithstanding Lord Newry saying the prince felt the picnic an event he seemingly 'don't half like'. Ultimately McLerie assigned 12 police to Clontarf, but not with any specific instruction. Alfred and the police chief seemingly shared enough confidence that the welcome procession had passed peacefully, there had been no subsequent incidents, and Irish conflict with English royalty was unlikely to descend on a beautiful picnic spot in the Empire's most remote outpost on one of the final days of the royal visit.

But amongst those making their way to the Clontarf picnic was one Irishman, with a passion and pistols.

9
TERROR AT CLONTARF

It plunged me into fever, the having to decide in loyalty to a Church or to Country.
— Henry O'Farrell

Henry O'Farrell had been denied his destiny to be a priest and his efforts to be re-embraced seemingly rejected. He retained his Bible and crucifix but also his disdain of church leadership on Irish freedom. He was passionate about the Irish cause, hateful toward British royalty.

The call for Irishmen to 'revolt' and seek 'vengeance' was in the air. A *Freeman's Journal* correspondent said 'my blood is boiling with indignation' at the death of the Manchester martyrs at the hands of British rule and oppression. Thousands of sons of Ireland would be strengthened in their resolve to rescue their country from the power that had ground it down for 700 years: 'Would to Heaven every Irishman were…so self-sacrificing, so nobly heroic, and so brave in death, and Ireland's freedom would not be far distant!'[1]

For the past year local Irishmen devoured reports of stirring speeches by Fenian leaders in Boston and New York about 'vengeance' and enthusiastic support for James Stephens, who O'Farrell had openly lauded. Father Jeremiah Vaughan, of Clare, Ireland, told a packed public meeting in New York that exile did not diminish Irishness, and it was time to end 'the evils (of)…English rule.' It was 'the duty of every Irishman to combine and revolt' against what was revolting to human nature and blasphemy against God'.[2]

The stirring words of 'vengeance' and 'duty' were not words O'Farrell had heard from his Catholic leaders in Australia, but they began to appear in the scrawled notes of his small pocket book, which he kept close along with his Douay-Rheims Bible and Roman Catholic missal and crucifix.

In the troubled creases of his mind a 'desperate deed' was unfolding: a Royal had to be sacrificed, and if that meant he too had to be sacrificed, then that was his mission and thinking, as he revealed in a letter to newspaper editors in Dublin.

About a week before Alfred's arrival in Sydney, O'Farrell wrote to the editors of *The Nation* and the *Irishman* in Dublin, 'an address to the people of Ireland' as he put it. His letter was addressed to Alexander Sullivan, who with brother Timothy, a future Lord Mayor of Dublin, had developed the newspaper into a potent Irish nationalist voice. They were also the brothers of Richard O'Sullivan, feisty editor of Sydney's *Freeman's Journal*. With Alexander Sullivan in prison for an article on the Manchester martyrs, Timothy opened the letter from Australia and 'found the communication was from one Henry James O'Farrell, informing us of his intention to shoot the Duke of Edinburgh, son of Queen Victoria. The deed would be done, he said, on an occasion which would present itself some three or four days after the date of that letter'. Sullivan said O'Farrell 'knew the act would cost him his life, which probably would be taken on the spot, but he adduced reasons and arguments, as he supposed them to be, to justify his engaging in this criminal enterprise'.

Sullivan told his brother about it as he walked with him in Richmond gaol yard, noting any such attempt must have occurred long before the letter even reached Dublin, and so 'consequently we could do nothing toward preventing the commission of the crime'.

'Take my advice' his lawyer-journalist brother said, 'and as soon as you get back to the office, burn that letter; you know what harm has already been done in this country by the keeping of "documents". I acted on his advice.'[3]

Beyond the pen, O'Farrell also had the power of a gun, two in fact, a six-chamber Colt and a six-chamber Smith and Wesson. He secured the Colt, known as a 'belt' or 'navy' model, from Henry Challener, a Sydney gunsmith, who advertised the country's largest stock of Colonel Samuel Colt pistols. This was the weapon favoured by many, including some colonial police, as better crafted, more portable and more reliable than English weapons. The Smith and Wesson had a barrel about 6 inches long and a smooth rosewood grip, it was capable of firing a 0.32 calibre copper cartridge; Loaded with black powder, it produced a lot of smoke and flame out the end of the barrel. Known as an 'Old Army' model, it was favoured by Indian fighter General George Custer and frontiersman James Butler ('Wild Bill') Hickok.

At the end of the Civil War, abandoned rifles, carbines, revolvers and pistols of American soldiers and farmers were snapped up by entrepreneurial Sydney merchants like Henry Challener and Frederic Lassetter, the son of a Wesley minister. They advertised to Australian miners and farmers keen to protect themselves and their property that the weapons 'during the late war, had proved most efficient and serviceable'. They were now available at cheap prices, but customers were warned to 'beware of counterfeits and base mongrel imitations' and buy only 'righteous' weapons.[4]

With his 'righteous' weapons, O'Farrell undertook target practice at Waverley, boasting about his marksmanship over a distance of about 10 yards. Over an ale he showed a Waverley publican a handkerchief with bullet holes in it. 'He put his finger through one and said "the washerwoman will think I have been doing something".' He also showed a landlady the handkerchief, 'riddled with bullets, boasting what a good marksman he was'.[5]

He told several people he was 'anxious' to see the Prince from the moment of *Galatea's* arrival. He took a room in the Custom House Hotel in Argyle Street in The Rocks, near the wharf where Alfred was due to ceremoniously land before a city welcome procession. The night before O'Farrell did not sleep. William Martin, a commission agent who had done business with O'Farrell in Ballarat, came across him several times in Sydney. 'He said he had been so anxious to see the Duke of Edinburgh…that he had sat up all night', Martin said.[6]

O'Farrell had Alfred 'covered'. 'I could have killed the whole four in that carriage…I could have shot him dead…and Lord Belmore'. But he wasn't sure, later saying his Fenian 'mission' was 'discretionary' on the question of killing anyone other than Alfred , and Belmore was patron of the St Patrick's Day Regatta.

In any event a little girl saw part of the brass cover of his pistol fall off, and cried 'There's a gun!' forcing him to quickly abandon his first opportunity. In addition, 'I said to myself, what is the use? They are prepared for all the sports in Sydney. Let them enjoy themselves, it would spoil everything…it would have spoiled everything; I intended to enjoy myself, the time was not specified.'[7]

O'Farrell moved to the Clarendon Hotel on the corner of George and Hunter Streets, from where he had seen Alfred pass several times, and then the Currency Lass Hotel—currency lads and lasses being a term for native-born colonists—on the corner of Hunter and Pitt Streets. He frequently wandered from the Currency Lass at night, sometimes not returning until the early morning, causing owner Daniel Tierney to say: 'Mr O'Farrell, you devil, you must have something bad in your head.'[8]

There were numerous opportunities for any devil deed, but O'Farrell said it was 'too soon, there were so many enjoyments going on…(people) were spending a deal of money; crowds had spent small fortunes on their dresses…it did not matter for a fortnight or so, it would do as well as just before his departure as at the very beginning.'[9]

As Sydney basked in royal sunshine, O'Farrell freely conversed in hotels about Alfred as a 'fine fellow' and 'a fine strapping young man'. He also spoke excitedly about Ireland and Fenianism. A Royal Naval surgeon was offended when he spoke 'in favour of Fenianism, and approved of the blowing up of Clerkenwell Gaol.' And when the surgeon said he hoped a Fenian vessel reportedly on its way to intercept a ship carrying Fenian prisoners to Perth would be sunk, O'Farrell said he hoped the ship of war would be sunk first.[10]

After his plan to shoot Alfred at Circular Quay was thwarted, he considered a Citizens Ball at a specially erected Pavilion in Hyde Park but claimed 'one of the Fenian circle wanted to fire the Pavilion…he said it had been erected in honour of English royalty and if they did these things (the people) would suffer for it' but he was not in favour of 'this miserable sort of thing'. The Sydney council was so worried the Pavilion would be fired by people 'disaffected to the prince' it burned off the surrounding grass and installed eight hydrants and 24-hour watchmen.[11]

He did take steps to attend the 'public fancy dress ball' at the Prince of Wales Theatre where he could easily mingle with 1000 others, buying a 20s ticket and visiting a tailor to order a dress-coat for the event, but claimed that when he returned the coat and ticket was missing. He was annoyed, telling one publican he was 'never so sucked in in his life'. He then asked 'what sort of place Clontarf was, but did not say why'.[12]

A few days later was Clontarf picnic day. O'Farrell made a morning visit to the University of Sydney's St John's College, the first Catholic college in a pre-existing, non-Catholic university in the English-speaking world since the Reformation, to collect some money and letters from his sisters and friends in Ballarat.

He had told them this was to support staying in Sydney to resume his religious studies but wrote in his notebook 'I cannot get money unless I lead them to believe I am studying for the church… the idea disgusts me…I did think of doing so once and it plunged me into fever, the having to decide in loyalty to a Church or to Country' and later referred to this 'system of deception'.[13] Some of the money went to ensuring he was suitably dressed for Clontarf. He needed a new hat. A fellow lodger, who talked cricket with him and found him 'highly intellectual and of good education'[14] suggested he go to Mountcastle's drapery, the country's first hat manufacturer. At first he selected a cheap 2s hat, but returned after 10 minutes saying it 'did not look gentlemanly', and spent 10s on a replacement.[15] He paid with a Bank of Victoria banknote, and happily left his name and address in case any Sydney bank had a query over it. Perhaps he was unconcerned about hiding his identity because, as he had written to the Dublin newspaper editors, he did not expect to survive this day.

Now, with his new hat to go with a dark coat, trousers and white waistcoat, he made his way to join those who had paid a guinea to attend the picnic and were now impatiently waiting at Circular Quay for the noon steamer.

Among the estimated crowd of 3000 at Clontarf, O'Farrell first visited the refreshment tent where he asked George Cunningham, a government clerk he had met at the Currency Lass Hotel, to have a glass of wine with him. While O'Farrell was having a fortifying drink—he later said he had 'two or three glasses of whisky and some wine'—[16] Alfred, accompanied by his equerries Haig, Yorke and Newry, two Naval commanders, Lord and Lady Belmore and their family and staff arrived on the steamer *Fairy* at 2.15pm.

The Prince, in uniform of blue frock-coat and white trousers, was met by Sir William Manning, prominent lawyer-politician and president of the Sailors Home Committee, and the Chief Justice, Sir Alfred Stephen, and escorted to the luncheon tent where a toast to the health of the Queen, 'was enthusiastically received'.[17]

Alfred's plan was to leave the event as early as possible so he could explore other inlets in Middle Harbour. After lunch he gave his arm to Lady Belmore and walked her to the ladies' tent, then called Sir William to his side. The two men walked across an open space, used for cricket and other sports, where the Prince paused to hand over a cheque for the Sailors' Home. They resumed walking toward the shoreline where 300 Aboriginals readied for a corroboree and boomerang exhibition.

O'Farrell now said to Charles Watkins, a man he had met on the steamer to Clontarf: 'Let us get behind the Duke, let us go round to the other side.' Watkins declined, not wanting to be conspicuous. O'Farrell went ahead alone, but not before insistently asking Watkins to 'swear that you will stick to me?' if there was a 'row'.[18]

O'Farrell steadily moved through the crowd following the Prince.

Now he made his move. He took some quick steps, suddenly emerged from the crowd and strode to within two yards of Alfred's back.

He raised his arm holding the Smith and Wesson revolver. Superintendent John Orridge, in charge of escorting Alfred, could see the revolver aimed at Alfred's back and began running toward the Prince.

But it was too late. Bang! The polite murmurings of the Royal picnic crowd were broken by a sharp noise. Then a few seconds later, another. Bang!

Lord Newry, talking to a woman and her daughter about 150 yards from Alfred, thought the sounds were Chinese fireworks, 'merely the reports of crackers and squibs',[19] while 16-year-old Emily Thorne, who had earlier received 'a good stare' from Newry, also talked of 'a sharp noise like a Chinese cracker.' Alfred heard the noise before he realised what had really happened. He felt himself lifted from the ground and it hit him, and everyone else, that he had been shot.

'The Prince is shot!' a woman cried out. Young Emily Thorne turned to where the cry had come from. 'I just saw the Prince fall. Then the whole flashed across our minds in a moment and we all exclaimed "The Prince is shot!"...It was an awful moment...our noble Prince falling first on his hands and knees and then over on his back and looking up and uttering two dreadful "oh's"'.[20]

Lord Belmore, who was about 70 yards away, heard others cry 'The Duke is shot!' and 'He is shot and has fallen down dead'.[21]

Beside Alfred, Sir William Manning turned to the direction from where the first shot had come from. He found himself looking straight at O'Farrell who was stepping backwards but still aiming in the direction of Alfred and saying 'stand back'. O'Farrell said 'I forced him back two or three steps...then was the time I would have (again) shot him (Alfred) but Sir William Manning prevented it.' Manning instinctively ducked as O'Farrell took aim again, but the gun misfired. O'Farrell aimed at Alfred a third time, despite feeling some 'irresolution, as though I would not like to shoot a man when he was down.'[22] But William Vial, a coach-builder and grand master of the Masonic lodge, jumped him from behind, forcing his right arm down just as the gun fired. The bullet hit former Sydney mayor and Rose Bay merchant George Thorne in the ankle. 'I am shot! I am shot!' Vial jumped on the back of O'Farrell who twisted around and tried to point the gun at him, saying 'You — b — b — '[23] before Vial and several other men managed to pinion his arms.

O'Farrell now began to ask himself why he had kept the Colt hidden under his jacket and not used both guns simultaneously. 'I did not shoot him with two pistols – two shots at once – that would have killed him.'[24]

Manning and Lord Belmore ran to the Prince, who by now had been carried to the ladies tent by Dr Alexander Watson, surgeon of *HMS Challenger*, a steward from one of the ferries, and some *Galatea* bandsmen. The women were cleared out and Belmore arranged cushions for the Duke.

The crowd immediately thought the Prince had been assassinated. 'The Duke is killed!'. Within moments the scene was one of 'almost indescribable confusion and distress'. Men and women were pale and in tears, some 'seized with hysterics.'[25]

The Royal party feared worse was to come. 'I cannot describe the feeling that came over me at that moment,' Lord Newry said. 'Every detail of all the Fenian outrages and shootings of royal personages seemed to flash through my mind in a minute…From the variety of expressions I heard…I fully expected to see a dozen or two men firing revolvers indiscriminately among the crowd.'[26]

There was no way of knowing if O'Farrell had armed accomplices, but he was set upon amid angry calls of 'Kill the wretch! Lynch him! Hang him! String him up.'

One woman recalled: 'They put up a rope to hang him a few yards from where we were and I really think I should not have noticed or cared if they did', telling a crying friend 'we had better turn our backs, they are going to hang him.'[27]

Lady Manning told Mrs Barker, wife of the Bishop of Sydney, the 'scene was…so instantaneous and stunning that people seemed to lose their senses…rushing about in all directions…men as well as women fainting. The culprit had the narrowest escape of being torn to pieces'.[28]

Even Vial was mistakenly kicked and beaten in what Lord Belmore described as a 'determined effort …to 'lynch' him' (O'Farrell) and if it wasn't for the efforts of Superintendent Orridge, Chief Justice Stephen, Lord Newry and band members of the *Galatea* and Her Majesty's 50th Regiment, 'he would probably have not left the ground alive'.[29]

Some said O'Farrell smelt of alcohol as he 'fought and kicked fiendishly' as he was pummelled by fist and foot, and a *Galatea* drummer beat him about the face with his drumsticks until he became 'insensible'.[30] The revolver was retrieved by a *Galatea* bandsman, and the fully loaded Colt pistol reprised from his left hand under his coat.

Commotion reigned. Rev. Creeny said, 'Ladies were fainting and lying almost neglected…some men fainted and "nearly all had shed tears or had red eyes"'.[31] The bishop's wife said it was 'like a horrible dream' to witness an assassin's bid to 'murder the son of our beloved Queen! Who could believe it or dream that an atrocity would be perpetrated in the midst of our universal demonstration of love and loyalty.'[32]

Chief Justice Sir Alfred Stephen 'could not speak for crying', while one of his sons described the staid Anglican politician and future Premier Alexander Stuart as 'running about with a large carving knife in his hand to stab O'Farrell' before Sir Alfred implored him 'No, no Stuart, let the law take its course!', to which the outraged MP said 'Damn you and the law, let me rip the – scoundrel up!' while several women shouted they would cut O'Farrell up with their scissors.

The Stephens thought the shots the beginning of 'a general massacre by the Fenians'[33] Shocked and outraged by the spilling of Royal blood on Australian soil, the crowd wanted immediate vengeance, the law of God on their side. 'The divine and unrepealed law of retribution is still in force, demanding blood for blood and life for life.'[34]

Superintendent Orridge, who had considerable experience pursuing and killing bushrangers, had to work hard with the assistance of Royal Navy Survey Lieutenant John Gowlland, *Galatea* bandsmen and members of the 50th Regiment, to keep the crowd at bay for 10 minutes while the Chief Justice and Lord Newry manoeuvred O'Farrell away from the milling crowd, still trying to kick and punch him, toward the shore.

Orridge told the crowd O'Farrell had said 'I did it just to frighten him'[35] but the crowd was outraged, as were the *Galatea* crew. William Bradley, Alfred's shooting aide, was 'in a fearful state of excitement', according to Newry, and 'would have hung him on board the steamer. They had the rope all ready.' While O'Farrell appeared 'more dead than alive' the crowd rushed towards the steamer where 'a number of sailors had a rope ready to string him up' on *Paterson's* yardarm. Newry intervened, repeatedly 'screaming out no, no over (and) over again'[36] and the *Paterson* was ordered to immediately cast off and await further orders.

By the time O'Farrell had been dragged across the decks of two steamers to reach the *Paterson*, his upper clothing had been torn away, his eyes, face and body bruised and swollen, his lips 'puffed out like those of a negro'. Blood flowed from his wounds, and 'he appeared to be utterly unconscious'.[37]

The crowd shouted to the captain to haul back in so they could 'dispatch him at the scene of the crime', crying out 'Lynch him! Up with him!'[38] The captain wavered, but was firmly told by former Parliamentary speaker John Hay, who was on the bridge, to haul off.

Superitendent Orridge said without the help for the small number of police, 'I doubt if I should have succeeded in removing him alive.'[39] When they learned the assassin had not been summarily lynched the Aboriginals reportedly asked for the shooter for the purpose of 'roasting him.' One of those seeking to avert the dispensing of immediate justice was the Rev. John Lang, a leading republican and opponent of Catholics. 'I addressed the enraged multitude, entreating them to do no violence to the assassin, as the preservation of his life was the likeliest means of enabling the Government to ferret out his accomplices.'[40]

When O'Farrell realised his mission had failed police reported various versions of what he said.

Senior Constable Robert Irvine, who had previously come across O'Farrell in the billiards room in a Glebe hotel, said he was the first policeman to seize him, telling those hitting O'Farrell 'leave him, he is my prisoner now...O'Farrell then said 'Oh, my God! what have I done?' I says "you scoundrel, you know". He then said, "God love old Ireland! Old Ireland forever".'

But Irvine's account was later ignored in favour of other police who alleged O'Farrell made more sensational statements. According to them O'Farrell said 'sorry I missed my aim' and 'I made a bloody mess of it but it can't be helped now', and more explosively 'I'm a bloody Fenian and will die for my country', 'May God save Ireland', and 'I can die for my country, I have done my duty.'[41]

While O'Farrell was under guard on his way back to Sydney, Alfred remained in the tent for about an hour, biting his hands in agony, his eyes rolling. When Lord Newry first arrived, Alfred said: 'Good God! I am shot…take hold…My back is broken!'[42] Newry was shocked. 'When I…saw his poor body covered with blood, heard him groaning and saw all the horror stricken doctors and attendants around him, I couldn't hold up any longer. I don't know what I did much for about the first hour but cry, like everybody else did.'[43]

Rev. Creeny saw 'the blood on his shirt of broad blue stripes and his face all pale and his light blue eyes rolling…he at first lost the use of his legs, and now at times there's great pain in his right leg and partial paralysis'. A groaning Alfred cried 'give me air', and Lord Belmore and Yorke lifted the sides of the tent and removed Alfred's neckcloth and opened his bloodied shirt and waistcoat. Elliot Yorke removed his watch and other valuables, and ice was put on the wound to try to stem the bleeding.

Dr Watson, with *Galatea* assistant surgeon, Dr William Powell, and a picnic guest, Dr Horatio Wright, assessed the injuries. They found the Prince had a miraculous escape, although he thought 'he had lost the use of his legs'.[44] O'Farrell had fired from close range, 'so close he might have picked his pocket when he fired',[45] according to *Galatea* bandmaster Charles Pritchard, but Alfred was saved by his braces.

The bullet deflected off some brass or thick rubber and entered his body half an inch from the spine, between the ninth and tenth ribs, travelled about a foot and finally lodged about 4½ inches below his right nipple.

Dr Wright had surgical instruments, but 'the shock was very considerable and it was thought advisable not to remove the ball at this time'.[46]

Governor Belmore's aide-de-camp was quickly despatched on the *Fairy* back to Sydney to find Dr James Young, the *Galatea* surgeon, and Lady Belmore sent to prepare a ground-floor drawing room at Government House for a Royal emergency.

Alfred sent a message to the anxious crowd standing in a cordon around his tent that he 'would be better presently'.[47] The crowd responded with 'great cheers' but became dead silent when the Prince emerged on a stretcher cobbled together from timber from one of the guests' gigs. Carried by six sailors and covered by one of the doctor's coats, he passed through the crowd to the small jetty and placed on the skylight of the after-cabin of *Morpeth*.

When the steamer arrived at Farm Cove a barge, rowed by 20 sailors, came alongside to transfer Alfred to the landing place near Government House.

Already 'at all appearance in a dead swoon,' he narrowly avoided further injury when *Morpeth's* mast struck the *HMS Charybdis* rigging. Broken spars crashed onto the deck of the steamer and into the water, barely a yard from the wounded Prince. 'The shrieks! The cries! The faintings!...the hysterics of the ladies (who were already in the most nervous state) were something to be remembered.'[48]

O'Farrell and Alfred were now leaving their vessels on Sydney harbour, both barely conscious, both their lives in the balance, one on his way to Darlinghurst Gaol, the other to Government House.

In Parliament, a late afternoon report that the Prince had been shot was not taken seriously until Superintendent Orridge personally went to the House to tell them he had a man in custody, followed by Premier Martin telling shocked MPs that 'a Dublin man drew a revolver and fired at his Royal Highness, and struck him in the back'. With the Prince's fate unknown, he moved the adjournment of the House.[49]

The final fate of O'Farrell and Alfred was still to come, but the instant outcome was that the shot at Clontarf killed the joy of greeting the first Royal blood on Australia's shores, killed any modest hope of Alfred soon becoming King of Australia, and killed the hopes of republicans wanting a break from England. Any transition to a new monarchical or republican country hinged on the pre-requisite of peaceful and unified colonies, and this went up in gun-smoke as the country descended into moral panic, shame, vengeance, bigotry and political division and opportunism.

10
ANGELS OVER ALFRED

God knows what is to become of us all. I believe we are all in danger of our lives.
— Lord Newry

Prince Alfred should have been dead. The bullet, fired from close range, just missed his spine and major organs after deflecting at the cross-over of his Indian rubber braces.

The *Medical Journal* said it was 'one of the most extraordinary escapes which has ever been recorded in the history of gunshot wounds.' In 999 cases out of 1000, the bullet would have fatally pierced his heart, lung, diaphragm, intestines or liver, so his survival was 'incredible', the bullet 'within a hair's breadth of causing instant death.'[1]

But the danger wasn't completely over. The Prince, 'rather hysterical and in much pain,'[2] needed quality care and nursing to ensure the bullet was safely removed with no fatal complications.

And now his second good fortune was presented. Just five days before the shooting, Lucy Osburn, the daughter of an English wine and spirits merchant and amateur Egyptologist, had arrived with four other women as the first trained nurses in Australia. They were despatched by Florence Nightingale following a request by Colonial Secretary Henry Parkes after a government committee condemned the Sydney infirmary as an over-crowded, vermin-infested, fever-ridden, unhygienic squalor little changed from convict days.

After a year's training at the Nightingale School of Nursing at St Thomas Hospital in London, Osburn was appointed Lady Superintendent of Nursing at the Sydney Infirmary. She was still getting over the first night shock of bed bugs and absorbing the enormity of the challenge of fulfilling her heroine's vision that 'the very first requirement in a hospital is that it should do the sick no harm'[3]. She was looking forward to a relaxing cup of tea when she heard the news racing around Sydney—'the Prince is shot'.

As a shocked city held its breath, Osburn was called to urgently bring two nurses to a makeshift ward at Government House, where they and the naval surgeons would face the most important assignment of their lives, to save a Prince by successfully extracting an assassin's bullet and ensure his recovery without complications.

Outside, authorities faced the most important assignment of their lives, to save the colony by safeguarding the Prince and the people from any further treasonous violence, and ensure the world was in no doubt the depth of shame was matched by unambiguous loyalty to Queen and Empire.

The unprecedented emotion of welcoming the Prince was the most unifying event in every city and town in colonial history. Now they were more emotional, and unified, in grief, shame and anger.

'Never before has any single event taken so powerful a hold on the public mind, never before has the national voice been so vehement, so unanimous, so full of rage, sorrow and vengeful bitterness.'[4]

With Alfred's fate in the balance, shops and businesses in Sydney posted 'God Save the Queen' posters on their windows and closed their doors. People flocked to newspaper offices for information and gathered in the streets of Paddington, Woollahra, Newtown, Waverley and Parramatta to talk about the shooting, the assassin, the Prince's health, and the consequences. All decorative bunting was taken down and public events, including a concert, cricket matches, horse races, St Patrick's regatta and ball, were cancelled 'in consequence of the diabolical attempt to assassinate HRH' and because any amusement 'seemed out of place'.

Some 20,000 people attended an 'indignation' meeting in Hyde Park about 'yesterday's outrage'. To minimise religious tension clergymen were forbidden to speak. The speaker of the Legislative Assembly, William Arnold, was loudly cheered when he told a public meeting that when the news broke the general surmise was that it was 'one of those Roman Catholics'.

When the news was announced at theatres in Melbourne and Ballarat, tearful audiences demanded the national anthem be played to 'deafening cheers'. Some 7000 people attended an indignation meeting at the Exhibition Building in Melbourne, 6000 in Hobart. Similar meetings and prayer services in all denominations rolled out on a daily basis in almost every community.

Amid the tears were fears more bloodshed or revolution was imminent. Colonial Secretary Parkes and his ministers, police, Royal Navy and Prince's party set about ensuring that Alfred, and themselves, remained safe and that Clontarf was not just the first shot in a broader uprising against the Empire and colonial rule.

Soldiers from the 50th Regiment and police were despatched to guard Government House and its grounds, 'the fear of more bloodshed and more assassinations...so great that all the orderlies, guards etc. are armed to the teeth.' Blue Jackets from the *Galatea* were posted outside Alfred's window,[5] because, a *Galatea* seaman said, they 'won't trust the soldiers' and news telegrams claimed some *Galatea* crew were 'most anxious to bombard Sydney, and were only deterred from turning their guns on the city by the strict orders of their officers'. Lord Newry armed himself with a revolver as did Premier Martin, who also had armed guards outside his home at Pott's Point and Colonial Secretary Parkes no longer walked anywhere alone.

The immediate government and Royal conclusion was a Fenian conspiracy was in operation. Alfred wrote that he was in 'no doubt that O'Farrell was a 'Fenian emissary' especially charged with the duty of murdering me to frighten all at home by showing how widely spread the conspiracy is'.[6]

Lord Newry, who expected O'Farrell's attack to be immediately followed by others shooting 'in the most approved Yankee-Irish style', felt if O'Farrell's words about doing his Irish duty were true 'God knows what is to become of us all. I believe we are all in danger of our lives.' He told his friend Candler in Melbourne he was in 'daily and hourly dread of new catastrophes, expecting anything' and 'very anxious about the English mail'.[7]

The dread of the Naval surgeons and nurses was something going amiss with Alfred on their watch. The three surgeons were cautious about Alfred's condition. Dr Alexander Watson, from *HMS Challenger*, said 'had it not been for the divergence of the bullet it would have killed High Royal Highness' and while they felt the wound would not prove fatal, they still had to remove the bullet and ensure no complications.[8]

After the surgery it would be up to Lucy Osburn to provide the Prince the highest standards of nursing care. Ensuring a Prince remained alive was not what Osburn expected to face on landing in Sydney. It was challenging enough to deliver Nightingale's brief for Australia's first nurses to evidence the highest standards of professionalism, hygiene and propriety. Now she had to do so with a member of the Royal family, one Nightingale was personally acquainted with, having met Alfred as a boy, telling Queen Victoria he was 'the darling' with 'higher spirits'.[9] The Queen had also sent 'the Lady with the Lamp' a personal thank-you letter after her pioneering work in the Crimea War, and a diamond brooch inscribed 'Blessed are the Merciful'. Now Nightingale's chosen one, the 31-year-old Osburn, had the responsibility of nursing the Queen's son. Resembling a nun in floor-length woollen black, with white linen collar, cuffs and muslin bonnet, she had to select which of her 'sisters', as she called them, could best meet the challenge.

She considered her nurses' varying experience and temperaments, deeming some unsuitable because they had a temper, or were too noisy or nosy to be at a Prince's bedside. Finally she selected two Scots in their early 30s as the two she could 'trust to say the least'.[10] Sister Haldane Turriff, the least experienced but clever and most socially presentable, as day nurse, and 'sensitive' Sister Annie Miller as night nurse.

During the first night of Friday 13 March the doctors said Alfred was in 'great pain'. He told Lord Newry he was in 'agony' and thought he had lost the use of his legs, complaining of 'painful spasms and twinges down the sciatic nerve', apparently grazed by the bullet, and his bottom feeling like a balloon.[11] The doctors were confident the Prince's lungs and spine had not been damaged, but he had 'lost the use of his limbs…some of his nerves are severed'.[12] It wasn't until 2am on Saturday that they felt confident enough to state 'no danger to life is anticipated' although the bullet had still not been removed.

They could readily see where it had lodged, and shortly before 8am, they prepared to operate. Without anaesthetic, Alfred sat almost upright in a chair, holding firmly onto the arms as the surgeons, using a gold probe, located and removed the bullet, originally half an inch long with a conical end but now 'an ugly rough slug, of size and shape of a small thimble.'[13] The surgeons did so 'without causing much pain or uneasiness' and while Alfred still 'suffered considerable pain in the track of the bullet' by Sunday evening he was 'almost free from pain or uneasiness. The wounds at the back and chest doing well.' Sedatives allowed him a few hours of sleep, and by the next morning, dressed in his fine silk night wear, he was able to get out of bed and on the Sunday 'enjoyed the open air, in a perambulator, propelled by two of his own sailors'.

Bulletins were posted at the Lodge Gates of Government House at regular intervals. On Monday at 2.30am he was 'sleeping tranquilly', at 11.10am he had 'enjoyed refreshing sleep since the ball was extracted. He is able to sit up this morning.' At 3.40pm he was 'suffering from pains in the back and along the course taken by the bullet'. At 5.48pm 'the duke is better'. Tuesday at 11.50am he had 'slept soundly last night' and the doctors reported 'no apprehensions are at present entertained of a full recovery' and, finally, on the night of Thursday the unambiguous news the whole country was desperate to hear: 'The physicians attending upon him do not consider that the wound is likely to prove fatal.'[14]

Relief swept the colonies, but tension remained high. The whole country fretted over the 'stain' on reputation and loyalty, fearing Queen Victoria and the Mother Country might think 'the democratic atmosphere of the colony had generated an indifference to the institutions and dynasty of the mother country'[15]—: 'What will they say of us in England when they hear the news? is the question everyone asks.'[16]

England would hear the news from Gov. Lord Belmore. He knew he had to report to the Duke of Buckingham, Secretary of State in the Colonial Office, as soon as possible, but faced unanswered questions about Alfred's recovery and Fenian uprisings, and it would also be some time before any message could reach Downing Street, as it had to be put on a steamer for a 5300 mile voyage to reach the nearest telegraph station at Galle in Ceylon (now Sri Lanka), about half-way to London.

With the fate of Alfred, Australia, or even the Empire, possibly changing dramatically before word got through to Buckingham

Palace, Belmore waited until he at least felt confident that he did not have to convey the news that the first Royal blood had been fatally spilled. Two days after the bullet was successfully removed, it was his 'painful duty' to send the news that Australia feared would shake the Empire to its foundations.

On 16 March Belmore wrote:

> On the 12th March a person named Offarell (sic) deliberately shot his Royal Highness the Duke of Edinburgh in the back at a public picnic, given in aid of the Sailor's Home at Clontarf Middle Harbour, Port Jackson. Providentially the wound was not fatal, and he is now able to go on board his ship, and hopes shortly to resume his duties…The ball was easily removed on Saturday 14 March by Drs Watson and Young, of HMS ships Challenger and Galatea. Offarell (sic) fired another shot the moment he was seized, which severely wounded a gentleman named Thorne in the foot; the ball has been extracted and he is doing well. The assassin, who avowed himself to be a Fenian, was arrested on the spot…In consequence of the report of a medical board, Commodore Lambert has ordered His Royal Highness to return to England as soon as he is sufficiently recovered, which will probably be next week.[17]

It wasn't until the early hours of Saturday April 25 that Belmore's telegram finally reached London. Whitehall was already in consternation, absorbing news from Canada of the Fenian assassination of D'Arcy McGee, an Irishman whose efforts to form a confederation of Canada embraced Protestantism and a close alliance with Britain; a confrontation with Ethiopia after its emperor imprisoned several missionaries and two representatives of the British Government, and the war in Abyssinia which would see the defeat and death of King Theodore.

The news about Alfred was shocking, but also unclear. By the time the Belmore telegram had passed through various telegraph stations from Ceylon to the Colonial Office, the contents were seen as 'incoherent, unintelligible and in many parts strangely contradictory', and numerous telegrams were sent back and forth to Galle on what an *Irish Times* correspondent described as an 'elucidation tour'.

By 3am word spread around London's gentleman's clubs and newspaper reporters rushed to the Colonial Office. The Duke of Buckingham and Chandos, roused from his bed, forbid the telegraphic cable being released until noon. He sent a brief message to Queen Victoria and ordered an express train so he could rush to her palatial holiday house, *Osborne*, on the Isle of Wight to personally deliver the full cable from Belmore.

Queen Victoria had only recently dismissed government and police concerns about Fenianism: 'Do not be alarmed about the Fenians. There has been a great deal of nonsense and foolish panic'—she told her daughter Vicky.[18] And only a few weeks before she wrote in her journal that Fenians, at least in England, 'have no money and no one thinks of them.' Now she was confronted with a brief but alarming cable from the Duke of Buckingham that Fenians had tried to assassinate her son on the other side of the world.

Colonial Office intelligence reached newspaper offices soon after 1pm Saturday. The *Pall Mall Gazette* reported 'a startling piece of news' as its evening edition was about to go to press, stating 'PRINCE ALFRED SHOT. A telegram was received by the Duke of Buckingham this morning that Prince Alfred had been shot in the back by a Fenian. Saturday 2 o'clock.'

When Victoria heard the Duke (of Buckingham) had arrived at *Osborne* it 'alarmed me and I dreaded the worst, However thank God! it was not.'[19]

She wrote: 'Dear Affie has been shot, at Sydney, but was going on well thereby showing however that he had been wounded! All greatly shocked.' The Fenian element shook her. It was 'shamefully wicked' as 'poor dear Affie is so entirely unconnected with anything political or Irish.' She told her daughter Vicky: 'I grieve to say it was again a Fenian – or an Irishman – though I hope an American Irishman.'

While the British newspapers assured readers Victoria received the news with 'becoming composure', she was anxious about Edward, who had not yet returned from a trip to Dublin with his pregnant wife, the Princess of Wales. Their trip had passed without incident—Alexandra charmed the locals by wearing green Irish poplin and putting shamrocks in her hat, and Edward was made a Knight of the Order of St Patrick—but the Queen was keen to have the heir home safely. She urged the news be told 'cautiously' to Edward and Alix when they landed at Holyhead, where the Prince asked railway officials to rush him to London, which they proudly did in record time at 70 mph.

Sir Thomas Larcom, Under-Secretary at Dublin Castle, was relieved the news came after the heir had left Ireland. 'Had it come while the Prince was here, go and do likewise would have been the first feeling in every Fenian heart.' Despite her dismissal of the Fenian threat, and her misgivings about her sons, the Queen's relief was evident. 'How easily Bertie might have been struck in Ireland!' Victoria told her daughter.[20] It was 'dreadful to think what danger (Alfred) was in, God has indeed mercifully spared him, for his escape is marvellous'.[21]

Home Secretary Gathorne Hardy received the shooting news while laying the foundation stone of Keble College at Oxford University. When he relayed it 'something between a groan and shriek rolled through the great assembly' until he said all indications were that the wound was not fatal, 'and ringing cheers and loyal cries filled the place.'[22] The Bishop of Oxford was applauded when he said Irish Church revenues were being confiscated to fund 'traitorous assassins', and the Establishment church was being done away with to satisfy the desires of a 'band of assassins – meaning of course the Fenians'.[23]

Victoria's 'becoming composure' may have been in part because she had wanted Alfred's voyage and distance from decadence of London and Paris would 'be for his good' and he might 'come back an altered being!'[24] rather than engage in more 'mischief', and a narrow escape might influence her son's priorities.

She also understood the value of a Royal attack. Her 'widow of Windsor' absence had eroded much of her popularity, raised questions about royalty's future, and saw a call in Parliament for her to abdicate. But a shooting engendered much 'enthusiasm, loyalty, sympathy and affection', she told Vicky, and 'it is worth being shot at to see how much one is loved.'[25]

How a shooting could deliver loyalty and affection was being experienced first-hand by Alfred, as any misgivings about his behaviour on tour were swamped by compassion and care.

Inside Government House in Sydney, he was attended to constantly by his surgeons, the Nightingale nurses, his Royal party and *Galatea* sailors. The ship's band played for him, and a 'piano mecanique' was installed for 'whiling away the tedium of the sick-room.' Sedatives helped overcome the pain in his back and leg, and his bed was carried from room to room as the sun moved. At night his companions Yorke and Newry joined those taking turns to use large fans to ward off the mosquitoes that were 'positively maddening'.[26]

Pushed around the Government House grounds in a perambulator, Alfred wondered why the assassination attack 'could have been done', saying he 'cannot remember having ever harmed a soul', recalled Captain James Banks,[27] a navigator at John Cuthbert's ship yard, which was preparing *Galatea* for its return journey.

Australia also could not understand why it had been done and worried that colonial loyalty was under serious question. An endless stream of messages of distress, sympathy, loyalty and devotion, along with prayers, bibles, patriotic songs and verse, poured into Government House. They came from community and town meetings across the colonies, bishops and clergy, civil servants and police magistrates, US and Chinese citizens of Sydney, foreign consuls from throughout Europe and the United States and Russia, the 'squatters' of Ten Mile Creek, and even the inmates of Liverpool lunatic asylum.

The Government Printer published an extraordinary Gazette of 14 pages of messages on 20 March, and another 18 pages a week later. Six special editions of the *Sydney Gazette* were printed to record the endless petitions of loyalty and expressions of shame. An address of condolence to the Queen was drawn up, quickly garnering 45,000 signatures on a document 700 yards long.

From the billiards room of Government House, Alfred was delighted to see the Naval squadron dressed with masthead flags to mark the 21st birthday of his sister Princess Louise. And when he was well enough to visit the *Galatea* he received rousing cheers, a reception which he later told his mother moved him deeply.

> I was very much overcome by it and had to go to my cabin and remain there some time to compose myself. I think it was the proudest moment of my life, to find that the nearly 600 men I command really loved me; they wrote me such a beautiful letter, signed by all the petty officers, which I will show you when I get home.[28]

Another person apparently overcome was his female companion from Melbourne, Sarah Saqui, who had perhaps been hoping her 'fortune' had been within reach. Lord Newry complained he had been in continual attendance 'on that poor unfortunate woman Sarah, who has been more like a maniac than anything else ever since the affair took place'.[29]

After the public announcement that he was likely to survive, Alfred responded to all the messages in a statement published in the *Government Gazette*. He received 'with sincere gratification the numerous addresses and desire to return my warm thanks for the expression of sympathy which they contain'. And he took the opportunity to reinforce the Britishness of the colony and its British subjects:

> The cowardly act of an individual has not, in any degree, shaken my confidence in the loyalty of the people of this colony towards the Throne and Person of Her Majesty, or in their affection for myself and I shall gladly convey to the Queen the universal expression of horror and indignation which the attempt to assassinate me has called from her Majesty's faithful subjects in Australia. Alfred.[30]

Fifteen days after the shooting, 'to everyone's joy', Alfred drove through Sydney in a carriage and four, 'and immediately up went the flags again and the City assumed quite a changed aspect'.[31]

It was only now that Alfred wrote to the Queen, on 11 pages of *HMS Galatea* notepaper: 'My Dearest Mama, I am sure it will reassure you after the shock you must have received in hearing of the attack made upon my life and the wound I received to get a letter written by myself.'

He was 'in no doubt that O'Farrell was a 'fenian emissary' especially charged with the duty of murdering me to frighten all at home by showing how widely spread the conspiracy is' but others could better describe the shooting. He could only say 'how strong my feeling of thankfulness is to the Almighty for my marvellous escape. No man who saw it could have believed that I had the slightest chance of escape'. He told he her had 'suffered a great deal of pain' in the first few days, especially in his back and right leg, it had been difficult to breathe. Writing was difficult due to rheumatism in his right arm. 'I cannot tell you how much I thought of you during my illness.'

Alfred was uncertain about whether he should continue the voyage which the Admiralty had planned for New Zealand, Tahiti, Hawaii, Callao in Peru, Valparaiso in Chile, Falkland Islands, Montevideo in Uruguay, Rio de Janeiro in Brazil and the West Indies.

But Commodore Rowley Lambert, Commander-in-Chief of the Royal Navy's Australia Station, felt Alfred should return to London. He was anxious about New Zealand, where a Fenian demonstration and mock funeral in honour of the Manchester martyrs had just been held, and he had heard O'Farrell had suggested the Prince risked being a likely target. After asking each of the naval surgeons for their opinion, the Commodore made the call: Alfred's voyage had to end, and for the sake of his recovery, and the wellbeing of Queen and Empire, it was time to go directly home.

So Alfred, in his 'Dearest Mama' letter, said he had been ordered home as soon as he was strong enough, possibly by early June. 'This determination was strengthened by a conviction that you would not feel comfortable until you saw me back again', and he hoped to 'soon be with you and all my brothers and sisters at home'. He signed off 'with the sincerest love and devotion, I remain, your dutiful and affectionate son Alfred'.[32]

No doubt he and his friends were also keen to resume their affections for the social life of London, around which their lives were built. Lord Newry told the *Times* editor he expected to return 'by next Ascot races'.[33]

In London, the Queen absorbed the despatches from Lord Belmore, including his account of the shooting at Clontarf, extracts from the *Sydney Morning Herald* and *Empire* on the shooting and its aftermath and accounts by Elliot Yorke and *Galatea* artist Oswald Brierley, the plans for a trial, and reports about O'Farrell and Fenians.

In late May she received 'a good telegraphic message from dear Affie, from Sydney. He had sailed April 6, his external wounds healed.' A relieved Victoria could not know if he would return an 'altered being'. But his 'dear affectionate letter' gave her some hope as 'he speaks so nicely and properly'.[34]

11
VENGEANCE OVER AUSTRALIA

The blow aimed at Prince Alfred's life is a dastard stab at the honour of this young community.
— Armidale Express and New England General Advertiser

Inside Government House, every effort was made to keep the mood as calm as possible as Sisters Turriff and Miller nursed a recovering Alfred, but outside the country was beside itself. The country was shamed, wounded, vengeful and fearful. Royal blood had been spilled—the royal family's most serious regicide attempt—which meant Australia, or perhaps even the Empire, was at risk.

The would-be assassin had been apprehended and would soon be on trial and face his judgment. But so too was the country on trial on matters of colonial security, empirical loyalty and royal devotion. The colonies, having evinced an unprecedented outpouring of loyalty when they greeted the Prince, now evinced a 'universal feeling of sorrow, shame and rage…the whole colony has been wounded in the person of its Royal guest'.[1]

One correspondent wrote:

> Never before has any single event taken so powerful a hold on the public mind never before has the national voice been so vehement, so unanimous, so full of rage, sorrow and vengeful bitterness…the blow aimed at Prince Alfred's life is a dastard stab at the honour of this young community, and all men say it will leave a stain behind even when the memory of the deed has ceased to excite anger or inflame popular rancour.[2]

The whole colony was also fearful of further uprising and violence, of what the Mother Country would think, and the consequences.

The Sydney Bishop's wife, Jane Barker, said everyone supposed that O'Farrell was part of a Fenian conflict which had now reached 'our side of the world…where or when it will end who can say? I feel that none of us are safe now'.[3] And a Queenslander spoke for many when he said colonists had quickly come to the conclusion the attack 'was part of an organised confederacy to overthrow the British Government'.[4]

The fear of Irish insurrection arrived with the first settlers 80 years before. Catholic convicts were forced to attend Church of England services and their children treated by authorities as Protestants. The first Catholic priests arrived as convicts for their complicity in the Irish 1798 uprising. Early governors warned Irish Catholics were unsuitable migrants and security risks, and a chain of events were portrayed as confirming their threat to empire, colonial authority, Protestantism and peace: Irish convicts had been involved in the first battle between Europeans on Australian soil in 1804, the Battle of Vinegar Hill, when plans to seize ships in Sydney Harbour and escape were put down by the infamous Rum Corps killing 11 rebels. Priests were not officially permitted into the colony until 1820, one who did arrive in 1817 was deemed an unauthorised and threatening presence and deported. An Irish Catholic protest against Orangemen in Melbourne in 1846 led to shootings and so-called 'Popish riots'. The 1848 Irish uprising's Young Irelander leaders were in the colonies as political exiles. Irishmen were among the leaders of the Eureka uprising in 1854. Catholic priests and Irish newspapers in the 1860s were seen as supporters of Fenian sedition and anti-British. Now 'one of those Roman Catholics' had shot a member of the Royal family.

Re-ignited were the passions and prejudices evident at public meetings about constitutional reform in the 1840s, described by the *Sydney Free Press* as 'the contest between antagonistic principles of democracy and aristocracy'. Conservative forces branded opponents as mobocrats, Jacobins, Chartists, anarchists, levellers, Robespierres, Papineaux, radicals and rebels.

'They are democrats of the muddiest water. They respect neither the aristocracy of rank, nor the aristocracy of wealth, nor the aristocracy of intellect, nor the aristocracy of character', declared the *Sydney Morning Herald.*

The *Australian* warned against 'infidel' and 'seditious' thinking, citing the lessons of France, 'a nation which got drunk with blood to vomit crime.' It was 'absolutely wicked' for revolutionary thoughts to be spread among an 'excitable and uneducated Irish mob to pour this moral poison into the ears of the rising youth of Australia.'[5] O'Farrell's gun had now re-ignited the battle. Irish Catholics were readily seen as Fenian sympathisers or conspirators. The Speaker of the Legislative Assembly, William Arnold, said it was incumbent on Irish Catholics to publicly 'disclaim being influenced by those disloyal feelings from which so vile an act had sprung.'[6] A North Sydney alderman, John Jago, declared it was 'the duty of every Englishman, if he heard of a disloyal person, to hunt him down like a rat',[7] and some newspapers said while it 'is to be regretted the culprit was not immolated on the spot', hanging was also too good for each miscreants and it was hoped legislation would change so 'every Fenian, capitally convicted, shall be torn to pieces by wild beasts'.[8] In the mindset of the First Fleet, those not aligned with British law, religion and values were seen as dangerous 'infidels', with Irish Catholics at the top of the 'most dangerous' list. The colonies' security still relied entirely on the British Navy and there was unsettling talk of the Fleet retreating from far-flung corners, including Australia, even as France and Germany were seen to retain territorial designs in the Pacific, and Melbourne had been recently shocked when Russian and Confederate war ships entered its harbour.

The security fears had not changed since newspaper editor Edward Smith wrote 60 years previously: 'If England were to withdraw her protecting arm our situation would be almost as helpless and pitiable as that of the embryo kangaroo, when its mother in her terror to escape from the hunter and in order to lighten her weight and aid her speed, casts out of her bag and leaves to shift for itself'. Australia was still 'an infant British society making its way in the Empire, too fragile for complete independence',[9] Colonial Secretary Parkes felt, and now faced its biggest security threat just after Irish nationalists in the United States launched abortive invasions of Canada and an unsuccessful uprising in Ireland.

The Fenians were the first face of a new crime, one in which rebels operating in various countries were seemingly ready to use guns and explosives to end what they saw as imperial and religious tyranny. Fenians were the first intercontinental group to operate in multiple countries and take advantage of unprecedented mobility due to steam-powered shipping, broader and faster communications due to the telegraph and printing presses, increasing modernisation of banking allowing a global flow of funds, and the American Civil War providing arms for patriots around the world.

The country was on edge. One letter to the government talked of 'an invasion of the colony' designed to convert the country 'into some enormous kingdom for the Pope'. Police pursued rumours that four Fenian 'head centre' men had arrived from Panama. Detectives regarded anyone who even drunkenly said 'Who is the bloody prince? He is only a damned German bastard' as Fenian sympathisers.[10]

There was more emotion than evidence, but Parkes was a shrewd reader of the public mood, and of pro-British and anti-Irish Catholic mood himself. He could see national security and conspiracy represented not just risk and crisis, but opportunity and reward.

It was not what Parkes could have foreseen growing up as an apprentice ivory turner in Birmingham. In his younger days he supported Chartism and its push for parliamentary reform and universal suffrage, even admiring some Irish rebels and admitting he had 'hung upon the voice of Daniel O'Connell with an unspeakable interest.'[11]

After his own ivory-turning business failed, 24-year-old Parkes pawned his tools and with his wife Clarinda, the first of three who would bear him 17 children, arrived in Sydney in 1839 as a bounty immigrant. After working as a labourer and foundry worker, he set up an 'Ivory Manufactory and Toy Warehouse' in Hunter Street. It also failed but his parlour became a favoured haunt for men debating matters of democracy, independence and constitution.

While his parents were illiterate and he received a limited education, Parkes developed his writing talents as the Sydney correspondent for the *Launceston Examiner*, co-founded and edited by future federation leader and *Sydney Morning Herald* editor Rev. John West. He turned his love of writing and politics to found the *Empire* newspaper as 'an independent power to vivify, elevate and direct the political life of the country', a magnet for the leading liberal minds of the colony.

Some of these minds, such as Rev. West, were pressing for a united Australia, and some, including Presbyterian clergyman Rev. Lang, for a republic. In the 1850s Parkes and Lang founded the Australia League to encourage a sense of national identity, end convict transportation, and emulate the United States in a single political federation of 'the United Provinces of Australia.'

Lang began a newspaper, *The Press,* with one of its aims to unite the colonies 'against imperial injustice' and advance a great 'Federation of United Providences' into 'one great Australian nation.'[12] Such sentiments were branded 'republican' by the Governor, Sir Charles FitzRoy, in letters to Earl Grey, Secretary of State for War and Colonies. London newspapers, including the *Times, Morning Chronicle, Spectator* and *Economist* analysed Lang's likely impact, and Parkes' *Empire* said Lang's re-election to the Legislative Council showed Sydney people had embraced him 'in the heat of his disloyalty, like a bolt of steel from the glowing coals,' and English people could only guess at what distant colonists would do with this 'red hot steel'.[13]

Parkes was initially a key player in efforts to transform the rival colonies into a 'Great Federal Republic' in place of what he and republicans described as the 'dung-hill aristocracy of Botany Bay'[14] and 'the bastard branches of the... accursed English aristocracy.'[15] His then appetite even extended to some support for 'Irish history and Irish wrongs', so impressed by exiled Irish rebel Gavan Duffy that 'if he had been placed in the same position, he would have been a rebel like him'.[16]

But Parke's *Empire* was another business failure. He survived bankruptcy with the help of friends, some occasional journalism income, and £1000 as a lecturer promoting emigration on an 18-month tour of England with lawyer William Bede Dalley during which he described himself as being 'as much an Englishman as an Australian'. He could see better prospects in politics than business—'I am wholly unfit for business, but the fittest of all men for Parliament'[17]—and realised that appealing to wealthy and influential men in Sydney, rather than 'rebel' republicanism, was his best hope of fulfilling his ambitions, which his critics described as becoming the 'Napoleon of Australia, the saviour of society'.

His strong oratory, prominent white beard, energy and burning ambition made him a force to be reckoned with as he shed any lingering republican interests in the pursuit of what he called 'respectability'. Vowing 'I will yield to no man in feelings of loyalty to the British Crown',[18] he prosecuted what he later termed 'the crimson thread of kinship' which bound the British Empire, Mother England and Young Australia. A kinship and vision which had little time for Irishmen, Catholicism or republicanism.

Republican Daniel Deniehy said Parkes could not be of serious comfort to republicans because he had 'too much, not of the Englishman, but of "Englishmanism" about him'[19] and wrote presciently in an 1855 editorial that the important question for Australia was 'whether Australia is for the Australians…and whether the Australian and English nationality are henceforth to be identical', or whether like America the similarity in colour and language would be 'an additional incentive to national hate, and to the intensity of national revenge'.[20]

With Parkes' rise to become Her Majesty's Colonial Secretary, his 'Englishmanism' and love of the 'crimson' was readily apparent from his sword and uniform welcome of Alfred, and his personal joy after Alfred's arrival procession around Sydney:

> The Prince sent for me in into his own room, and I was the only member of Parliament or of the Government who was introduced to him personally. HRH was alone and handed me a chair in a very pleasant way…who would have dreamed…(I would) live to dine with Princes and be led in by Earls.[21]

But now, just a few weeks later, that crimson blood had been spilled! For a loyal Royal with 'Napoleonic' ambitions, having an Irish Catholic and apparent Fenian agent thinking it his divine mission to assassinate a Prince was a God-sent political providence to seize the approbation of his English masters, royalty and Australia.

Parkes, like Alfred, was immediately accepting O'Farrell was a Fenian and part of a broader conspiracy which threatened the colony. In his mind, the *Freeman's Journal* articles about the implications of the Manchester hangings soon becoming clear was 'accomplishment of this prophecy.' Everything Parkes heard, or chose to hear, reinforced his conviction as he set out to almost single-handedly deliver redemption by saving the colonies and helping preserve the Empire. He was fortified by politicians, newspapers and community leaders defending 'loyal' society, building a national fear that a real threat to country and Empire existed, and demonising the 'them' posing the threat. The government claimed it had 'intelligence' from police, but much of it came from Parkes who described it as 'various rumours (which) reached the Government, through different channels…which appeared to call upon the Government to take every precaution', 'innumerable' letters from citizens, including some 'occupying respectable positions of society', such as his own Attorney-General and a magistrate, as well as anonymous citizens giving information about 'who might be suspected of disloyalty and treasonable purposes'.[22]

In the wave of shame, sectarianism and loyalty which some described as 'almost run mad', guards and soldiers with fixed bayonets protected senior government officials, Government House, Darlinghurst Gaol, Victoria barracks and munitions stores.

Parkes took charge of the hunting down of any disloyal person 'like a rat'. As Minister for the Police as well as Colonial Secretary, Parkes felt entitled to direct police operations, reprising a role he took the year before when he armed himself and headed a mounted pursuit of a gang of bushrangers. He had the full support of police Inspector-General John McLerie, known to his troops as 'The General', and his department head, Edmund Fosbery, son of a Royal Navy commander.

But he was not fully confident in the constabulary. There was already public muttering about how police had failed to keep a more vigilant eye on O'Farrell. As Parkes' former paper the *Empire* posed, given an apparent Fenian agent had been 'almost publicly talking treason and meddling with murderous weapons in two hotels in the very heart of Sydney for at least three months before the outrage, what were the police about?' And the police force, not unfamiliar with drinking and corruption, had an Irish hue: half of the dozen detectives had Irish names, and McLerie quickly sacked two officers and suspended several others for not acting with 'promptitude and energy in the late emergency.' Parkes went to Darlinghurst Gaol to personally question O'Farrell, who told him: 'The Prince will live, you need not fear for him…it's only a side wound…I shall be hanged…but the Prince will live.'

But it was O'Farrell's alleged comments at Clontarf that he was a Fenian which was Parkes' focus. He absorbed O'Farrell's tale of joining the Fenian organisation, being part of a series of clandestine and secret groups, describing how a 'cell' of 10 or 11 Fenians reported to a 'circle' who in turn reported to a head centre chairman, or 'senex', and how his cell had received the death 'warrant' in the form of a 'sealed parchment' from the 'Fenian government' and of drawing lots for the assignment and giving his oath to deliver the death of a Prince.

'A programme was issued that three men were to be shot for the three men executed at Manchester' and it was 'imperative' to kill Alfred, O'Farrell told Parkes. The more obvious target, the Prince of Wales, was being spared as he was useful to the republican cause as he already 'disgraces royalty' and 'turning England against royalty'. William Chapman, a prison warder, similarly reported O'Farrell telling him he had 'got word from London…to do away with the Prince' as Edward was 'drinking himself to death', so Alfred was in line to be the next King. As O'Farrell told it, he had questioned why Alfred could not have been assassinated in England, but his Fenian superiors called Australia a 'shambles, or convict station…they said "let one of the Royal family die out here"' and the Fenian 'central council' knew 'the oligarchy would be awfully savage if the prince were killed out here'.

Principal warder Frederick Barnard, who knew O'Farrell in Victoria and visited him the day after the shooting, said O'Farrell told him that 'immediately after the news arrived here of the Manchester executions, a Fenian body was organised in Melbourne composed of some Ballarat men under the leadership of a person who came out from England for that purpose…when it was agreed that Prince Alfred was to be shot.' From two dozen recruits the band was reduced to 10, who 'drew lots' to decide who would 'assassinate the Prince and Earl of Belmore', but after discovering Belmore's links with the St Patrick's Society regatta, they drew lots again to 'shoot the Prince only'. The decision was made two months ago and the most prominent members of the group had returned to England.[23]

This was enough for Parkes to hastily post a reward of £1000 for 'accomplices'. A day after the shooting, a notice in 78 publications throughout the colonies in Australia and New Zealand said an attempt had been made to assassinate the Duke of Edinburgh, and a second shot had wounded a bystander, and 'a man giving the name of H. J. O'Farrell has been arrested for the crimes, and there is reason to believe the offender was acting in concert with or by direction of others not in custody, organised and associated together for treasonable purposes.' The reward was for any information leading to the conviction of each and every accomplice of O'Farrell, whether they resided in New South Wales or elsewhere, and a free pardon from the Governor for the first accomplice to provide such information.[24]

Not everyone shared Parkes' conviction co-conspirators would be found. One newspaper in Melbourne, the reported heartland of the Fenian plot, asserted immediately after the shooting: 'We believe we are perfectly safe in predicting that the police of Sydney will discover that the assassin was without associate, and that the crime was not arranged by any body of conspirators, but was the act of a solitary monomaniac.'[25]

And the *Ballarat Star* said its investigations of 'those who were most capable of forming a judgment' indicated O'Farrell was 'no more than a monomaniac, an individual who for some years past was scarcely responsible for his actions, and...should have been kept under restraint as a decided if not dangerous lunatic'.[26]

But Parkes was on a mission. After hearing O'Farrell's Fenian 'confession', he rushed from Darlinghurst Gaol with Chief of Detectives, Henry Wager, and Sergeant Alexander Baikie to the Sydney hotel rooms where O'Farrell had stayed.

At the Currency Lass Hotel they found letters connected to O'Farrell's sisters in Melbourne. And at the Clarendon Hotel they found a Catholic Douay-Rheims bible and other religious books, with O'Farrell's name inscribed, along with percussion caps, detonating cartridges and wadding for revolvers. And several articles about recent Fenian–British violence from the French journal *L'univers Illustre*, which was sympathetic to the Irish cause.

More explosively, inside a waistcoat pocket at the Clarendon they found some leaves torn from a notebook sitting on a dressing table. Some of the writing was barely decipherable scratching and not entirely coherent, but some words and phrases leapt off the pages:

> This thing I have to do for vengeance, and to rouse the Irish here...vengeance for Ireland is sweet...if I had my will every English ship in these colonial ports should have been destroyed...I know I could have done so much more in England. But it is my duty to the R, and I will, if able, do it...oh destiny! it must be done! Fate, fate!...If I should fail I should never forgive myself...to think that I have not one relation that knows of my proceedings...I am to die in two weeks from this...grim satisfaction in thinking of the vengeance...how the nobility of the three countries will curse me and the toadying lickspittle press hunt the dictionaries over for terms of abhorrence...woe to you England when the glorious "nine" carry out their programme...[27]

The notes were extraordinary but Parkes resolved to keep them to himself in his pursuit of Fenian co-conspirators, one which went beyond overseeing official police work. Parkes formed his own private posse, engaging a political ally, his Under-Secretary and Public Works Minister, James Byrnes, to recruit and swear in eight government and bank clerks as 'special constables' to find evidence of Irish sedition.

O'Farrell's oral and written words, information coming from his private 'bloodhounds', concerned citizens, and newspaper reports all convinced Parkes and his police chiefs that a number of Fenians had come to the Australian colonies. Under the cloak of fundraising for the widows of Fenian 'martyrs', they corresponded with colleagues in Ireland and America and sought to recruit accomplices like O'Farrell, who told the Darlinghurst principal warder the funding drive was a 'sham' and 'humbug' and all proceeds went to 'the cause'. Seditious meetings had been held before the attack, they believed, and it was 'improbable that an assassination of that kind could be committed by one man, avowing himself Fenian, without the connivance and assistance of other Fenians'. In Chief McLerie's mind, 'the attempted assassination...was not the unaided act of one individual but the fruits of a treasonable organisation commonly known as Fenianism; this opinion has been strengthened by after occurrences and disclosures'.

Fosbery, his department head, said the conclusion was based on 'the nature of the crime itself, the statements made by the convict, and the similarity that the crime bore to others of the same class committed by avowed Fenian agents.' There were obvious questions over O'Farrell's words and the circumstantial nature of alleged treasonous activity—Fosbery later described it as 'the prevailing impression'[28]—but within 48 hours Parkes advised Lord Belmore he was satisfied there was 'a treacherous spirit of disloyalty instigating small knots of men to displays of criminal intentions.'[29] He told the Governor that 'Americanised Irishmen' from gold rush

California and Irish emigrants had fuelled Fenianism, and it was 'not uncommon thing to hear of persons of this class who openly boast that the time is not far distant when they will possess the government of this country'.[30]

Parkes wrote to all the colonies to tell them that:

> there is sufficient evidence...before this Government to justify the belief that disloyal organisations exist in the Australian colonies, and that these bodies are in treasonable correspondence with agents of the Fenian conspirators in the United Kingdom. It appears to be beyond doubt that the man O'Farrell...acted throughout as the appointed agent of a diabolical organisation of this kind.

He called on the colonies to fully support efforts to 'bring to justice all accomplices in the great crime which has been committed', and warned the New Zealand Colonial Secretary that according to O'Farrell, 'if Alfred continued on his tour he would be in much greater danger in New Zealand'.

His Victorian peer, James McCulloch, said he would assist if Parkes had any information showing O'Farrell had accomplices in Victoria, and his police chief Frederick Standish quickly replied that one of his detectives knew O'Farrell well: 'He...drank very hard and was subject to fits of delirium tremens. Upon one occasion he asked Detective Berrill for a pair of pistols to blow out his brains' and his police superintendent suggested he was a 'dissipated drunken man'.

Despite the suggestion of mental and alcoholism issues, and the erratic nature of O'Farrell's notebook and conversations, Parkes was in no doubt his man was Fenian, truthful and sane. In a minute, Parkes wrote that O'Farrell provided information 'unhesitatingly', had no appearance of an 'invented' story, and where his truthfulness could be tested 'in all these cases it was ascertained that he spoke the truth'.[31] The streets of every town and the corridors of power were awash with the 'truth', much of it of the most 'exciting', 'startling' and 'painful' kind, including the government possessing 'secret intelligence' of Fenian plots, conspiracies, organisation, papers and weapons.

An *Empire* report on 16 March, headlined 'Political Origin of the Crime', was widely reprinted:

> We believe we are correct in stating that the Government are in possession of abundant evidence to prove that the act as the result of deliberate political organisation and appointment, originating in Ireland; and assuming that the information is reliable and authentic, serious apprehensions are entertained that the next or succeeding mail from home may convey the intelligence of attempts to perpetrate corresponding outrages in Great Britain. For obvious reasons we are not at liberty to stay more.

There was widespread coverage of claims by a prominent Tasmanian parliamentarian, William Langdon, that O'Farrell was 'an uncle of the assassin Allen', William Allen, one of the Irish Republican Brotherhood martyr hanged for the murder of a policeman in Manchester.[32]

Other 'evidence' reported to police was of similarly doubtful quality: someone at Penrith 'heard' someone else warn that a black flag would wave over Alfred, another 'heard' that explosive materials had been imported, another that a *Galatea* sailor said 30 men had originally been involved in the plot, of whom 10 had gone back to England, 10 to Ballarat 'and the rest are here'.

One said a man called McBurney had commented that 'the villain is a better man than the Prince' and suggested the Prince had taken away his wife, 'as he is a rare boy for the girls'. The American consul Hayden Hall told of a man who had made 'violent expressions against the Queen and his Royal Highness...and knew that it had fallen to the lot of O'Farrell to shoot the Prince'. When a former Victorian policeman, Harry Benedict, claimed he had evidence of O'Farrell's 'four confederate' accomplices in Melbourne, Parkes quickly put him on the colonial payroll as a secret agent, gave him a train ticket and £30 to travel south to investigate further and hire more agents, quietly promising £1000 for every accomplice he could help arrest, despite Victoria's chief warning Benedict was 'not to be trusted'[33] and a detective saying that when 'when the case was being got up against O'Farrell he (Benedict) was working with O'Farrell's solicitors for the defence'.[34]

Benedict kept promising he was close to securing 'important documentary evidence' but repeatedly sought additional funds to pay for his 'heavy' expenses on travel and 'informants'. He told Parkes that 'unless the great inducement, money, is forthcoming, information becomes scarce', before, three months later, the disappointed Colonial Secretary stopped signing vouchers for 'special services' and ended the arrangement. Parkes also embraced Charles Miller, who wrote to him from Darlinghurst prison claiming to be a former Fenian who knew the assassination had been planned and could infiltrate his old circle. Miller had a string of aliases and convictions and had just begun an 18 months hard labour sentence for stealing a gold watch, and police regarded him as an 'infernal rogue' but Parkes was unfazed. He interviewed Miller in Darlinghurst, and citing 'very important information',[35] arranged to have Premier and Attorney-General James Martin secure the Governor's quashing of his gaol sentence, an immediate release and some advance funds to pursue evidence. Like Benedict, Miller produced more requests for funds than evidence.

Parkes also recruited the *Sydney Morning Herald's* parliamentary reporter, Samuel Cook, pioneer of Pitman's shorthand in Australia, to sit outside O'Farrell's Darlinghurst cell and record his conversations. The fee of £16.10s was useful income for Cook, and the inside knowledge of O'Farrell's comments was advantageous for his newspaper, however prejudicial it might be to the forthcoming trial. O'Farrell suspected what was happening: the Gaol Governor

John Read said 'O'Farrell could not see him (Cook) but seemed to be trying to get a glimpse round the door'.

Whatever the soundness of information from O'Farrell or anyone else, Parkes was of no mind to hesitate, even when some police expressed doubts. Some said they had not heard any suggestion of any plot against Alfred, and while there were Fenian sympathisers they had not seen any treasonable evidence. Detective Daniel McGlone's judgment was that the Fenian conspiracy was 'a concoction of the greatest falsehoods ever known' and after seeing O'Farrell was convinced 'the man is mad'. This led police department head Fosbery to describe McGlone as 'a good Catholic' and dismiss him for resisting an order to stop residing at Shalvey's public house, which was 'nothing but a nest of Fenians' who drilled with revolvers in the Domain. 'If I had my will I would bring the guns from the *Galatea* and blow some of the wretches' houses down', Fosbery said.[36] McGlone felt he was dismissed 'because I was too truthful'.[37]

And when his eight special constables resigned after finding no evidence of seditious activity, Parkes signed up two more to keep searching. He and his acolytes could only see conspiracy, not concoction.

And the Colonial Secretary had long seen Irish Catholics as a threat to his equating of Protestantism and Empirical loyalty with prosperity, security and progress. He had frequently used the *Empire* to attack Rome and rivals like Archdeacon John McEnroe, who dared to support a Catholic candidate for the Legislative Council. The *Freemans Journal* rated the *Empire* as more vindictive than anything seen in the worst days of racial bigotry and Orange ascendancy in Ireland, and Archbishop Polding described Parkes as 'hateful' and 'the heaviest curse that could befall this country'[38],

Parkes in turn complained he was 'pursued with a sleepless and relentless hostility' by the *Journal,* which he described as 'the organ of the Irish and Roman Catholic body in NSW'[39] and often described Irish Catholics as 'jabbering baboons', 'disruptive troublemakers', 'not the best people' as immigrants, declaring their drinking, gambling and other vices had supplied America with 'a criminal and pauper class'.[40] His argument was supported by the Protestant establishment—one newspaper said if Irish immigrants were taxed at the rate in which they cost the country for gaols, poor-houses, watch-houses, and police it would be a 'relief'.[41]

Parkes had caused bitter Catholic resentment with his state education control and funding at the expense of the historically dominant church schools, and now his political rivals like William Macleay accused him of using the Clontarf shooting to have the country believe 'that abominable secret association denominated Fenianism was a kind of Catholic conspiracy'.[42]

Infused with distrust of Rome, disdain for Irish Catholics, and despair of treason and revolution, Parkes knew the eyes of an Empire and country were on him as Australia dealt with its first act of intercontinental terror.

12

LOYALTY AND ROYALTY

These laws are large enough to embrace any attempts at deposing the Queen or establishing a republic...here or elsewhere.
— James Martin, Premier New South Wales

A moral panic gripped the country after the 'one short minute (which) converted the loyal land of Australia from one of rejoicing to one of shame, grief and indignation'[1] a panic which was later described as the 'Australian Reign of Terror'.

As Henry Parkes and the police aggressively set out to 'prove' the Fenian conspiracy, Premier and Attorney-General James Martin, while preparing for O'Farrell's trial, hurriedly drafted and introduced a new *Treason Felony Act* 'for the better security of the Crown and Government of the United Kingdom and for the better suppression and punishment of seditious practices and attempts'.

Freedom of speech and *habeas corpus* rights were abandoned, because, Martin explained, 'There are persons here, agents of persons in other parts of the world, and in correspondence with societies that have entered into a conspiracy against the British Crown. We have been informed these persons have their places of meeting where there are, no doubt, papers connected with the conspiracy or where such papers are supposed to exist.' Proclaimed by and signed 'Henry Parkes. God Save the Queen!'—although Parkes later distanced himself and asserted it was the sole work of Martin—the legislation adapted 1848 British laws, introduced in the wake of Irish and French uprisings, to allow treason trials to have the same standards of evidence as other crimes.

But Australia went much further. Any person who would 'imagine, invent or devise or intend to deprive or depose Our Most Gracious Lady the Queen', her heirs or successors, from the style, honour or Royal name of the Imperial Cron of the United Kingdom', through war, force or constraint, by printing, writing or speaking, would be guilty of felony and convicted to hard labour for the term of his natural life or any term not less than seven years.

People could be prosecuted if their intent or language was proven by two credible witnesses, and Justices of the Peace were empowered to issue warrants allowing police to enter a suspected person's house, by force if necessary, to search for papers or weapons.

The legislation also targeted anyone 'who shall move or induce any foreigner to invade the Queen's dominions', with such intentions to be judged on 'writings or open and advised speaking.' In the latter case this merely required someone to give information on oath within six days and a warrant to be issued within 10 days. Accessories before and after the fact and principals alike were liable to two years hard labour on the roads.

In a clause which even Downing Street and Buckingham Palace thought excessive, it became a criminal offence to be disrespectful to the Queen, or not join a loyal toast to the Queen. Specifically, anyone using 'any language disrespectful to Her Most Gracious Majesty or shall factiously avow a determination to refuse to join in any loyal toast or demonstration in honour of Her Majesty', or anyone who should 'write or publish any words disrespectful to Her Most Gracious Majesty or expressing sympathy' was now deemed guilty of treason. The sale of foreign or local newspaper content deemed 'seditious' became a criminal offence.

Anyone who committed such offences, or expressed any sympathy for anyone found guilty of treason, risked apprehension without warrant and imprisonment with hard labour for up to two years. Parkes placed advertisements in newspapers and posted placards urging citizens to provide information about any offenders, and utilise the provision for any offenders to be apprehended not just by constables, but 'any other person without warrant for such purpose'.

Martin made it clear the law was intended to be sufficiently 'large' to embrace 'any attempts at deposing the Queen or establishing a republic…here or elsewhere'. One MP said that regardless of any drafting issues it was 'morally a crime to talk disloyally or seditiously'.

The extraordinary legislation passed through both parliamentary houses in seven hours in a single day and given assent by the Governor the next day. Political leaders, including opponents of Parkes, were swept up in the reign of loyalty and panic. Future premier John Robertson, a critic of the aristocratic notions of the British constitution and supportedr of the 'just claims' of Ireland, initially doubted the Fenian fears but now quickly said he had been persuaded there were Fenians in the country, and for anyone declining the Royal toast 'the best thing would be to lock him up'. John Macleay, another Parkes critic, said the only way to suppress such 'odious principles' as Fenianism was by 'complete extermination by hunting them out of the country like a venomous reptile'.

Republicans and moderates could do little except question why such draconian laws had to be passed so hurriedly, and why Australia needed more restrictions on liberty and speech than England. When republican John Lang said the legislation did not clarify whether it was targeting seditious speech in public or private, Martin interjected 'anywhere'. Former Colonial Secretary William Forster reminded Lang the legislation could be used as a 'dangerous power' by the government to punish political opponents, and his republican rhetoric put him at risk of punishment and in 'circumstances of danger'.[2] But Lang was against Roman Catholicism as much as he was for a republic, and in his mind O'Farrell's crime was yet another example of political assassinations 'perpetrated by certain fanatics in the interest of Romanism' and to 'subvert and ruin the interests of Protestantism.' Lang would continue to remind everyone that the Catholic Church had ordained O'Farrell as a deacon, and called him 'the reverend assassin'.[3]

While London had urged colonial governments to adopt its 1848 law, New South Wales was deemed to have gone too far. The *Spectator* was particularly scathing, describing the 'loyalty in convulsion fits' as a form of 'cerebral disease' and 'political delirium.'

> It is obvious that at present a live Prince acts upon the starved appetite for rank which is dormant in our Australian colonists, like a draught of neat brandy on an empty stomach entirely unused to alcohol, completely intoxicating and furiously stimulating it into acts of rude and frantic idolatry. If a whole colony could be put under medical care, the colony of NSW seems to have been in the most urgent need. The response to Alfred's shooting was 'equivalent to those religious orgies which certain savage tribes celebrate around their favourite idols or festivals of extreme importance as they strip, wound and gash themselves with an enthusiasm that would seem to indicate a physical enjoyment…if we did not know how easily a pain is sublimed into pleasure by the ecstasy of certain passions.

The New South Wales rulers had committed a 'political orgy' by stripping away cherished liberties and freedoms 'in a frenzy of excitement which no one can study without amazement and compassion', as if the laws were enacted upon 'the whole colony would be guilty of crimes even greater than O'Farrell's'.

The Treason Laws were 'insane' or 'cruel, brutal, and silly', the *Spectator* said, and urged Queen Victoria to withhold Royal assent, and suggested 'a little more Prince would be a capital thing for the Colonies'. She could make Alfred Governor of New South Wales, send Royal Princes out as Governor-Generals, or ensure a Prince of the Blood visited at least once every three years: 'the cure for fanaticism is a little more knowledge of the object which excites it.'[4]

The *Star* called the laws a 'grotesque outrage upon the spirit of law.' Dublin's *Nation* said the 'idiotic display of delirious loyalty' would one day lead the people of New South Wales to be 'ashamed' of the 'madness' and 'vile and dishonoured' role of their 'political eunuchs of England'. Others called the laws 'monstrous', 'servile' and 'un-English'.

The reaction upset some Australian newspapers. 'When we thought we were doing the correct thing, in offering up our liberty at the shrine of loyalty, it is rather hard to be told now that we are simply making fools of ourselves,' the *Illustrated Sydney News* commented. 'The only excuse they seem inclined to allow us is the not very complimentary one of 'cerebral excitement, occasioned by over-indulgence in unaccustomed stimulants...we had had a little too much Prince, and didn't know what we were doing.'[5]

And one reader told the *Spectator* its savage criticism showed a misunderstanding of the 'vein of personal sentiment' which ran through the colonies, the feeling 'we are all of kin, held together by a bond of family relationship' which was wounded by O'Farrell's pistol shot. And because the community was resolved to ensure the spirit of Fenianism 'should be crushed at any cost...we consented to a temporary sacrifice in order that we might...crush a new evil in its infancy...we were in no mood to haggle about the temporary cost of crushing it'.[6]

Serious consideration was given to withholding royal assent to the more extreme anti-treason laws. The Secretary of State for the Colonies, the Duke of Buckingham, diplomatically told Gov. Belmore that while Queen Victoria was 'very sensible of the feelings of loyalty and devotion', some of the clauses 'appear to me...extreme in their scope and in the severity of their penalties. I rely on the discretion and prudence of your Government to prevent any abuse of such unusual powers. I abstain from submitting the Act, in its present shape, to her Majesty; and I should learn with satisfaction that your Government had thought well to propose modifications of those clauses.'[7]

The *Empire*, one of the few Australian papers critical of aspects of the *Treason Felony Act*, said London's hesitancy represented some security against the 'colonial blunders...to be derived from the connection of the colonies with the mother country'.[8]

Gov. Belmore asked Parkes what course 'my responsible advisers' would recommend in response to the Duke of Buckingham's blunt reproach. The Executive Council met, undoubtedly under the strong influence of Parkes who was not to be moved. He was still leading the pursuit of treason and in the process of closing government departments on 6 August to commemorate Prince Alfred's 22nd birthday, and of no mind to concede any 'blunder'. The Council rebuffed London.

In a strongly worded self-serving defence, the Council said it was 'unable to recognise any force in the objections which have been raised', and there was nothing approaching the severity of the suspension of the *Habeas Corpus Act* which had operated in Ireland for more than a year. 'The local legislature, it may be fairly presumed, is better qualified to judge the exigency which called for such special laws than persons residing in England.' It was 'a matter of regret' that the Secretary of State should have expressed doubts about the propriety of the course taken 'when prompt and vigorous action was universally admitted to be necessary for the preservation of public order'.

It said seditious articles had been published in an organ of people calling themselves Fenians, the atrocities of Fenians had been held up for the admiration 'of the most ignorant and excitable classes of the population', the British Government openly 'denounced' British connections 'contemptuously derided', and people had 'ostentatiously' said they would leave the room if a toast was to be made to the Queen.

> When the attempted assassination became known, the disloyalty which had previously existed found new vent; and from the sympathy manifested with the assassin, the Government were convinced that some strong measures ought to be taken, not so much to punish as to prevent crime.
>
> The Government and the Legislature...desired only to preserve the public peace, and the Council are in a position to say that the object has been accomplished without injury or oppression of any kind...the clauses objected to have had the effect of...preserving the public peace by preventing, in a time of great excitement, the open and habitual expression of disloyal sentiments and the making of disloyal demonstrations.

In a final self-congratulatory flourish, the Council 'upon the fullest reflection' was of the opinion that 'a great public good was achieved by the passing of the *Treason Felony Act*'.[9]

The Colonial Secretary of State reluctantly accepted New South Wales was not going to back down.. He advised the Queen would not exercise her 'power of disallowance' but made it clear her signing off on the law 'must not be taken as indicating any approval on the part of her Majesty' of sections relating to royal toasts writing or publishing disrespectful material, and sympathising with anyone committing a seditious felony.[10]

With the extraordinary powers set in place for two years, the colonial lawmakers wanted to prosecute some particular 'sedition' targets, especially the *Freeman's Journal* and its editor and part-proprietor Richard O'Sullivan. The *Journal*'s rivals, the *Sydney Morning Herald* and *Sydney Mail*, were in full support: 'Anyone taking it in hand would pronounce it to be for sacred purposes as a Catholic journal' which defended murderers as martyrs, predicted reprisals, reviled English people and the British Government, and spoke of the Sovereign with ribaldry. While informed people would read and forget its content there were 'some who burn to act out the schemes they approve. They make themselves the executive of what they believe is a common counsel. They mean to stimulate a sale and they find they have inspired an assassin.'[11]

The *Sydney Morning Herald* said the big lesson from the O'Farrell assassination attempt was the importance 'of not allowing non-Australian questions to rise to any prominence in Australian affairs.' Any immigrant, Irish or otherwise, who could not leave feuds behind were not welcome, and Fenians had no right to 'pollute the soil of this colony with…blood-shedding atrocities…if Irishmen could not leave their hereditary feuds behind them, they would not make good Australians'. American politics had demonstrated the 'evil' when immigrants hated England more than they loved their new country.

O'Sullivan lambasted his 'anti-Irish' rivals for promoting 'a new kind of crime…the introduction of foreign politics into New South Wales', a wicked notion 'capable of transcending even the Treason Felony (Act) in enormity'. This was a free country, he said, where anyone of any nationality could profess their views, but 'not so for an Irishman. The very first requisite for his peaceable living here is that he denationalise himself and lay aside every vestige of manliness and independence'. Otherwise he would be seen as disloyal, a rebel, assassin, murderer or demon.[12]

Fearing attack, O'Sullivan ensured he never went anywhere alone. His brothers in Dublin did not believe he was a member of the Fenian Brotherhood 'but in every way possible...he befriended and defended his 'advanced' compatriots...as a consequence the loyalist party regarded him as practically one of the conspirators'.[13] Ultimately the government did not pursue its sedition prosecution, merely fining the newspaper on a registration technicality, but his business partners wanted an end to his activism and he was forced to leave the colony for San Francisco.

While one journal described O'Farrell's 'smashing of the country into atoms by religious discord'[14], the discord erupted from long-standing colonial and sectarian rivalry and put the whole 'public mind ...in a feverish state.'

Sydney newspapers were never shy of painting rival Melbourne as home to 'a large number of the vilest of the vile...the gathering of old seditions'. While the 'assassin has been a stranger' in Australia that had been changed by O'Farrell, who came from Melbourne and meetings at Randwick and Redfern condemned a crime of 'foreign importation.' Victorians in turn objected to Sydney's 'jesuitical' effort to 'fasten upon Victoria the stigma of being the headquarters of the Fenian organisation from which he had received his orders to assassinate the Prince'.[15]

Victoria's *Age* outraged Catholics by citing Irish 'disloyalty' of the *Advocate* in raising murder 'to the dignity of heroism by the priesthood in Ireland', and declaring it 'certain that the worst class of Fenians and the Roman Catholic priesthood are in accord, and our readers will now be able to appraise at their proper value the denials of the truth of our statements respecting the doings in St Francis's schoolroom.'[16]

The *Age* was accused of 'jeopardising the peace of the country', by setting 'creed against creed' and risking 'riot and bloodshed' and 'the future of Australia...but a reproduction of European fanaticisms.'[17]

On the first reports of the shooting the *Freeman's Journal* said 'the prayer which was fervently uttered by thousands of our countrymen...was "Pray, God, that he is not an Irishman"'.[18] But the prayers were not answered, and Irish Catholics were under immediate suspicion, deemed guilty by association.

The loyalty forces of government, business, churches and newspapers promoted a national narrative: unambiguous loyalty to the Mother Country, of which royalty was the embodiment, delivered safety, stability and security to Australia; conversely, republicanism and disloyalty, especially by Irish Catholics, was the path to bloodshed, uncertainty and risk. A Protestant Political Association was formed for the 'self defence and maintenance of Protestant principles'[19] and membership of the Orange movement boomed; within a decade there were 19,000 Orangemen in more than 120 lodges in New South Wales. Parkes' electoral base of Kiama alone had nine Orange lodges, and named part of its local farmland 'Loyal Valley'. A Sydney alderman, William Pritchard, said if Irishmen continued to agitate he would advocate a poll-tax to restrict Irish immigration.[20]

Armed with the *Treason Felony Act*, and a deluge of allegations of Fenianism and sedition, authorities questioned, arrested and charged numerous individuals. While many reports were not much more than gossip or trouble-making, anyone heard making a comment, sober or otherwise, indicating empathy with O'Farrell, or antagonism to the Royal family, risked arrest.

At a meeting in Sydney, a man who said he was glad of the Prince's shooting and hoped he would die was rushed by the angry crowd before being seized by soldiers and roughly dragged away and charged. A Victorian was charged with being an accomplice after being heard to say four months previously that Fenians in Sydney would try to seize Alfred him and keep him as a hostage for prisoners in Ireland, 'and (he) would be finished', making a bet 'the Duke don't leave Sydney' alive.[21]

Two men were arrested for saying in a public house in Cowra 'there was no more harm in shooting the b—Prince than a blackfellow of this country'.[22] In Goulburn, a man was committed for trial for saying 'it served the Prince right, he had no business in this country', in Yass another was committed for trial for saying 'I am a Fenian', in Orange another arrested for using 'seditious' language towards the Queen; an elderly man charged after being heard at Gundagai races to cry 'up with the green'.

Those in government service were under particular scrutiny. The Council of Education wrote to police about 'certain disloyal conduct'[23] by a teacher at the Roman Catholic school in Currajong. The captain of the Ballarat Rifle Rangers urged his colonel-commandant to court-martial a junior captain who had allegedly avowed himself 'a Fenian'. A Brisbane warder was dismissed for 'fenian sympathies', a customs officer in Albury faced an inquiry for 'complicity in Fenian practices', and another dismissed for using 'highly improper language' toward Alfred and Lord Belmore. Four Sydney policemen were dismissed or suspended for 'evincing sympathy with the Fenian movement'.

Those who refused to join Royal toasts were roughly forced out of events. The Greville Telegraph Company reported: 'Two parties had to leave Sydney on Saturday to escape the vengeance of the people for refusing on a public occasion to drink the Queen's health'.[24] Gov. Belmore withdrew his patronage of the St Patrick's Day regatta after learning at least two men refused to toast Queen Victoria.

Police searched the baggage of an Irish-born American about to sail from Sydney and found numerous letters relating to fundraising for the widows of the Manchester martyrs and other Irish 'matters', which police department secretary Fosbery said 'fully proved that he was an active Fenian agent' but there was insufficient grounds to detain him.[25]

Those arrested were generally discharged by courts after police admitted they lacked firm evidence, or magistrates were content to issue stern warnings about the dangers of 'drunken bluster' and the risks of voicing national or party cries.

Some likened the 'wickedness' of suspicion to the aftermath of

John Wilkes Booth's assassination of President Lincoln three years before and were at pains to distance themselves from O'Farrell and Fenianism.

Charles Duffy, a leading Young Irelander nationalist arrested in 1848 for high treason over a plot to kidnap Queen Victoria before migrating to Australia to become a successful lawyer-politician, fulsomely lauded Alfred in a toast to his recovery at a St Patrick's Society supper in Melbourne, saluting his recovery from 'the foul and cruel attempt to murder him…I do not believe that there is in history a crime more bereft of all possible excuse or palliation…the killing of a child in its mother's arms would not be a more cruel and unprovoked crime'.

He rejected Irishmen 'being held accountable for a crime which they abhor'[26] when Ireland was one of the few countries to not experience a political assassination. It was only Englishmen who had shot at Queen Victoria, but the English thought 'the worst' of any offence connected to Ireland.

Fellow Young Irelander and Queensland MP Dr Kevin O'Doherty, proposing a condolences address to Prince Alfred, said his years in exile meant no man had a greater right to speak on Irish sentiment and he deplored O'Farrell's crime because it would 'attach to thousands of innocent persons a share of the infamy.'[27] In his view 'no greater crime has ever been committed against the cause of Ireland than this miserable crime'. O'Farrell, he said, was to the Irish case as Marat and Robespierre were to the French Revolution, and Booth was to the Southern cause.[28]

Irish Catholics were urged to 'patiently wait till the good sense of the people returns', but many were outraged their loyalty was under suspicion and questioning, especially when its genesis was statements by O'Farrell, a 'mendacious ruffian…telling lies'[29]. Irish men and women were being dismissed from workshops and domestic service. Advertisements in the *Argus* and *Examiner* proclaimed 'No Irish need apply', 'Wanted a Parlor Maid, Protestant',

'Wanted, protestant nurse', and 'Wanted a Cook (protestant)' and it was reported 'many Irish and catholic labourers, mechanics and others are leaving the colony for other countries day after day'[30]. And because the colour green was now such an odious and ready source of accusations of 'being one of those demons let loose upon earth – a Fenian' no woman should wear the colour 'if not forever, at least until the name of Fenianism has no more power to agitate society'.[31]

Archbishop John Polding endeavoured to guide and defend his faith. In a pastoral letter, he lamented that some had ignored his previous warnings about the dangers of religious activism—the 'ill-instructed and ill-advised (who) have kept up those separating, alienating, misplaced recollections and associations'[32]—and ignored the church's age-old principles opposing secret societies as 'a foci of sedition and rebellion'.[33]

'The unhappy creature who attempted the life of our Prince and guest professes to be a Catholic. Be it so. But will any man of sense believe that his crime was Catholic?'[34]

The Archbishop did not publicly acknowledge the 'unhappy creature' had been a deacon in priestly training, or that he had visited O'Farrell in gaol. But he said the Church would disown any clergy who evinced any sympathy with public criminals, and urged all clergymen and followers to resist any notion of sympathy or lukewarm indignation, and 'set your faces like flint' against anything which might excite others or 'wickedly import miseries and enmities'.[35]

He also wrote personally to Alfred to express the 'horror and detestation' and that there should be no doubt in his mind that Catholics had 'affectionate respect' for him and 'dutiful loyalty' to the Queen. He also added that while O'Farrell had 'signally disappointed' him, the mercy of God meant some good had come out of 'a monstrous evil'.[36]

O'Farrell's Melbourne mentor Bishop James Goold did not receive news of the shooting until the next month in Paris, where he promptly sought out the British Ambassador, Lord Lyons, and in 'a long conversation…I begged him to convey my sympathy and that of the clergy to her Majesty'.[37]

Goold painted O'Farrell as 'notoriously labouring under insanity for a long period'. According to one Paris correspondent, Goold 'had personal cognisance of that fact, that he was continually under supervision to guard against the violence to which he has become addicted'.[38]

Irish sympathisers were warned off public activity or statements. Plans for a mock funeral procession in Melbourne to support the Manchester Fenians were abandoned after the *Argus* warned that any display of 'sedition' could lead a 'feverish and excitable' community to become 'ungovernable' when it was already impatient at the 'slow' processes by which 'justice will be done' to O'Farrell. In Sydney, St Patrick's Day celebrations were called off but rumours were rife that Government House would be attacked that night and the Ministry massacred, and police warned the 'the gaol would be attacked and O'Farrell would be released'.[39] Extra gaol guards and all available military forces patrolled the city, but came across nothing more than the night cart men doing their work.

But not all Irish sympathisers were silenced. There were numerous reports of Fenian meetings being held in hotels, and threatening letters were sent to those speaking against Fenianism. Editors received threats from 'patriots' resenting any 'malignant spirit towards the Fenian cause…we have the means at hand to accomplish our goals'.[40] A Brisbane banker received a letter saying his comments 'aroused in the minds of the Fenians a murderous hatred against you…they intend to have your life when an opportunity offers them' and the 'lot' had fallen to the author to shoot him.[41]

The Mayor of Ballarat received an anonymous letter from a 'Fenian brother' threatening that 'what the hero in Sydney failed to do others will yet accomplish. We must be avenged for the death of the three Irish patriots'; a running street brawl broke out in Rutherglen in a clash between Irishmen and 'lankies' expressing disgust at the crime, and 'rowdies' brawled at the Marengo races in Victoria and roared 'we're bloody Fenians. Come on! We'd soon kill a man as look at him.'

A police magistrate reported an effigy of Prince Alfred, with a paper fastened on the breast of the figure stating 'The last of Prince Alfred, Duke of Edinburgh', had been hung at the Tyagong gold field, 'chiefly inhabited by Irish storekeepers and miners'.[42]

And in Cork, during a visit by Alfred's younger brother, Prince Arthur, the Mayor, Daniel O'Sullivan, told a cheering banquet for released Fenian prisoners that 'when that noble Irishman fired at the prince in Australia he was imbued with as noble and patriotic feelings' as the three Manchester martyrs, and the same motive for liberty as the Polish assassin of the Russian Tsar.[43] Queen Victoria demanded her Prime Minister take action against such 'atrocious language'. Opposition leader Disraeli supported the Irish Government efforts to have O'Sullivan removed as Mayor for his 'disgraceful' comments, blaming Gladstone's 'clemency' towards Fenians. O'Sullivan explained he did not approve of O'Farrell but 'would not deny him credit for pure and honourable motives'.[44]

Those loyal to the Crown and Church of England saw British people and their Protestantism, headed by the Queen, as being under the 'special protection' of the Lord. The view of Sydney Bishop Frederic Barker, was that it was their 'duty' to ensure this 'protection' and primacy was not under attack. The Bishop said the Clontarf crime was so sinful many fathers could not look their own children in the face 'for very shame to think that their children should have been born in a country the shores of which had been stained with the blood of the Queen's son, so bitterly did they feel the outrage, so acutely did they feel the disgrace'.[45]

But drawing Catholics under Fenian suspicion was seen by some, even among Parkes' long-standing friends, to have gone too far. The founding editor of the *Australasian Chronicle,* William

Duncan, wrote to him:

> I wish to God you could manage to conciliate the Irish (in some manly way of course) on that cursed Fenian business...it would be a grievous injustice to confound the whole body with a few noisy characters...a few conciliatory words, and an admission that an atrocious crime committed may have led you to a too easy belief in the existence of a conspiracy connected therewith – and the amende to a wounded nationality would be generally accepted.[46]

But conciliatory words would not be forthcoming. While professing to have never been prejudiced against Roman Catholics, Parkes' view was firm:

> I do not want to see this colony...converted into a province of the Pope of Rome! I do not want to see the majority of the people of this colony of the Roman Catholic faith! I do not wish to forget that I belong to a nation that is eminently Protestant, where a person who is not a Protestant cannot ascend to the Throne![47]

His eldest daughter Clarinda, the wife of a Presbyterian clergyman, supported his 'resistance', saying an increase in Roman Catholic numbers 'and therefore political power, would mean, I fear, an eventual blood-struggle for predominance.'[48]

While Parkes and the government were aggressively pursuing criminal and security issues and defending loyalty and faith, they also sought to urgently contain reputational damage , to avert the fear, as expressed by the wife of the Bishop of Sydney, that 'Poor Australia will never recover this blow to its reputation' from a crime'worthy of the early history of Botany Bay!'[49]

The ides of March would forever be etched deep, as the *Illustrated Sydney News* lamented:

> The 12th of March will ever be a memorable day, one to be thought of with feelings of the deepest humiliation...

> and regret that on the soil of New South Wales...a ruffian could be found base enough to attempt the life of the son and representative of the most virtuous and most beloved sovereign that ever graced the throne of our mother isle.[50]

Having struggled to dilute its convict stain, Australia would now forever labour under the additional odium of a royal shooting. 'In England even now a man who hails from Australia is regarded with disfavour...we shall now have fresh cause for blushing', wrote one correspondent. England was already aware, he said, of convictism, bushrangers, drunkenness, dark crimes and pugilism even in the Legislative Assembly, but the descent into 'ruffianism' now extended to a 'horrible, base, cowardly, treacherous, traitorous, diabolical attempt' on Prince Alfred.[51]

The *Empire* appreciated 'The nature of the calamity...cannot fail to draw towards us the eyes of all nations'. And especially the eyes of the Mother Country.

Every community and colony, joined in competitive loyalty to welcome Alfred with the biggest and most united assemblies ever seen, now gathered again, united by even deeper emotion. At indignation meetings in parks, mechanics institutes, town halls, churches and pavilions they strived to ensure the Prince, Queen Victoria, British Parliament and the world were in no doubt they were shocked, outraged, horrified, sad, hurt, grief-stricken, paralysed with shame and humiliated. And more resolutely and eternally loyal to Queen and 'home', forever thankful to God's Providence they were congratulating Alfred on his miraculous escape rather than assembling at Government House for his Royal funeral.

All denominations held prayer and thanksgiving services. Reverend Samuel Kent, principal of Camden College, told his Newtown congregation O'Farrell's bullet

> entered the very heart of the people...it seemed impossible to get relief from the sense of shame, disgrace and indignation which has raged within our hearts. If Alfred had been killed, nothing could wipe out 'the stain' which defiled the colony.

> As men shame and refuse to tenant a home in which a deed of violence and blood has been committed, so would they have shamed and refused to emigrate to a land in which such a monstrous crime had been perpetrated. Cain like we should have been marked through the whole of our future existence.[52]

Newspapers feverishly amplified the message in the hope there would be no reflection on colonial loyalty. As the *Empire* said, when the electric telegraph did eventually announce the assassination attempt in the cities of Britain, Europe and America, there would be questions as to why the colony was not 'more vigilantly guarding the Prince' and so it was vital to 'send forth to the world' the strongest and fastest expressions of sympathy for Alfred, devotion to the Queen, and horror at the crime. The national prayer was that once people in those countries reflected that they had experienced similar crimes they would not 'cast a stain upon the loyalty and honour' of Australia.

Editors rushed additional copies to the docks of Melbourne to go aboard the next available ship sailing, the *Great Britain,* the largest passenger ship in the world. It sailed three days after the shooting, but not before a team of detectives raced on board after hearing rumours O'Farrell accomplices were on board.

In the aftershock of emotions, dismay over Alfred's 'unprincely' behaviour on tour was forgotten. Numerous church leaders and others now lauded this 'unoffending' young man of 'many amiable and excellent qualities'.

Some thought New South Wales had suffered from an unending association with its criminal origins, and the Prince's shooting was the 'culminating result of its (criminal) origin'. It was too much of a burden to bear. Joseph Docker, the Postmaster-General, told the Legislative Council that as people called their children Australians, the oldest colony was entitled to take the name Australia to help 'efface as much as possible the memory of the crime' and entitled to ask the Queen to 'change the name of this colony to Australia'.

Others felt it too late to usurp Australia, and said Alfred ought to be asked to allow the colony to be named in his honour. Alfredland, said Rev. Kent, would 'prove to the world...we have no sympathy with the dark deed', and it was appropriate for the land sprinkled with his blood to be called by his name. Others favoured adding the initials of his other names, Ernest Albert, to create Alfredea, others favoured Prince Alfred Land. Alfred's name was not adopted but one newspaper reported 'nearly every baby born in the colony during the last 3 months' had been named Alfred or Alfredia. His name began to adorn numerous towns, parks, streets and buildings, and was embraced in fundraising for a 'thanksgiving' infirmary in his name in Sydney (ultimately the Royal Prince Alfred Hospital) and Melbourne (the Alfred Hospital).

The reaction in England was less excitable when it received Australian newspaper accounts of the shooting eight weeks after the event, although the Greville Telegraph Company reported they were devoured with 'indescribable excitement' and 'electric reaction' and only after a special squad of detectives versed in Fenian affairs in Liverpool, Dublin and Cork were despatched on a Naval ship, along with a famous Fenian informer, to search the *Great Britain* to see if any O'Farrell co-conspirators were also on board.

The news coincided with the alleged Fenian shootings of D'Arcy McGee in Canada and a magistrate in Westmeath on his way home from welcoming the Prince of Wales, and the trials of the Clerkenwell bombers and the arrest of men with alleged Fenian 'fire' near Buckingham Palace. But the shock was quickly mitigated by the realisation Alfred had survived and would recover.

It was not clear whether O'Farrell was part of a broader Irish Fenian conspiracy or what Russians referred to as a 'lone wolf', but the press was quick to denounce Fenianism and assert that anyone thinking such an attack would impact British Government thinking was insane or delusional.

The *Manchester Guardian* said the idea that 'making war' by shooting Alfred would impact government thinking was 'fanciful', but there ought to be 'unrelenting severity' towards those who classed themselves, by their own conduct, 'as enemies of the human race.'[53] The *Morning Post* said the Fenian movement was a 'malignant madness' and a fatal shooting of Alfred could only have brought it into 'greater odium.' The *Standard* described the shooting as 'political, treasonable', but perpetrating such crimes to promote the cause 'so far from precluding the assumption of insanity, furnish proof positive of it'.

The *Newcastle Daily Chronicle* hoped it would be found O'Farrell 'laboured under mental delusion', the *Morning Star* that he would be proven 'a mere lunatic', otherwise 'we must only hope and believe, for the credit of human nature, that his crime is all his own.' The *Daily Telegraph* assured the Queen that even 'the least contented of her subjects must...shrink with horror from the factious name that can be assumed as the cloak for a pitiless insanity'.

Political leaders were more restrained than those in New South Wales. New Prime Minister Benjamin Disraeli, not known as a supporter of the Irish, said while it was suggested 'some dark confederacy...is spreading over empires...all I can say is that for a moment such acts should have been associated with the name of Ireland I am convinced myself...that the imputation is unjust',[54] while his predecessor William Gladstone also said that based on telegraphic intelligence it did not seem 'wise or safe' for him to assume, as others had, 'that this foul and loathsome deed is connected with Fenians'.

Of greater import to the colonies, the extravagant sentiments of loyalty and shame paid dividends. To the immense relief of Her Majesty's appointees and subjects in Australia, Queen Victoria commented that O'Farrell's act had 'only further roused' the loyalty of the Australian people, and *The Times* concluded that 'no slur can for a moment be cast...upon even the most insignificant body of British subjects'.

The *Times* said it was understandable the colonies were 'stirred to their depth by such an outrage on hospitality and loyalty', given 'the first occasion that a Prince of the Blood had ever set foot in one of these colonies' and the Duke was much more than a Royal guest. It was the 'first opportunity ever offered to them of displaying to a representative of the Royal Family their loyalty to the Queen and their attachment to the British connexion…to bind afresh the links which unite them to the Crown and the Empire'. If the design of the Prince's visit was to bind the 'insignificant' colonies more closely to the Crown, the *Times* opined, the shooting had ensured this more completely than would otherwise have been the case, making the Royal visit 'the most uncheckered success'. The 'colonists may dismiss from their minds the least shade of anxiety respecting the reception of the news in England.' Moreover, it said, Australians had done themselves 'an infinite honour' with the depth of their sentiments.[55]

The *Telegraph* concurred: 'No wound taken in hatred ever helped to win a more beautiful reward than this, the hurt endured by Prince Alfred has added to the stability and unity of his royal mother's dominions.' The 'wicked pistol shot' had awakened a vast echo of shame and sorrow 'from all the many English people who live the word's breadth off the mother land, but as close as ever in heart'.

The Australian colonies breathed a sigh of relief. Their loyalty and devotion was not being questioned, the failure to protect Alfred not denounced, the certainty of Naval security not in doubt.

Happily, as a number of newspapers declared, 'the loyalty of Australia is more assured now than before the act was committed'. But the demonstration of loyalty was not universally applauded in London. *The Times* scoffed at the 'excess' and *Reynolds's Newspaper* said the shooting had opened 'the flood gates of flunkeyism' and 'sycophancy' and dismissed the 'lip loyalty' of Australians who 'swell and plume yourselves on a "loyalty" which costs you nothing, either in the way of hard cash or political independence.' One reader told

Reynolds's that the lesson from New South Wales was to 'warn the world of the evil tendencies of royalty' and its influence. While America had burst the chains of royal tyranny, Australians 'tender their necks as a pavement for any prince or royal personage to walk over', even someone like Alfred, 'a royal Billy Taylor'. Australians made 'great British flunkeyism…comparatively tame and feeble', but it was their choice to make themselves ridiculous to the world, 'more servile than the belly-crawling courtiers of Siam', and more judicially vindictive than Russia.[56]

Henry O'Farrell's 'wicked pistol shot' had shaken Australia to its foundations as panicked authorities turned freedoms and justice upside down to repress anything which challenged their authority and a reverential attachment to, and reliance on, Queen and Empire. The freedom of Irishmen to freely pursue their religious and political values was under question. Freedom of the press was proscribed.

While the firestorm raged, O'Farrell waited quietly and calmly in Darlinghurst Gaol, receiving authorities, police, clergy and family. While he had been the fulcrum on which much was swinging, a judgment loomed on his crime, his mind and his fate.

8 *PALL MALL*

Saturday, 2 o'clock.

This Evening's News.

PRINCE ALFRED SHOT BY A FENIAN.

A startling piece of news reaches us just as we are going to press. A telegram was received by the Duke of Buckingham this morning, announcing that Prince Alfred had been shot in the back by a Fenian. We have however, the gratification of adding that the wound was not fatal. The ball was successfully extracted, and the Prince is reported to be doing well.

The following is the telegram which conveys this intelligence :—

"*Earl of Belmore, Sydney, to Secretary of State, Colonial Office.*

"On the 12th of March a person named Offarell (*sic*) deliberately shot his Royal Highness the Duke of Edinburgh in the back at a public picnic given in aid of the Sailors' Home at Clontarf Nidle Harbour, Port Jackson. Providentially the wound was not fatal, and he is now able to go on board his ship, and hopes shortly to resume his duties.

"The ball was easily removed on Saturday the 14th of March, by Drs. Watson and Young, of H.M.'s ships *Challenger* and *Galatea*. Offarell fired another shot the moment he was seized, which severely wounded a gentleman named Thorne in the foot ; the ball has been extracted, and he is doing well. The assassin, who avowed himself to be a Fenian, was arrested on the spot.

"In consequence of the report of a medical board, Commodore Lambert has ordered his Royal Highness to return to England as soon as he is sufficiently recovered, which will probably be next week."

A British newspaper article in regards to the attempted assassination of Prince Alfred. The article includes a telegram which was sent to the from Sydney to the Secretary of State informing them of the shooting. *Pall Mall Gazette*, 1873, *This Evening's News*, The British Newspaper Archive.

WANTED—A respectable woman as cook and housemaid for a gentleman' family in the country. Must be strong, clean, and active, and have a good character. Wages £20 per annum. A laundress kept. No Irish need apply. Address L. S., Hamilton Post Office, River Forth. (a

UNIQUE CURIOSITY.

O'FARRELL,

the most terrible spectre in sunny Australia's annals, modelled from life by one of the best modern sculptors at an enormous cost, and rendered in wax by Madame Sohier, will be added TO-NIGHT (Thursday), at seven o'clock p.m.

This faithful and thoroughly life-like likeness has been vouched for here by several gentlemen well acquainted with the infatuated maniac, and who have kindly permitted reference to be made to them.

In order to enable the most timid ladies to have a look at this extraordinary portrait model, it will be placed in the ground floor room, just behind H.R.H. Prince Alfred; his revolver in hand, and every detail of toilet, &c., conscientiously represented.

Notwithstanding the great outlay attending the production of this fac simile, no extra charge will be made, but only

1s, and children half-price.
Vivat Regina!
Waxworks Exhibition,
97 Bourke-street east. 46 3785

top: A job advertisement after the attempted assassination attempt by Henry James O'Farrell declaring that 'No Irish need apply'. *Anti-Irish Advertising*, *Launceston Examiner* (Tas: 1842–1899), 1868, p. 5. Image courtesy National Library of Australia, nla.news-article36696699.

bottom: An advertisement for a waxworks exhibition of Henry O'Farrell. *Unique Curiosity*, *The Age* (Melbourne: 1854–1954), 2 April 1868. Image courtesy National Library of Australia, nla.news-article177001528.

13

TRIAL OF MAN AND COUNTRY

The task of executing the Prince was sent out to me, but I failed.
— Henry O'Farrell

Henry O'Farrell was about to face the young country's biggest trial. But so too was the country on trial, with its reputation and values on the line.

O'Farrell's fate was seen as inevitable. Many thought he should have been lynched on the spot and a trial unnecessary. Authorities too had no doubt about O'Farrell's guilt and deserved punishment, but understood that the shame of the assassination attempt might be offset by being seen to adhere to proper English process and justice.

A preliminary inquiry began the day after the shooting, in the debtors section of Darlinghurst Gaol before Magistrate Houlton Voss. He was usually in charge of the Water Police, which originated from the 'row board guard' which Governor Arthur Phillip instituted in 1789 to police convict crime on the harbour. Now he presided over an inquiry into the biggest crime seen on the harbour.

O'Farrell, dressed in white calico prison garb, was charged with 'wounding, with intent to kill, His Royal Highness the Duke of Edinburgh on 12 March at Clontarf, near Sydney'. He entered a plea of not guilty.

Watched closely by Gov. Lord Belmore, Premier-Attorney-General James Martin and other government ministers, Alfred's colleagues Lord Newry, Elliot Yorke, and artist Oswald Brierley, and Naval officers, O'Farrell presented a 'sickening sight' after his narrow escape at Clontarf. His left side was 'very much swelled' with an eye 'livid with bruises' and partially closed; his right side was 'cut and bruised' with an eye black and closed. His nose was considerably swollen and he was 'unable to see except with difficulty'.

Police Superintendent John Orridge recounted the events at Clontarf, supported by witnesses including two sergeants, coach-maker William Vial, a leading merchant, a magistrate, several *Galatea* crewmen and Alfred's gun aide William Bradley.

O'Farrell was not represented but allowed to question witnesses. In doing so, he was 'never disturbed from…almost stolid indifference' and said little to help himself. When Sergeant Richard Musgrove said that when he grabbed O'Farrell by the hair and shoulder he had said 'I'm a bloody Fenian, and I'll die for my country'. O'Farrell told the court, 'I never used the word bloody.'

After a weekend break, the inquiry resumed on Monday 16 March, again with strong government and British Navy presence. O'Farrell's appearance had improved, but there was again 'nothing remarkable in the expression of his countenance, and well-dressed as he was when his crime was committed, he would have passed as an individual of respectable intelligent aspect'.

Sir William Manning recounted how he had seen Alfred fall and turned to see O'Farrell still pointing his pistol. After Manning's testimony, O'Farrell stunned the court: 'I have no question to ask, but would make a remark. If he had not come forward I would have shot the Duke a second time.'

The Crown Solicitor, John Williams, was stunned: 'Will the prisoner repeat what he has just said?'

> O'Farrell: If Sir William Manning had not rushed between me and the Duke, the Duke would have received a second shot. He rushed at me. The Prince would have received a second shot and I should have shot myself, but I had no time to do it.

Waverley publican William Glading told of O'Farrell's shooting practice, and Dr Watson produced the ball which he had extracted from Alfred's body over the weekend, satisified it probably came from the revolver produced in court.

Magistrate Voss followed usual practice at the conclusion of the evidence to listen as it was all read to him before he called O'Farrell to stand and asked whether he wanted to say anything before making his judgment.

O'Farrell shocked the courtroom. 'I have nothing to say but that the task of executing the Duke was sent out and allotted to me.'

> Crown Solicitor: Will you repeat what you have just said?
>
> O'Farrell: The task of executing the Prince was sent out to me, but I failed, and I am not very sorry that I did fail. That is all I have to say.

O'Farrell was committed to stand trial 10 days later at the Central Criminal Court on 26 March and to remain in custody at in Darlinghurst Gaol.

While O'Farrell waited in Darlinghurst Gaol for his judgment day, his sisters in Melbourne, Caroline and Catherine, had to make a heavy one of their own. When they first heard about the shooting, they did not immediately realise their brother and the Royal assassin were one and the same. Absorbing the reality and the family shame they wrestled over whether they should get involved.

The sisters finally resolved they had to do their best to keep their younger brother from walking the scaffold. They engaged lawyer and Melbourne Club player, Butler Cole Aspinall, who had been known to their solicitor brother Peter. The son of a rector and former parliamentary reporter for London's *Morning Chronicle*, Aspinall had migrated, like the O'Farrells, from Liverpool. He quickly made his name in Melbourne as a newspaper writer and editor before turning to law, and agreed to take the case on a 500 guinea retainer, with the assistance of Sydney barrister William Bede Dalley, the son of Irish convicts, and Melbourne solicitor Thomas Pavey.

It was not a popular decision. Aspinall was warned of plans in Sydney 'to hoot and hiss me on my arrival' and make him an object of 'popular displeasure', but he argued in a letter to the *Sydney Morning Herald* that the principles of English jurisprudence demanded the defence of 'a fellow creature accused of even the most heinous offence'.

> The community will be outraged at the supposition that O'Farrell would not be allowed professional aid, but simply lynched. As to a professional man's taking a brief in a case such as O'Farrell's, I have no doubt that the royal sufferer by O'Farrell's act would justly have despised me if I had refused to do my duty in my profession, and turned coward because the prosecutor was a prince.

Aspinall felt obliged to emphasise that 'the Queen has no more loyal subject, the Prince no more sincere or respectful admirer', and hoped he and Dalley had not forfeited their friendship with those whose 'loyalty and attachment are as well known to the Prince as (I have reason to believe) the purity of our motives'.

Not everyone in Sydney was persuaded, seeing him as an outsider offered 'a large fee'—perhaps by a Fenian organisation in the assassin's home of Melbourne, which the *Herald* believed housed a large number of 'vile seditionists'[1]—to defend the indefensible. Despite Melbourne Club members' entitlement to visit the Australian Club while in Sydney, Aspinall was black-balled.

A son of Chief Justice Sir Alfred Stephen, solicitor Montagu Stephen, told his wife that solicitor-politician James Norton 'says if the jury finds O'Farrell to be insane neither they nor Aspinall nor the prisoner will live through the day – and from the way he speaks about it I have no doubt he would lend most willingly a helping hand to murder the lot – and I have not spoken to anyone who I believe would not do the same. They are all as bloodthirsty as Fenians.'[2]

The bloodthirst was a contrast to what even Henry Parkes had said just three years before about those wanting a harsher approach to bushrangers, including the empowerment of ordinary citizens to apprehend them, dead or alive, for a £100 reward: 'The evil which has grown up is very great and alarming, but the remedy appears to many reasonable minds to have that fatal flaw so often derived from times of extreme excitement, of going too far and in too fierce a spirit.'[3]

But now in the extreme excitement of the assassination attempt, the remedy for O'Farrell's crime could not go too far or too fiercely, despite some timely advice from Parkes' idol William Gladstone, on dealing with evil crimes, even those threatening the Throne. 'When crimes are horrible,' he told an election rally in Lancashire,

> we begin to suppose...that because the charges are dreadful, therefore we might be less particular about the proof; but depend upon it, there cannot be a more fatal error. It is absolutely necessary that in every case against men...who are to be tried for outrages that make our blood run cold, they should have precisely the same advantages, precisely the same favour and indulgence as in ordinary time is given to the most ordinary, the slightest offence. It is a solemn duty for us to keep the balance of mind. If the public are excited the excitement will find its way to the jury box. Aye,

> it will affect even the benches of justice…you must look at nothing but the sufficiency of the evidence.[4]

Now, less than two weeks after a shooting which made the public and political blood 'run cold', Gladstone's 'balance of mind', judicial fairness and 'sufficiency of evidence' was to be visited on a colonial government, judge and jury.

The angry eyes of a whole country were on the Supreme Court on Thursday 26 March, with a large police contingent inside and outside the sandstone Darlinghurst courtroom, and in surrounding streets. Henry James O'Farrell, the first assassin in Australia, was charged with having 'feloniously and with malice aforethought, wounded Alfred Ernest Albert, Duke of Edinburgh, with intent to kill', a charge originally aimed at bushrangers, and not a capital offence in other colonies or in England.

The most hated man in the Empire was a man of slight build, 5 foot 10 inches tall, in his mid-30s, with a fair complexion, slight beard and moustache. At the preliminary hearing he was seen to have a 'stolidity of manner', but now 'so much more keenly alive to things going on around him…an evident uneasiness…his attorney apparently had some difficulty in engaging his fixed attention'.

The biggest trial in Australia's history would be heard by 58-year-old Justice Alfred Cheeke, supported in his Supreme Court appointment by Sir Alfred Stephen two years earlier against the wishes of the Bar and to the astonishment of the *Sydney Morning Herald*, which said he was 'about the last person that anyone really expected…nobody admired him for his legal profundity'. Cheeke was more respected as a horse man, having bred and trained the first recorded AJC Derby winner just three years before. But the Irish-born Cheeke did have a reputation for common-sense, and first-hand experience with criminals of Irish background: as a travelling District Court judge he and his party were held up by the Ned Kelly gang, which stole his gold watch before reading his inscribed name and position and hurriedly returning it before galloping off.[5]

The jury was selected from a panel of 72, much larger than the customary 48. The Crown challenged four jurors with Irish-sounding names, an O'Regan and three O'Briens, before 12 men were empanelled.

The prosecution was headed by Cork-born Attorney-General James Martin, 47, and Solicitor-General Robert Isaacs, 58. Martin, the son of a castle steward, began his life in Australia as a writer, publishing the first book of Australian essays, *The Australian Sketch Book* at age 18, and the next year was acting editor of the *Australian* before qualifying as a solicitor. He controversially became Attorney-General at age 35, despite not yet having his barrister qualification, and had his first of three terms as Premier at age 42. Isaacs, originally from the Virgin Islands, was educated in London and practised at Middle Temple before migrating, and been Solicitor-General for two years.

Martin's mission was to deliver the noose for O'Farrell to sate political and public appetite—poet Henry Kendall said it was time to show Alfred 'we punish those who dare to plant distrust's rank thorn between a loving people and their well loved Queen',—but punish in a manner which demonstrated not pure vengeance but the proper process of British law.[6]

O'Farrell's defence team mission, to keep the noose from O'Farrell's neck, was headed by Butler Aspinall, 37, the witty, sharp-tongued lawyer and bon vivant from the Melbourne Club who made his name when he helped secure the acquittals of several men charged with treason after the Eureka uprising. In support, he had Sydney-born William Dalley, 36, who like O'Farrell, had enjoyed the patronage of Archbishop Polding at St Mary's seminary, been editor and part-owner of *Freeman's Journal*, and had a term as Solicitor-General at 27. Short and thick-set, he was a colourful dresser who jovially greeted everyone as 'old boy', and was a popular after-dinner speaker. He led moves to abolish capital punishment for rape and would become the first Australian appointed to the Privy Council.

Aspinall and Dalley's instructing solicitor was Thomas Pavey, 36, whose career had just taken off after he led the prosecution in a major Melbourne fraud case.

The indictment was read and O'Farrell was called to plead. He responded, low and indistinctly: 'Not guilty'.[7]

It had been reported Aspinall intended to move for a postponement and change of venue, but apparently he decided, or was quietly told, this was a waste of time: most witnesses, at least on the prosecution side, were from Sydney, and no one was of a mind to assist the defence or delay a verdict.

Aspinall did press for a modest adjournment, explaining the defence had only been engaged by O'Farrell's sisters the previous Friday, who had taken some time to accept that the assassin was indeed their sometimes estranged brother and decide it was 'their duty to place the case before the court…in order than something might be said in reference to his state of mind'.[8]

The defence team had immediately gone to Ballarat to pursue potential witnesses, especially doctors who had attended O'Farrell, and then left Melbourne by steamer to arrive in Sydney at 4am, just hours before the trial was due to begin. Dalley, telegrammed in Mudgee, and had also only just arrived. It had been simply impossible to secure all desired witnesses from either Victoria or New South Wales.

Aspinall also made clear his strategy. It was not to attempt to dispute the facts: 'The defence to be made on behalf of the prisoner is that he is, and was at the time the act was committed, a person of unsound mind.'

His key witness thus far was O'Farrell's sister Caroline Allan, who had observed her brother's insanity 'at an early age'. Doctors in Ballarat had been unable or unwilling to testify, he said, and it was impossible to subpoena them. (Until Federation, colonial boundaries made subpoena processes difficult, and even the leave of a Supreme Court not necessarily enforceable).

In an echo of the trial of Edward Oxford, who shot twice at Queen Victorian in 1840 as she sat in her carriage at Windsor railway station, Aspinall knew he would rely heavily on family to evidence his client's mental state, and would argue, just like Oxford's lawyer, that anyone who shot at a Royal in broad daylight and admitted his crime at the scene must be mad.

Judge Cheeke had little option, but wasn't going to give Aspinall much relief. After 35 minutes of proceedings, he agreed to an adjournment until Monday, giving the defence just the weekend to prepare.

The courtroom was again packed on Monday 30 March, many turned away. Inside were numerous government ministers, several judges, the Sheriff of Victoria, some foreign consuls and Prince Alfred's support team of Lord Newry, Elliot Yorke, Lieutenant Haig and other British Navy officers, artist Oscar Brierley and actor-friend Walter Montgomery.

Attorney-General Martin was conscious of evidencing at least the perception of justice. It was important, he said, that 'the British Empire and the world might have an example not of our vengeance but of our justice'.

He told the jury that scarcely any crime was more likely to enlist the feelings of 'Englishmen', but this ought not be a case heard in a 'spirit of vengeance and partiality', but in a calm, cool and dispassionate manner. He avoided talk of Fenian conspiracies or the prominence of the victim. In considering O'Farrell, the jury 'must deal with him in the same impartial spirit as that they would show in regard to any other case brought before them'.[9]

The law, he said, threw no greater protection around one of Her Majesty's Princes than even the meanest of other subjects. This was not a crime against the Duke of Edinburgh but a crime against the law.

But it would become clear that O'Farrell's trial, in environment, process and outcome, was more vengeance than impartiality. The extensive reportage of the crime and O'Farrell was prejudicial, the heat of anger infected the whole community from which the jury was selected, and the trial was held as quickly as possible with minimal time for the defence to prepare.

The *Sydney Morning Herald* had set the scene, and the expectation, immediately after the shooting. A 'universal feeling of sorrow, shame and rage pervades the community. The whole country has been wounded in the person of its Royal Guest...assassination is a new crime amongst us...the assassin has hitherto been a stranger... we repudiate it.' And not just young and excitable men wanted to repudiate it, but others 'grave and grey-headed...(were) happy for an instant application of lynch law'.[10]

Irish-Catholic leaders, churchmen and even opponents of capital punishment were of the same judgment. Charles Duffy said there was no crime in history 'more bereft of all possible excuse or palliation', and if any others were involved 'I pray that they may be speedily associated with him on the gallows'. The Bishop of Sydney, Frederic Barker's view was that the shooting was 'much worse than any other sin and crime ever committed in the colony'.[11]

The president of the NSW Legislative Council, Sir Terence Manning was also president of the Society for the Abolition of Capital Punishment, but as long as a single Fenian existed he would not press for the end of capital punishment, and hoped 'the assassin in this case would be hung on a gallows 50 cubits high so that everyone might see him' and the gibbet remain standing 'for as long as any man like this man remained'.

The judgment against O'Farrell, and his fate, seemed inevitable. Martin's prosecution case was not challenged by the defence: the Prince had been shot; O'Farrell had fired the gun in front of numerous witnesses; and he had made various statements, before and after the crime, of his intent and deed.

The only possible way O'Farrell's neck would not soon be in a noose was a successful insanity defence, so the prosecution pre-emptively produced any witnesses who could cast doubts over any linkage of epilepsy, delirium tremens and insanity.

A Sydney baker, Henry Lewis, recalling many chats with O'Farrell in a hotel, considered him merely 'eccentric'. Dr Joseph Colville, a Royal Navy officer staying at the same hotel as O'Farrell, thought him 'perfectly sane...exceedingly intelligent', and only when speaking in favour of Fenianism and the blowing up of Clerkenwell Gaol did he become 'excited'. Another surgeon, Dr Horatio Wright, who conversed with O'Farrell on the harbour journey to Clontarf, thought there was nothing peculiar in his manner or conversation.

Neither doctor had expertise in mental disorders, but to the jury they were medical men. And just in case it needed reminding about the gravity of the charge, *Challenger* surgeon Dr Alexander Watson said that 'had it not been for the divergence of the bullet it would have killed His Royal Highness' and despite issuing bulletins a week previously that the wounds were not likely to prove fatal, added that 'I consider his Royal Highness is not entirely free from danger yet' as he produced the extracted bullet for the jury to inspect.

Aspinall's defence task was almost impossible. There was no disputing O'Farrell had shot Prince Alfred, or that O'Farrell had incriminated himself, and no disputing the jury would find it difficult to deny universal expectations about the verdict.

His only strategy to save O'Farrell from the scaffold was to question the fairness of the trial and the overwhelming disadvantage visited on his client, especially on the primary defence that O'Farrell was not of sound mind, and do his best to cast doubts on that mind. The trial had been rushed, the environment was hostile, there was insufficient time to secure desired defence testimony.

To hold the trial so quickly, when public anger was 'so obviously unabated', meant it was almost impossible for any jury to 'consider the whole case as calmly as was desirable for the furtherance of the true ends of justice'.[12] Few people would have not devoured the prejudicial newspaper reportage, including the secretly recorded conversations O'Farrell was having while in custody where he talked of Fenianism and the order for Alfred's assassination as reprisal for the 'Manchester patriots', and his 'obligation' to undertake the assignment or risk being shot by fellow Fenians.

And the jury would not hear evidence from three doctors and a pharmacist who had attended O'Farrell in Ballarat. None was prepared to testify at the trial, which Aspinall said 'very materially prejudiced the prisoner's defence'.[13] All found a reason to not get involved. The hospital's resident surgeon, Dr William Owen, who was reported to have felt O'Farrell was 'bordering on madness', not a safe person to be at large and 'a much fitter subject for a lunatic asylum than a hospital', claimed his board would not permit him leave to travel to Sydney, and he did not want to be absent from his patients. Dr William Heisse, a non-resident surgeon at Ballarat Benevolent Asylum, also regretted he could not travel, despite some financial inducement, and would not even tell the *Argus* his opinion because the family had not paid for it.[14] Dr William Whitcombe, one of the first surgeons at Ballarat Hospital, initially agreed to attend for a fee of £25 and £10 daily allowance before discovering a patient he could not abandon. Ballarat chemist, Irish-born Joseph Usher, maintained he could not leave his family and business.

There was no calling of Ballarat police, such as Detective William Berrill, who knew O'Farrell as a hard drinker subject to fits of delirium tremens who once asked him for pistols to 'blow out his brains'. This was not known to the defence, and while Berrill had strong views about the trial he was not going to volunteer to give evidence in a colony which wanted to 'hang a man to show their loyalty to the throne'. A newspaper said the respected detective, who had worked at the Yarra Bend Asylum, regarded O'Farrell as 'a shingle short…a lunatic'. He and a colleague 'could have saved the man's life I do believe…the man was not really responsible for his actions'.[15]

Caroline Allan was the only witness to O'Farrell's mental state. Telling the court 'I am the prisoner's sister' and the wife of a Victorian government officer, she detailed how her brother had spent long periods away from family, including his time abroad from the age of 17 'training in the Roman Catholic Church'.

She and her sister Catherine had observed their brother's periods of restlessness and excitability. He often 'could not sit still', spoke irrationally and bitterly about his financial losses saying he 'did not know how he should get on after my brother's losses' and they had received frequent letters from him asking for money.

The sisters had witnessed his epileptic fits and his armoury of pistols, swords and daggers, and heard his fears of being poisoned and claims of being kidnapped. And his threats to kill himself. In the past two years Caroline noticed he 'took too much drink', and was 'labouring' under the influence of brandy and port wine. His 'softening of the brain' as doctors had called it, was, in her mind, due to alcohol.

'The doctors said he should have a strait-jacket at once,' she said. The sisters initially resisted him being sent to a lunatic asylum, but Caroline said she also eventually came to the view that her brother was 'unsound in his intellect – that he was mad'.

Aspinall painted a picture of a man unhinged by drink, epilepsy, delusion and paranoia. But he lacked medical witnesses, so could only endeavour to cast doubt on the expertise of prosecution witnesses, and questioned why Dr Isaac Aaron, the Darlinghurst Gaol doctor, had not been called. Perhaps he hoped that with more experience with deranged prisoners Dr Aaron would characterise O'Farrell as one of them. Or perhaps he was aware Dr Aaron had talked to O'Farrell about helping to bring in an insanity verdict.

Aspinall also endeavoured to appeal to the jury's humanity, saying the evidence

> must have almost brought tears into their eyes…here is a man actually attacked again and again with epileptic fits, and they not tending most assuredly to anything but insanity… at Ballarat one might learn how he came to drink, how he

> was robbed in mining speculations, and how in the whirl of excitement his mind got worse, latent insanity developing itself quietly until it led him to the point when this attempt on the Prince's life occurred.
>
> Coming to other symptoms of insanity, did we not find that there were always associates connected with political crimes? Had not this Government done all they could to find associates in this crime, and had they found one?…A man with madness in his brain seized the prominent idea that presented itself, and imagined himself to be the agent for carrying it out.

Aspinall said the foulest of deeds had been committed by a person 'without moral responsibility', and the jury should not 'hurry out of the world a person who might not be responsible before God'. He questioned the probability of a sane man endeavouring such an outrage and what would motivate any sane man to do so. If a man fell into insanity, through ill-behaviour or intoxication, and his mind became 'unbalanced and unhinged, and no longer under his controlling power, that person…was not legally responsible'. Aspinall, himself only three years away from a mental breakdown which ended his career, conceded the law decreed it was up to the defence to prove insanity at the time of the act, but O'Farrell's admissions meant this would be 'like calling on a lunatic to prove his insanity'. It was a mark of lunacy in itself to accept that O'Farrell could be so intelligent, fluent, fearless and cool before and after a shooting 'which must result in his own seizure and death'.[16]

He cited the similarities with Edward Oxford, who shot at Queen Victoria and Prince Albert: he too claimed links with a secret society, practised his shooting and studied the bible, was alternately rational and irrational and seen to be 'absent'. He was found guilty on the grounds of insanity and sent to a lunatic asylum. (Unknown to Aspinall Oxford had arrived in Australia just a few weeks before in an exile deal struck with the British Government, many years after *The Times* had said that of all the asylum inmates of Bethlehem Hospital, also known as 'bedlam', the only one not showing the most remote symptoms of insanity was Oxford. An unhappy Queen also felt Oxford was not 'in the least mad', and should have been made an example of).[17]

Aspinall characterised O'Farrell as a man whose life fell apart when his destiny of becoming a priest was lost when he returned from training in Europe. 'He returned to the world neither a layman nor a churchman. He was banished from the priesthood and he banished himself from the world.'

In conclusion, while O'Farrell had 'shaken a great Australian society to its foundations, and the news of the deed will fall like a thunderbolt upon Europe', his life was now in the hands of the jury to decide if he would be consigned 'to an ignominious death, or to a doom still more appalling in the dread solitude of a lunatic asylum'.[18]

In reply, the Attorney-General said a person was responsible for their act if they knew they were doing wrong. The defence had not proven insanity and to suggest it was impossible for any sane person to commit such a crime suggested 'the greater the crime, the greater the impunity'.[19]

The insanity argument would have stood more chance if the jury had heard from Ballarat medical and police witnesses who had advocated a strait-jacket. And if it been aware of material found by Sir Henry Parkes, notably O'Farrell's notebook, suggestive of a disturbed mind. But no one was to know of this, as Parkes and the prosecution kept the material secret.

It wasn't as if the Colonial Secretary was unaware of mental illness and madness: he was closely involved with the Lunacy Act's provision of lunatic reception facilities instead of gaols while mental assessments were made, an Act given Queen Victoria's assent just two months prior to O'Farrell's attack.

But in Parkes' mind there was no use for evidence from the notebook and his gaol conversations 'for the case against him was already complete'.[20] And very aware that as he was yet to prove the Fenian conspiracy theory, one that he, his police chief and Prince Alfred subscribed to, the material was more valuable to that pursuit and so better kept secret than possibly assist O'Farrell's defence team.

The notebook material, and the full transcripts of gaol conversations, would have shown O'Farrell's capacity to be coherent and intelligent, but also erratic and wild. In his conversations with Parkes, he was also selective, mischievous and elusive. Perhaps even manipulative, with a 'method in his madness' as the *Freeman's Journal* thought.[21]

When Parkes pressed O'Farrell on his co-conspirators, saying he ought to name accomplices so innocent people might not be unjustly suspected, he responded: 'Perhaps so, but you see that if I were to do that I should deprive you or someone else of the credit of finding them out, you must excuse me I could not be so unkind.'

In another exchange which Parkes sought to keep out of the newspapers he put to O'Farrell: You have said something about a great Fenian conspiracy in Sydney?

> O'Farrell: Yes but you must not say anything about it just yet, it's a big conspiracy and some of the principal men of Sydney are mixed up in it.
>
> Parkes: Of course, I knew all along this conspiracy was in existence. But tell me, my good man, who are these conspirators and where do they meet?'
>
> O'Farrell: They meet in Macquarie Street.
>
> Parkes: Yes go on, what place in Macquarie Street and who are they?
>
> O'Farrell: This is a great secret but I may as well tell you, they are members of parliament and the meet at Parliament House.
>
> Parkes: Yes, who are they and who is the leader?

> O'Farrell: Let me whisper, the leader is Henry Parkes and he will be able to tell you the names of the others![22]

The Crown Solicitor, John Williams, later denied vital evidence had been deliberately withheld. The notebook material would have been presented if O'Farrell had not been defended because 'every facility is given', but O'Farrell was represented and it was the defence's job to present material to the jury and 'it is not the duty of the Crown to suggest defences'. He argued there was a difference between 'keeping back evidence and volunteering information'. As to whether the state had 'industriously concealed' the evidence of Constable Irvine about O'Farrell's statements at Clontarf, which lacked the 'fenian' elements of other police statements, Williams simply said the defence counsel 'ought to have been aware of it' without explanation as to how that was possible. And as to whether the pre-trial reportage of some of O'Farrell's gaol cell conversations was prejudicial and calculated, he steadfastly said 'I have not the slightest doubt…that he had a perfectly fair trial'.[23]

Before handing the case over to the jury, Justice Cheeke adjusted his fur-edged red robes and reviewed the basic facts and outlined the applicable law on insanity, developed in an 1843 case involving a delusional Glasgow wood-turner, Daniel M'Naghten.[24] Believing there was a widespread conspiracy against him, M'Naghten attempted to assassinate Prime Minister Sir Robert Peel but mistakenly killed his private secretary instead. The verdict of insanity caused uproar, and Queen Victoria complained to the Prime Minister about it.

Under what became known as the M'Naghten defence, everyone was presumed sane and responsible until the contrary was shown to the jury's satisfaction, with insanity and irresponsibility to be proved by the defence. The question for a jury was whether it was satisfied an accused did not have sufficient reason to know he was committing a wrong, and whether it had been proved they laboured under such a defective or diseased mind as to not know, or be unconscious of, their act being criminal.

For Aspinall's insanity defence to succeed it had to be shown O'Farrell was legally insane at the time of his crime. More than 10 prosecution witnesses testified that immediately prior to the shooting O'Farrell had not been anxious or strange. 'He was always perfectly rational and coherent', Judge Cheeke said, telling the jury if it was convinced of sufficient evidence O'Farrell had been insane for 18 month and this had continued up to the time of shooting, then it could render a verdict of not guilty, on the ground of insanity. But if they believed that when O'Farrell committed the act 'he knew the difference between right and wrong, that he was not then labouring under the effects of prior insanity, they would bring in a verdict accordingly'.

Perhaps helpfully, or deliberately, Judge Cheeke told the jury of various English cases where an insanity defence had been run but executions had still followed, such as Edward Arnold for shooting at Lord Onslow, and even when the accused was, like Lord Ferrers, a peer of the realm.[25] And as for the argument of disadvantage due the lack of medical evidence from Ballarat, the judge misleadingly said it could not have done no more than corroborate the testimony of O'Farrell's sister 'to the facts that the prisoner had had fits of epilepsy, and that he had been affected with delirium tremens'.[26]

With a judicial inclination to bring in a hanging, and government and public sentiment clear, the jury retired at 2.34pm to consider its verdict on the biggest crime in Australia's history. After just 54 minutes, a court official announced the jury had reached a verdict. The feverish courtroom was silenced and everyone rose as one, standing expectantly. After some embarrassed puzzlement, the crowd resumed their seats and an escort of police and gaol warders brought O'Farrell back into court.

The judge's associate asked: 'How say you, gentlemen of the jury, is the prisoner at the bar guilty or not guilty?'

Amid profound silence, the foreman, Charles Pitt, replied: 'Guilty.'

Judge Cheeke asked O'Farrell if he had anything to say as to why the sentence of the court should not be passed upon him. He replied 'in a clear and firm tone—"No, sir, nothing"'.[27] Only then did he evidence his sole 'quiver of emotion' as the judge turned to address him. Underscoring his own loyalty to Her Majesty ran deep, Cheeke contradicted the government prosecution's opening remarks that the law did not concern itself with a Prince more than an ordinary citizen, and evidenced Gladstone's warning that excitability about evil crimes could infect even the judiciary.

This was, he said, a 'cruel and deliberate attempt to take the life of a favourite young son of our beloved Queen', one which would have caused large sorrow and suffering in Europe, and 'horror and shame…throughout the civilised world'.

> Contemplate the awful grief and anguish of the Queen if one of her beloved and innocent children, innocent even of any evil thought against you or any other human being, had been thus torn by your ruthless hand from her widowed heart. Reflect also how the fair fame of this colony would have been tarnished by the consummation of this fearful deed. Consider what unutterable horror and shame would have fallen upon this colony…tarnished by the consummation of this fearful deed…if the providential care of Almighty God had not defeated your attempt.

Despite the speed of the trial and prejudicial newspaper reports which made it impossible to empanel an impartial jury and secure medically qualified witnesses for the defence, the suppression of key evidence and the non-calling of key witnesses, the judge reassured O'Farrell he had been 'ably' defended and the jury, on their oaths and consciences, gave 'calm and impartial' deliberation but had 'altogether discarded the proposition that at the time you committed the offence you were an insane man'.

He held out 'not the least hope of remission of the sentence of death'. Not only could he find no reason to make such a recommendation, it was manifest 'to the whole world that all men like you, whose evil hearts may now be harbouring and nurturing similar murderous intentions and similar traitorous designs, should be taught by your sad fate how swift, unerring and stern is the punishment which all civilised nations must inflict upon such a terrible crime as yours'.

O'Farrell's defence had put his downfall to being 'banished' from his Church, but Judge Cheeke now urged the man in front of him to use the short time left in his life to seek religious help in his sorrowful meditation.

He then reached for his black cap to pronounce his own banishment, the traditional sentence of death: 'You will be taken to the place from whence you came, and thence to execution, at such time and place as His Excellency the Governor may think fit to appoint, and there be hanged by the neck until your body be dead and may the Almighty God have mercy upon your soul.'[28]

O'Farrell reportedly 'gasped for breath twice'[29] when he heard the sentence, while others said he appeared 'but little moved; the only perceptible change being a tremulousness of the muscles of his face'.[30]

What O'Farrell thought of the judge's advice to seek religious help, or hope for the Lord's mercy, was known only to him.

14
JUDGMENT OF MADNESS

His sanity or insanity may in days to come be as fertile a field for critical investigation as that of Hamlet.
— Portland Guardian

The judgment of judge and jury, government and public was clear: Henry O'Farrell was an Irish Fenian, perhaps a little eccentric at times but legally sane and thoroughly deserving of having his head put in a noose.

From the first seconds of the shooting at Clontarf, the universal view was that it was the work of an Irish Fenian, 'one of those Roman Catholics'.

> Every man that heard of the occurrence guessed in a moment that the assassin was an Irish Fenian…long before the facts were known, people said that the ruffian who

> fired the shot must be one of these detestable miscreants who are forever wrangling about 'the wrongs of Ireland'... No other hypothesis was accepted for a moment, and the mere suggestion the man was a lunatic was scouted with derision. No, he was a rebellious Irishman.[1]

A unanimity of opinion, as the correspondent wrote, one forcefully pursued by Parkes and other loyalists, but there was a *but*.

Those who knew O'Farrell best, his family, were convinced an injustice would be done if their brother was hanged for committing the crime of a madman, and for a crime that no longer carried the death sentence in any other colony or in the Mother Country. And supporting medical and police evidence, and O'Farrell's notebook, was suppressed or not available to challenge the 'unanimity of opinion'.

Remarkably, Prince Alfred was the only key player to seemingly shift his thinking. Initially, and reflecting all he had heard, he had written to Queen Victoria that he was certain 'O'Farrell was a "fenian emissary"...especially charged with the duty of murdering me to frighten all at home by showing how widely spread the conspiracy is'.[2] But he now seemed convinced O'Farrell had no personal ill-feeling toward him, and questioned whether an execution was warranted. The man who had become known to some as 'The Dirty Dook' was now, in the very heat of a colony's desire for vengeance in the name of Her Majesty, a Decent Duke.

After her unsuccessful efforts at the trial to save her brother, Caroline Allan worked on a clemency appeal. With lawyer Butler Aspinall's help she drafted a petition to Lord Belmore, with a copy to Prince Alfred.

As the sister of the 'unhappy man' condemned for shooting the Duke, she 'ventures to approach your Excellency with the prayer that you will mercifully consider his case'. While the court had not heard medical evidence to satisfy it otherwise, 'from the bottom of her heart' she believed her brother, despite the absence of legal proof, was ordinarily the gentlest of men and 'was absolutely and entirely out of his mind…when he fired upon the prince'.

The family were 'grieved to the last degree' by the thought that if they had taken Ballarat doctors' advice and sent their bother to an asylum it would have avoided this 'terrible catastrophe', and spared their anguish that 'love of her brother had rendered them blind to the danger of allowing him to go unrestrained'.

If the trial had been delayed a month or two, she said, more evidence about his 'outburst of insanity' could have been produced, and without the 'spirit of vengeance and the thirst for his blood' the jury would have recognised the evidence justified a more merciful view and found him not guilty on the ground of insanity.

From personal knowledge she knew that if her brother had, in his sane moments, contemplated the shooting, he would 'for days beforehand have been excited, disquieted and restless' whereas the trial evidence showed him to have been quite calm right up to shooting the Prince.

She forwarded a letter from Dr William Whitcombe, one of the Ballarat doctors who had attended O'Farrell. He did not give evidence in the trial but in a letter to lawyer Butler Aspinall dated 22 March, apparently received too late to be of use in the trial, said: 'From my knowledge of him I have no doubt but that I could convince any reasonable person that he is a man of unsound mind.'

He had formed this opinion after several years of seeing 'sundry eccentricities in his conduct'. In January 1867 he attended O'Farrell after he suffered a severe attack of delirium tremens, and two months later he had seen him several times in Ballarat Hospital 'suffering from dementia'.

'He was then not suffering from delirium tremens, nor, as far as I could learn, from the effects of drink in any of its forms. And I may say that I recommended that he should be placed under restraint, as not being a man who was safe to be at large.'

And, Caroline Allan told the Governor, there were others who could have testified that O'Farrell 'had been, and was liable at any moment to become again, mad'. If they had been compelled to attend, she was sure that however prejudiced the jury was against her brother, they could have not resisted the evidence of former insanity 'liable at any moment again the break out'.

Her brother was 'a lunatic' and had acted alone. While there was no sympathy for him, if he was to be 'made a sacrifice to the popular indignation at Fenianism' it would convey the impression to the whole world he was a member of a permanent Fenian organisation, which would 'greatly encourage the Fenians themselves' and allow Fenians to 'make of a maniac a martyr'.

A commutation of the death sentence, she said, would be 'a death-blow' to those who would make her brother a martyr. It would be acceptable to all good and loyal men if he was kept under restraint in an asylum for life.

And it was a minor consideration but she was 'afflicted, agonized and sorrowful' and an execution would bring the deepest shame and infamy to the family.

Pleading for the prerogative of mercy 'in favour of this unhappy lunatic', she sent Alfred a copy of her petition and Dr Whitcombe's letter, and shortly after on 1 April she wrote directly to Alfred.

'I feel sure from your known kindness that you will excuse me for again writing on behalf of my poor unfortunate brother,' she told Alfred. 'I would not do so were I not thoroughly convinced that he is unsound of mind, and has been for some time past.'

She again enclosed a copy of the Dr Whitcombe letter:

> I earnestly beg and beseech of you, Your Royal Highness, to intercede for a commutation of sentence, for my poor insane brother.
>
> I feel confident, if the case were tried in England, your Royal Mother the Queen, with her usual clemency, would pardon him, although he attempted the life of her beloved son.
>
> If the trial could have taken place at Ballarat, sufficient

> evidence could have been brought forward to prove my brother's insanity...I again beseech Your Royal Highness to intercede...for the sake of his unhappy relatives than whom Her Majesty the Queen has not more loyal subjects.
>
> I would feel very grateful should Your Royal Highness think it desirable if you would grant me an interview, as there are many little details I would like to relate to you. With fervent congratulations on your recovery, I remain, Caroline Allan.[3]

Alfred initially indicated privately it was not his intention to attempt to influence the final decision of the Executive Council, but newspapers began speculating that Alfred believed O'Farrell was 'not motivated by any personal ill-feeling towards himself, and it was his intention to intercede with the authorities on the prisoner's behalf, so that they may not carry into effect the capital sentence, which will doubtless be passed on O'Farrell for his crime'.[4]

Rumours he had visited Darlinghurst Gaol to personally visit O'Farrell were refuted, but Alfred had met Lord Belmore on 24 March, on the eve of the trial. A news telegram reported he 'strongly interceded in favour of O'Farrell, and wished his Excellency to promise him (O'Farrell) a pardon, on condition of his becoming a voluntary exile', similar to the deal which British authorities did with Edward Oxford after he had been committed to an asylum.

Belmore, who would not have relished Alfred's pre-trial intervention, 'stated his inability to move in the matter at the present stage of proceedings, but promised that the wishes of his Royal Highness should receive every consideration at the proper time'.[5]

The 'proper time' had arrived with the pronouncement of the death sentence, and the Governor and Executive Council faced conflicting forces: the public will for vengeance versus the Prince's will for commutation; and the political need to demonstrate unambiguous loyalty to both Her Majesty and her son, and preserve local autonomy and reputations.

A day before his scheduled departure on Monday 6 April, Alfred again made his views known to Gov. Belmore.

> Having received an appeal from the sister of Henry O'Farrell, at present under sentence of death for 'wounding with intent to kill me', to intercede for the commutation of the prisoner's sentence; although I feel it is not within my province to interfere with the action of decisions of the Executive Government, I still consider that as this was an attack upon a member of the Royal Family, and that through the merciful interposition of Providence, it failed in its object, that the trial took place, by a special meeting of the court, within a very short time of the occurrence, and further that in England 'wounding with intent to kill' is no longer a capital offence, I am warranted in asking Your Excellency to submit to the Executive Council, when this case comes under its consideration, whether there are not sufficient grounds under such special circumstances – circumstances which from the nature of the case most nearly affect the Queen, to justify its being referred home with a view to obtain Her Majesty's pleasure thereon. I remain, My Lord, Your Excellency's obedient servant, Alfred.

While Alfred said it was not within his province to influence the government's decision on hanging O'Farrell, his letter was a potent Royal message: he was making it clear he thought the trial had been held in haste, the crime ought not carry a death penalty if it was no longer applicable in England, and as this was an attack on a member of the Royal Family the execution ought to be stayed while the Queen's views were obtained.

And to add to the Royal pressure, he asked Lord Belmore to send the original of his letter to the Colonial Secretary of State in London, along with another letter requesting that regardless of the Executive Council decision his views be made public, unless the Council 'have urgent reasons to the contrary'.[6]

Prince Alfred's leaning towards clemency was not supported by his close friend Lord Newry. After his initial fear of a Yankee-style uprising he was now also unconvinced O'Farrell was part of a broader Fenian plot, but still felt he should hang. Newry wrote to his friend John Delane, editor of *The Times*, urging him to publish 'a strong article' making it clear there was 'no proof whatsoever' to corroborate O'Farrell's statements about Fenian plotting, and the effort to discover Fenian co-conspirators 'has been utterly fruitless'.

> I consider the poor devil to be of unsound mind to begin with: to be suffering from the effects of hard drinking, and a…monomania which has developed…that he is an Irishman there is no doubt, but it is also fully understood he is a man of good education, gentleman-like appearance and manners, but moreover he is a bigoted and superstitious Catholic.
>
> No doubt this poor wretch has gloated over every particular atrocity that has been recorded of late in English newspapers (and) has worked himself up into the popular belief that the Irish race are unfairly treated and trodden down.

Newry said O'Farrell had this

> peculiar idea that takes so strong a hold in all persons who have shot at Royal personages, viz that he will become forever famous…this false feeling of heroism is evident throughout…in every case except that of (John Wilkes) Booth the would be assassin has prepared publicity in order that they might obtain their full measure of notoriety.

As to O'Farrell's claim he had been allotted the assassination assignment, Newry said O'Farrell had twice refused to repeat it, and had 'a malicious wanton way of trying to frighten others into believing that the secret of some organisation…would die with him'. His various stories, such as there being a cell of 10 who drew lots for the assignment, were in response to 'nervous and fussy questions' from Henry Parkes 'who had no right to speak to him at all'.

But of O'Farrell's fate he had no doubt: 'I hope the brute will get hung, mad or sane. I think he is quite sane enough to be guilty of murder, and not mad enough to save him from hanging.'[7]

Delane completely adopted Lord Newry's views. In an about-face, the *Times* said the Fenian conspiracy theory had 'no foundation'. O'Farrell exhibited the same 'vain, excitable and overwrought temperament which has so often been observed in assassins... (who) work themselves up into a belief that they are the destined agents of some imaginary doom and the fated avengers of some fancied oppression'.[8]

To hang or not to hang was a decision in the hands of Lord Belmore. As the Prince prepared to leave Australia, hoping to arrive in England as soon as possible after the arrival of the *Great Britain* carrying the first detailed accounts of the shooting, Belmore prepared to meet with the Executive Council to consider the death sentence and the Royal plea for clemency.

As Her Majesty's Governor he was the final arbiter in cases of capital sentences and execution, after listening to the advice of Ministers, led by Parkes. In this case, he also had the views of Prince Alfred, O'Farrell's sister, Justice Cheeke, and police.

The judge, unsurprisingly, was not resiling from the trial verdict.

> The evidence for the Crown was very clear and conclusive as to the guilt of the prisoner, the principal matter of inquiry being whether the prisoner when he committed the atrocious act was of sane mind...The prisoner was ably defended by counsel and several witnesses were called who gave evidence with reference to the mental state of the prisoner. The jury upon consultation for some time returned a verdict of guilty, negativing therefore the defence, and believing that the prisoner was of sane mind at the time of the committal of the offence. I passed sentence of death.[9]

There was no public or government sentiment for leniency, or for the matter to be deferred to home authorities, or mercy to be shown. The prevailing public view was that if anyone thought, like the Fenians, that ends justify means, then such crimes going unpunished would 'soon dissolve society into its original elements, when every man would execute his own vengeance'[10] and the law ought to deliver 'a solemn example'.[11] The government view was unwavering: reputations were at stake and it was the colony's right to administer its own justice and punishment.

But some were less certain about whether justice was being served. A 72-page letter to the *Evening News*, signed 'Justice and Mercy', intelligently and forcefully spelled out reasons why the trial was a miscarriage of justice. There was nothing incompatible with O'Farrell being insane and also exhibiting more than usual 'intellectuality', typical of monomania arising from brain disease. Too much reliance was placed on the fallacy of casual external appearances being 'indubitable evidence' of the sanity of men 'labouring under a peculiar form of cerebral disease. And there was no opportunity at the trial for evidence about O'Farrell's 'epileptic paroxysms which his delirium tremens had complicated'. In conclusion, 'by every consideration of justice and humanity (O'Farrell) should have been spared on the score of his insanity'.[12]

The Society for the Abolition of Capital Punishment, whose members included ministers and MPs, barristers, magistrates, church leaders and doctors, also raised concerns about the insanity issue, writing to the Governor on 18 April seeking a medical board inquiry. Expressing concern about jury expertise and judgments on insanity, the Society said a verdict which ignored medical evidence

> can scarcely be deemed conclusive…Public opinion is much divided…as to O'Farrell's sanity and should the execution take place without this point being cleared up those who believe in the insanity will feel that the Colony is

> really disgraced by...a fellow creature, although a criminal, who is irresponsible for his actions being consigned to a disgraceful death instead of being incarcerated in a lunatic asylum.

A non-execution would not endanger the city, and in the Mother Country the offence of wounding with intent was not a capital offence, so no possible harm could come from a deferral 'until these matters could be well and seriously considered'.[13]

The Society could not fathom why Australia's colonies still had 16 crimes punishable by death, despite these having been obsolete in England for up to 26 years.

Questions of sanity and justice were set aside while Lord Belmore gave a farewell luncheon for Alfred, but after the guns at Dawes Point Battery fired to announce that the Prince was making his final readiness to depart and the *Galatea* disappeared through the Heads in late afternoon, the Executive Council—comprising Lord Belmore, Parkes, Martin and four other Ministers—knew it had clean air to decide O'Farrell's fate.

On the table at Government House were Prince Alfred's doubts about the appropriateness of the death sentence and his urging that the matter ought to be referred to the Imperial Government and Queen Victoria, the pleas of O'Farrell's sister and lawyer on clemency and sanity, and the counter judgements of all those on the colonial payroll: Justice Cheeke, Premier and Attorney-General Martin—who as a lawyer had previously tried to save a bushranger from the gallows—Colonial Secretary Parkes—who had previously opposed death sentences—and police and gaol staff.

Lord Belmore weighed the biggest decision of his vice-regal career, and the disparate forces of colonial and empirical politics, royalty, law, public feeling and reputations. A tall imposing man, the Eton and Cambridge-educated Belmore was more composed than many, and been one of the few to realise the risk of over-reaction to the assassination bid. He had quietly advised caution in applying the extraordinary powers of the *Treason Felony Act*. He alerted troops but kept them out of sight at Irish Catholic gatherings, and cautioned the Orange Lodges there were many reasons why anyone acting as Her Majesty's representative ought not receive their political entreaties. He was also not entirely comfortable with Parkes' conduct, feeling that in his 'zeal' he had said and done things which appeared 'irregular'.[14]

While he considered the Society for Abolition of Capital Punishment and 'Justice and Mercy' material, he also sought the opinion of the Darlinghurst Gaol visiting surgeon, Dr Isaac Aaron.

Dr Aaron had not been called to give evidence at the trial. He had a reputation for his 'peculiar view' of those suspected of madness, often recommending prisoners be 'flogged and blistered' if he felt they were feigning insanity.[15] And the Darlinghurst Gaol Governor thought him an improper person to hold his position after warders heard him tell O'Farrell he would 'be called as a witness to prove your sanity – you are as sane as I am' but 'the more atrocious the crime, insanity is always the plea…Now what would you give me if I brought you in insane, and get you out of this?'[16]

The Gaol Governor described the behaviour as 'monstrous' and called for his dismissal in a report which went to Parkes. Aaron described his conversation as 'jocular' and was duly 'slightly censured' but not fully investigated. Now, he told Lord Belmore, his assessment of O'Farrell was based on conversations, 'some lasting five minutes', and a certainty it was possible to fairly form a view without knowing his previous history. He told the Governor he had seen O'Farrell within a few minutes of his arrival at Darlinghurst, and then almost every day as he 'considered it my duty to take measures for qualifying myself to give an authoritative and conscientious opinion on that point.' Initially, 'my impression was that he was excited by drink; that he afterwards acknowledged, in reply to my observation that I supposed he had been imbibing "Dutch courage" for the purpose, that he had taken a glass or two of whiskey and some wine.' But after his conversations 'my deliberate opinion is <u>that</u>

he is perfectly sane', underscoring the final words.[17]

Dr Aaron's behaviour and qualifications on mental health matters notithstanding, his 'sane' verdict was precisely what Parkes wanted, although he was still concerned about Belmore's juggling of Her Majesty's preference for hanging Fenians—they 'should be lynched-lawed and on the spot'[18]—and her son favouring O'Farrell being spared the noose. Parkes told his sister in England:

> At the last moment before his departure the Prince himself wrote a letter to Lord Belmore requesting that the fate of the prisoner might be left for the pleasure of Her Majesty. I am not sure but that Lord Belmore would have fallen into this view, but my colleagues and myself were unanimous that the sentence should be carried out.
>
> We did not think that His Royal Highness should interfere in the administration of our colony. We could not on principle consent to referring a question so purely local and which is ultimately related to the lives of our own citizens for the decision of the Imperial authorities.[19]

Parkes had much vested in the decision, and ultimately his view prevailed. The decision was declared 'unanimous'. O'Farrell would hang.

Lord Belmore waited until the day before the hanging to advise the Society for Abolition of Capital Punishment that O'Farrell was 'perfectly responsible' for his actions at Clontarf and the verdict 'quite right'. There would no medical board inquiry.[20]

In a minute, the Executive Council said:

> ...after the most earnest deliberation on the case...we are all of the opinion that no reasons exist to prevent the sentence being carried out in his case in the same manner as it has been carried out in other recent matters of the same kind.
>
> We think that an attempt to take the life of His Royal Highness, the Duke of Edinburgh, is in the eye of the law

> the same as an attempt to take the life of any other person, and that the Prisoner in this case should therefore be dealt with as in any other case of conviction for the like crime.
>
> By the law of this colony, 'wounding with intent to murder' is still a capital offence, and we think that this being the law, the sentence should be carried out in all such cases when the determination to deliberately take a life is clearly manifested and the means adopted to carry out such a design are such as in all human probability are likely to be successful. In extent of criminality such a case differs in no respect from murder.
>
> Believing as we do that the evidence against the Prisoner shewed that he had resolved to take the life of His Royal Highness under circumstances denoting the fullest deliberation, we think that a due respect for the law and a provident regard for the lives of Her Majesty's subjects in this community, demand that he should undergo the penalty attached to his crime.
>
> The Council therefore advises that the sentence of death passed upon O'Farrell should be carried into effect.[21]

Parkes wrote a note to the Sheriff the next day, telling him no one else outside the Council knew of the decision but 'it is desirable that the unhappy prisoner himself should be informed without delay'. He impressed on the Sheriff he had to prevent others knowing about it for the rest of the day, and 'it will be your duty to impress upon the prisoner not to entertain the slightest hope of mercy. The day of execution is fixed for Tuesday the 21st instant'.

The government made no formal announcement, but news telegrams began to race around the country, and the following day, Wednesday 8 April, the *Sydney Morning Herald* reported: 'THE PRISONER O'FARRELL – At a meeting of the Executive Council held on Monday, it was decided that O'Farrell should be hanged on the 21st instant.'

Parkes told O'Farrell's sister it was not felt appropriate the Prince should interfere in local matters of law. But following a request from gaol chaplain Fr. Michael Dwyer that 'it would be very hard for the first outburst of affliction to be witnessed by strangers', he would allow her one private visit to her brother. Father Dwyer would act as 'warder', but Parkes told the Gaol governor 'every precaution must be taken to prevent the possibility of the means of suicide'.[22]

Alfred's request for his views to be made public was ignored—MP William Macleay said it was kept 'a profound secret'[23] along with other documents which had been removed from the offices of the Colonial Secretary's Department because, Parkes deemed them 'private' or 'unofficial'.

But word of Alfred's intercession leaked out. Some newspapers said it spoke well for the 'noble' Alfred that he thought his assassin might be spared until the will of the Queen was known. But most felt that if any man deserved death it was O'Farrell, and the *Daily Telegraph* congratulated the colony for the spirit of its legal treatment as being 'what we at home…call English'.[24] It was seen to be impossible for any colonial governor to deem it in the public interest to pardon or reprieve an offender simply because a crime was committed on a member of the royal family, and a relief the Queen was not asked to consider the prerogative of mercy.

'We are glad…the Governor and his advisors…have affirmed the principle that the life of a prince is as sacred as the life of a beggar. A Sovereign extending a pardon would be a personal act of grace, but for a Sovereign representative to do so would be seen as an act of weakness and partiality.'[25] Others said while Alfred 'deserves credit for a forgiving and kindly nature', it would have been 'quite impossible for Lord Belmore to put the Queen in such an anomalous position as that of having to decide on the fate of the intending murdered or her own son'.[26]

The *Adelaide Observer* said a reference to the Home Government would have risked O'Farrell being raised above the ordinary category of criminals, or prevent the law taking its course, and it was 'better to encounter the risk of being thought precipitate' by hanging O'Farrell to save the government 'from the most painful situation in which a Government can be placed'.[27]

The *Empire*, in an effusive editorial about the 'distinguishing glory' of the Royal Family, said Alfred's action was more than ordinary benevolence: 'There is something in this which stamps the Prince as a true king among men, a king whose title no just man will dispute, a king whose way will be acknowledged wherever there beats a manly and magnanimous heart.'[28]

If Gov. Belmore had deferred to Queen Victoria she would have had to reject her son's views or her own. She had long been unimpressed that her would-be assassins like Edward Oxford had been found insane, urging Prime Minister Gladstone to change the law to 'guilty but insane'. She was convinced if Oxford had been hanged his death would have acted as a deterrent to other potential assassins, all perfectly cognizant of their crimes. Even Oxford himself was said to have remarked: 'If only they had hanged me, the dear Queen would not have had all this bother.'[29]

And if asked for her judgment on the most serious 'Fenian' attack on the Royal family, it would have been in the wake of the first political assassination in the new Dominion of Canada, on the day of Alfred's departure one of its confederate fathers, Thomas D'Arcy McGee, was shot by a Fenian Brotherhood sympathiser. As the *Times* said, before Lord Newry convinced it otherwise, the Canadian assassination and the attack on Alfred would 'bring home to the most doubting minds the true character of the Fenian conspiracy'.[30]

Queen Victoria had little time for insanity pleas, reflecting the limited public and medical understanding of mental disorders. It was only just becoming accepted that epilepsy was a 'neurological disease', and that disturbed brain activity could be caused by many factors, including seizures and the effects of alcohol abuse and withdrawal. Alcoholic excess and epilepsy was cited as the cause of half of colonial asylum admissions.

Many were adamant O'Farrell's 'alleged mania is not a mental but a moral disease'.[31] But whether his issue was mental or moral, and whether he was 'Fenian or moonstruck miscreant',[32] or 'liar or lunatic'[33] most colonial and British newspapers felt O'Farrell deserved to be the only one of eight men who tried to assassinate Queen Victoria or her family to be executed.

As the *Sydney Morning Herald* declared, the hanging was 'a terrible warning to evil-doers',[34] although one Victorian newspaper, the *Portland Guardian* presciently said: 'It will always be a moot point with the public whether O'Farrell was mad or the contrary… his sanity or insanity may in days to come be as fertile a field for critical investigation as that of Hamlet.'[35]

15
DELUSION AND DECEPTION

Play the fool like Brutus.
— Henry O'Farrell

Whether Henry O'Farrell was truly part of a Fenian conspiracy or a 'liar or lunatic' was not fully known, but it was not going to stop him walking to the gallows. As a verse posed in the *Sydney Morning Herald* said 'Fenian, or moonstruck miscreant – one or both – What matter?'[1]

But it mattered to O'Farrell's sisters, lawyers and others who felt the trial and sentence was a perversion of justice and the sanity question had not been satisfactorily answered, and those who saw the Parkes-led efforts to prove and punish any hint of Fenian conspiracy or disloyalty as an intellectual madness.

Former Attorney-General John Plunkett thought the Society for the Abolition of Capital Punishment wise to not agitate during the 'panic of overflowing loyalty' following the assassination attempt. But 'every principle of English justice ought to have suggested a postponement of the trial until the public furore had so subsided as to allow a jury to be obtained, free from the prejudice of the occasion, a thing quite impossible at the time.

'I regarded the trial as a mockery of justice under the circumstances. It was, in truth, lynching him under the colour of British law, and great as was his crime, justice required more sobriety and calmness in its investigation and judgment.'[2]

The Society said the colony had acquired the unenviable notoriety of being the only country in which the law permitted the punishment of death for a crime of which O'Farrell had been found guilty and when it was entirely possible he was a monomaniac. As the 'Justice and Mercy' author said there was nothing incompatible with O'Farrell being insane and also exhibiting, as with Edward Oxford, an unusual level of intellectuality.

Parkes placed a high reliance on the 'more than ordinary intelligence' he observed in O'Farrell's conversations. O'Farrell's entries in his suppressed notebook also evidenced an educated man who could write about Irish and royal affairs with Latin phrases and historical references to Roman history and the American Civil War, including whether George Washington was 'criminal' for hanging Major John Andre, an Englishman convicted of Civil War spying: 'He did it for his country, and it checked the cruelty of the English.'

But they were not all coherent, or legible, with many words and phrases rambling and indecipherable, featuring numerous exclamation marks and angry terms. The Royal family's 'ugly nose will get a tweak it little dreams of'. He hoped his actions would cause 'English capitalists' to lose money when the Colonies fell into 'a state of anarchy…if I had my will, every English ship in these colonial ports should have been destroyed'. He also slated what he called the 'toadying, lickspittle Press' and a government that was 'wicked, filthy, corrupt'.

On the hanging of the three Manchester martyrs, he wrote: 'Three of us butchered in Manchester? So some hundreds of the '98 patriots were shot down like dogs…woe to thee England, or rather to your accursed oligarchy'.

Apparently referencing his own design on Alfred it would 'rouse up the apathetic Irish of these parts…who think more of the fleshpots than of the allegiance they owe to their own country'.

'This thing I have to do for vengeance, and to rouse the Irish here, will cost too dear as I know I could have done so much more in England. But it is my duty to the R (sic) and I will, if able, do it.'

He indicated some reluctance about the task of assassinating the Prince. 'Oh for a gallant cavalry charge, not such a thing as this! Oh destiny! It must be done! And it must be done! fate, fate!'

And 'if I should fail, *quo a verta deno*, I should never forgive myself. Fail but I cannot, I am alone. Surely I can trust myself'.

Asking himself what might prevent his plan, O'Farrell wrote:

> Suppose the police come suddenly upon you, and taken unawares these papers found upon on you? True – but this last six months I have passed through so many dangers of the sort that immunity is begetting a kind of fatalism in my own invincibility.

Obviously familiar with the writings of Machiavelli about Brutus, who simulated madness and gave the impression of being a simpleton:

> You must play the fool like Brutus, and often you play the madman…contrary to your purpose, to please the Prince. Play the fool like Brutus – the simpleton – the ready laugh for all. Shew yourself incapable of entertaining serious ideas, least of all a sentiment of patriotism. Be…a good-natured tender fool and mountebank. Do excessively silly things in small matters.[3]

Was O'Farrell a Brutus 'playing the madman'? Was he intelligent but with lapses of delusion and derangement? Was he mad? How much delusion and deception was really involved in his own mind and his dealings with others?

Those who later became aware of the notebook described its often incoherent and rambling style as that of a sensational French novel written by someone not of sane mind. Lawyers wrote to newspapers saying the notebook contained 'improbabilities, incoherencies and extravagancies suggestive of insanity', and slating the 'alarming precedent' of such crucial evidence being withheld from a trial. 'The object of the Attorney-General is...not to arrive at the truth by producing all the evidence which is material for that purpose but...to ensure a verdict of guilty even against the truth'.[4] One newspaper described much of the notebook as 'the lines of a half-mad drunkard'[5] and the *Freeman's Journal* concluded: 'A medical man, if handed this sample document, and told to draw from it an impression of the writer's state of mind, would, we are sure, without any hesitation, declare the author as mad as a March hare, completely destitute of reasoning power.'[6]

Outside Parkes and his dutiful police and gaol staff, the only 'independent' person permitted any opportunity to assess O'Farrell's mind was a phrenologist, Dr T. Guthrie Carr, who made his living from studies of 'mental sciences' and demonstrations of mesmerism (hypnotism) and nitrous oxide (laughing gas). He was granted permission by Parkes to interview and examine O'Farrell a few days before his hanging for 'scientific interest'.

The gaol chaplain Michael Dwyer, a grandson of Michael Dwyer, exiled for his role in an Irish uprising, was firmly told by Archbishop Polding that Carr was not to discuss religious matters as it would be unwise to 'disturb the peace of mind which the prisoner had acquired from religious consolation'.[7]

But O'Farrell protested 'Oh no, this is not a religious but a metaphysical argument'.[8] He had heard Carr lecture in Ballarat and it was 'with pleasure' that his head be examined, asking if would not look better 'graced with a chignon'.

Carr talked with O'Farrell for one-and-a-half hours about literature, history and mental philosophy, and was impressed with his intelligence, pleasant manner and humour. In an address to the School of Arts, Carr said O'Farrell showed 'great wit and humour... preserving the same calm demeanour which had characterised from the time of his arrest'.

Notwithstanding his priestly training, and the efforts of the Archbishop and chaplain to prepare him for his passing into eternity, Carr said O'Farrell's longstanding discontent toward the Catholic hierarchy was clear: 'They are not friends of mine.' They had 'been opposed to every movement that would benefit Ireland...the Fenians are against them. The Pope prefers England to Ireland. He sent his directions to Ireland...the Catholics must not join the movement'.

In his report, Carr declared O'Farrell's 'size of brain more than average' but associated with an 'extremely sensitive organisation' exhibiting 'very small hope'. This and a nervous temperament meant such a person was 'subject to extreme reactions, to periods of deep melancholy, faith struggling with despair'.

He thought O'Farrell a man of 'extraordinary impulses'. He was apt to

> think one-sidedly...sensitive to the least annoyance... Forming hasty conclusions, false ideas of honour, irritable of temper, having indomitable will, great personal conceit, inflexibility of purpose and great concentration – these qualities made him an opponent to be feared...His purpose must be carried out – prayers, tears and smiles loss of friends, of reputation, of life even, must give way to such inexorable determination.

Whatever 'Dr' Carr's medical expertise, he tellingly described O'Farrell as 'in politics a radical, in spirit a revolutionist...he would have died alike for those he loved and those he hated'.[9]

And he had a sharper sense of O'Farrell than Henry Parkes, who never resiled from his views on Fenian conspiracy and O'Farrell's sanity, either out of conviction, stubbornness or political convenience. And neither did his police department chiefs John McLerie and Edmund Fosbery, gaol Gov. John Read, who was later knighted, and visiting gaol surgeon Dr Aaron, soon promoted to medical officer at the new Darlinghurst Lunatic Reception House. All steadfastly maintained O'Farrell was 'sane'.

In a subsequent minute, Parkes wrote:

> His explanations of the circumstances which led to the attempted murder were made unhesitatingly; they had no appearance of an invented story, and his casual allusions... to the main topic were all consistent with one another. In the course of his conversations, O'Farrell made various incidental statements where his truthfulness could be tested, and in all these cases it was ascertained that he spoke the truth.[10]

But Parkes' minute also revealed the weakness of his approach to O'Farrell, which itself was legally inappropriate: one political opponent, John Stewart, said 'you might ransack the annals of any British colony and you would not find another instance of a person high in the confidence of the Government going to the cell of a prisoner and with a concealed reporter trying to obtain evidence'.[11]

Parkes had only one motive: 'The case against him was already complete, but it was thought that some clue might be thus obtained, which would lead to the discovery of accomplices.' He had ears only for 'evidence' of a broader Fenian conspiracy against the Prince, colony and Empire. There was no effort to ascertain whether O'Farrell was deranged or deluding himself or his inquisitor. Beyond his ready acceptance that O'Farrell was unhesitatingly and consistently telling the truth, the Irishman's manner was calm, lucid and articulate. In Parkes' mind: 'His manner and language...were precisely what might be expected in a man relieved, as he described himself to be, from the horrible obligation to commit a crime.'[12]

O'Farrell's truthfulness, manner and intelligence could only mean one conclusion in Parkes' mind: O'Farrell was quite sane and had not evidenced any madness to those around him in the days leading up to the assassination attempt, or the days since; and he was clearly part of a Fenian conspiracy and could not possibly have planned and committed the crime on his own.

Parkes was likened to 'an old Bailey counsel engrossed in a very exciting cross-examination...(seeking) to elicit what suited him' by posing 'very suggestive questions...some of them almost answer themselves...they unmistakably indicate the reply which will be most acceptable'.[13] What he could not see, or chose to ignore, was any sign of insanity or inconsistency. In a colony fearful of losing its authority and Mother Country's protection, and with Irish Catholics and republicans seen as the biggest security threat, he absorbed only what served his conviction. And his politics, Parkes having one of the sharpest ears for the prevailing public mood.

Anything in O'Farrell's notebook which suggested more than eccentricity was simply ignored, as were the contradictions, evasion and mischief in his conversations.

O'Farrell outlined to Parkes and principal gaol warder Frederick Bernard how 'a Fenian body was organised in Melbourne, comprised of some Ballarat men, under the leadership of a person who came out from England for that purpose, when it was agreed upon that Prince Alfred was to be shot. They came over here and recruited to their ranks some two dozen, but losing confidence in some of their members, the band was reduced to ten, who drew lots to whose part it should fall to assassinate the Prince and the Earl of Belmore', but because Belmore had supported the St Patrick's Day Regatta the Prince became the sole target 'and lots were drawn to shoot him... It was agreed to put him to the most ignominious death, as Maximilian prayed to be shot in the back'.

O'Farrell told them a 'warrant', which came as parchment with a seal and signature, 'came out from England to execute the prince', that he and nine or 10 others had met in Sydney to consider the task, taken an oath binding each to abide by their decision to undertake the mission, drawn lots to decide the killer, and then taken a second oath to take the life of the chosen killer if he failed.

He painted a plausible picture of an organised and direct Fenian response to the Manchester martyr hangings: 'A programme was issued that three men were to be shot for the three men executed at Manchester. It was imperative to shoot the Prince...What I have done I could die for now...at the same time I was bound to it.'

But O'Farrell also gave less plausible and convincing answers. Asked if the 'warrant' was executed like a state instrument, O'Farrell replied: 'Yes...There are two ways of liberty, on the sea and on the scaffold – which would you prefer? I suppose you would prefer to be over the ocean waves?...yet the reporters say "he was launched into eternity" as if he were a ship going out into the sea'.

And despite his accounts of an assassination bid being carefully planned in Ballarat, Melbourne and Sydney, and his own involvement, he told Parkes his intention of killing the Prince 'came on by chance...it came on by a strange concurrence of circumstances'. He had 'not the slightest thought' of attacking the Prince when he left Melbourne, only joining the organisation in support of the redress of the wrongs of Ireland.

On one hand, O'Farrell indicated he had argued against shooting Alfred in Australia, 'Let them take his life in England. There were plenty of chances there', did not like the idea of shooting the Prince—'who would?...I had no stomach for it' and did not like taking the oaths 'to tell you the truth'. Moreover, he thought there was 'something genial' about Alfred. 'He was a good-hearted soul altogether...he seemed to be a nice winning fellow'.

But he also said he had no hesitation. 'As to the matter of fear I did not give a fig, and 'I took the oath to shoot any man that did not fulfil the particular obligation which devolved to him' even though he knew it would lead to his own death.

And while he freely related how a warrant had been issued to 'execute' Alfred, he oddly corrected Parkes when asked about how the Fenian cell decided whose lot if would 'to murder the prince', saying 'to kill the prince, not to commit murder'.

On his shooting plans, O'Farrell claimed he had once trained with the French artillery, and of his practise shooting at Waverley: 'I was pleased with the place, some of those gullies are very beautiful.'

On the shooting itself, he told Parkes…'it is strange that I did not shoot him with two pistols, two shots at once, that would have killed him' but after the first shot with the Prince was on the ground there was 'an irresolution to shoot him…it was all the same shooting, but still I had a repugnance, and before I could get the thing out of my mind I was jumped upon.' And while he portrayed a Fenian organisation and personal intent on bloodthirsty vengeance O'Farrell thought they 'might think of the anxiety of his mother… they might think that to shoot a man who had been shot at once would look cowardly'.

Some police said he declared at Clontarf 'I'm sorry I missed my aim, I made a bloody mess of it', but he later told Parkes 'I am delighted he is recovering, because I did my best, and I am not sorry that I failed' and it was 'by good fortune that the ball was stopped'.

He also hoped Alfred would not risk 'running the gauntlet' with his scheduled visit to New Zealand. 'Why can't he go straight home? I think he has had enough of suffering…I would like to beg them not to molest him, he has sustained so much injury.'

Of his own fate, 'I made up my mind to leave this world' and expected to be killed by the crowd at Clontarf.

> Parkes: Did it never appear to you, when you looked at the sunny waters and the blue sky and the green trees, that it would be better to live?
>
> O'Farrell: No, I was not very much enchanted by them. They are very well in their way. I was a little ennui'd.

And he accepted Parkes' observation that he seemed 'cheerful'. Asked by Parkes if Alfred's assassination was expected in England by anyone, he said: 'Oh yes…it is known now what has taken place', even though the first news reports had only just left by ship. If he was alluding to his letter to the Irish newspaper editors, he also told a warder 'ten to one the letters have been stopped' by Post Office authorities who were 'scrupulous'.

O'Farrell detailed the Fenian organisation as having a central council, with different circles in every town and capital city with its own 'senex' or chairman, and 'of course one circle could not know another', and said his group was aligned to the American Fenian movement. But while he outlined a detailed process by which the kill warrant was issued, he also said 'we know very little beyond us'. And his version of Fenian aims, such as 'a republic as much for England as Ireland' was much grander than any known Fenian ambition.

To all of Parkes' questions about specifics, such as the size of the Fenian cell in Australia, where and when the cell was formed, whether members were from Sydney or elsewhere, the delivery of the warrant, where and when the oaths were taken, or whether any cell members had gone on to New Zealand, O'Farrell's replies were invariably 'I will not say anything about that', 'I would not say', 'I would not mention', 'you can form your own conclusions' and 'I most decidedly object to assist you'.[14]

Or he would simply amuse himself at Parkes' expense, as when Parkes asked about Fenian conspirators in Sydney and O'Farrell said he could not deprive the Colonial Secretary of the credit of finding them, before revealing the 'great secret' that the conspirators were all MPs who met in Macquarie Street, and 'let me whisper, the leader is Henry Parkes'.[15]

O'Farrell was aware of the government's anti-treason blitz. He thought charges of sedition for abstaining from toasts to the Queen was 'going rather far', but was pleased because it 'this suits us to a T. It is one of the very things we want. It will stir up those who are always professing and professing and never doing anything. There are lots of Irish who profess and never do anything. Let them drink the Queen's health, and send home plenty of money. They want stirring up here, a great number of them'.

And he was dismissive of those, including Irishmen and senior Catholic clergy, joining the wave of indignation: 'This they will do as long as the place is attached to England'. Irishmen might not like the state of Ireland but felt 'we are so comfortable here', and under the Pope's orders clergymen would not join the republican movement and 'have been opposed to every movement that would benefit Ireland'.

In his notebook O'Farrell wrote 'what nonsense it is to write like this'. Perhaps he was seeing his own demons on the page, or perhaps heeding his own advice to 'play the good-natured fool like Brutus'.

Brutus or deluded patriot, Parkes admired his intelligence: 'It is a thousand pities to see a man like you, in the prime of life, in such a place as this – a man of more than ordinary intelligence'.[16] Parkes could not, or would not, see beyond the intelligence what others saw as insanity—'Posterity is more likely to regard his Fenianism as an element in his lunacy than to accept his lunacy as a proof of advanced Fenianism'[17]—or the possibility that at times he was being 'played', as the gaol chaplain and other opponents and critics would later argue.

Parkes was convinced he not only had his man, he had the 'truth'. But he was about to face O'Farrell's last words on earth. Would this be a confession revealing the final and absolute truth. Or a final delusion or deception?

16

HENRY SAILS TO ETERNITY

We are saved from the spectacle of an assassin transformed by the perversity of a faction into a patriot, and an execution raised into a martyrdom.
— Sydney Morning Herald

The hope of his father that Henry O'Farrell would make his mark as a man of the cloth had long dissipated. Instead he was to have a calico cloth hood over his head and be sent into eternity as the most hated Roman Catholic in the country.

Newspapers rushed to produce special supplements to feed the public appetite for information about the crime of the century. *The Illustrated Sydney News* advertised a supplement, price 1s, with eight engravings to visually tell the story of the day an assassin came to town: people starting for the picnic from Circular Quay, Alfred's arrival at Clontarf and handing over a cheque, O'Farrell being seized, people rushing to get at O'Farrell, Alfred after being shot and landing back at Government House, and a portrait of O'Farrell.

About 30 engravings were produced in various supplements, special reports and portraits of O'Farrell were 'now ready for transmission by the English mail'. Booksellers sold a 64-page pamphlet featuring a 'full report of attempted assassination, with Portrait of O'Farrell, from photographs taken in Darlinghurst Gaol' for a shilling.[1]

And just as Edward Oxford had been a star attraction at Madame Tussaud's waxworks in London after he shot at Queen Victoria and was sent to a lunatic asylum, now Henry O'Farrell stood alongside his victim, Prince Alfred, as the big drawcard at Philemon and Ellen Sohier's popular waxwork exhibits in Pitt Street, Sydney, and Bourke Street, Melbourne. Within days of the shooting they announced O'Farrell would be created by Ellen, 'the most distinguished modern sculptor, regardless of expense', and by 2 April O'Farrell had been immortalised. From 10am to 10pm adults could meet this 'unique curiosity' for just 1s, 6d for children.

> The most terrible spectre in sunny Australia's annals...is now added. This faithful and thoroughly life-likeness has been vouched for by several gentlemen well acquainted with the infatuated maniac. In order to enable the most timid ladies to have a look at this extraordinary portrait model, it will be displayed in the ground floor room, just behind HRH Prince Alfred, his revolver in hand and every detail of toilet etc. conscientiously represented...Vivat Regina![2]

There was no sign of timidity in O'Farrell. He knew his fate from the moment he fired the shot. 'I calculated that I would have been dead', he told Parkes. 'I expected to be dead...I had two plans, one to fire into my mouth, that is very certain; and the other to fire just above the ear.' He understood the Christian doctrine on suicide as a grave sin and his thinking was 'very awful, very unchristian'...but we have latitudinarian views'. And when he had been tackled to the ground at Clontarf before he could take his own life, he was sure he would die at the hands of the angry crowd. 'I would have done myself in the same case, Fenian or not Fenian, I would have done just what they did.'

He was spared the people's lynch law, but now he would soon face Her Majesty's executioner. When Parkes told him it was 'a thousand pities' such an intelligent man was in the condemned cell, O'Farrell replied: 'We must all die once.'[3]

When the gaol warden conveyed the confirmation he would be hanged, O'Farrell 'by no means allowed it to disturb the habitual firmness of manner'.[4] And when gaol surgeon Dr Aaron told him that as hangings were now more private than public he might not have any 'admiring' crowd or public martyrdom, O'Farrell replied: 'Well doctor, when you are hanged I hope there will be an admiring crowd.'[5]

Throughout his final three weeks at Darlinghurst, later dubbed 'starvinghurst gaol' by Henry Lawson, the *Sydney Empire* said O'Farrell 'preserved the same undeviating, calm and apparently unconcerned demeanour' as he had throughout his trial. 'His behaviour has in nowise seemed to affirm the presumption that he was in the slightest degree insane when he committed the deed that shocked and horrified the inhabitants of these colonies.' The only apparent breaking of his calmness came on a visit by his sisters Caroline and Catherine when 'he seemed to feel the degradation in which he had plunged his family'.[6]

O'Farrell did not want his sisters to fight for a reprieve. His fear was not death—the gaol governor thought he was 'gay and happy, particularly so for a man in his circumstances'—but that his sentence might be commuted. 'All I am frightened about now is that the Prince might exercise what is called royal magnanimity, and that the sentence will be commuted...the worst punishment on earth would be a long weary imprisonment. Better send a man to a madhouse.'

He would rather lose his life than being imprisoned for even 10 years: 'It strikes me as something terrible—ten years! What would it be for life?'

As he counted down his final days, hoping Alfred would not intervene, O'Farrell had final say on which visitors could sign the Darlinghurst Visitors Book and talk to him: the Colonial Secretary, judges, magistrates, a phrenologist, Prince Alfred's official photographer Montagu Scott—because, Parkes claimed, 'the Duke is desirous of having O'Farrell's photograph'[7]—and Colonial Architect James Barnet who had been in charge of Alfred's Royal reception, Archdeacon McEnroe and Archbishop Polding.

O'Farrell's expressed disdain for the Catholic Church and its leadership did not preclude visits by the Archbishop and Archdeacon, the attendance of gaol chaplain Fr. Michael Dwyer, and the support of two members of the Sisters of Charity, the first religious order to come to Australia from Dublin.

The Archbishop would have been uncomfortably aware he had confirmed O'Farrell at St Francis Church in 1845, and observed, if not supported, a 'star pupil' trajectory to priesthood. He was said to be 'deeply affected at seeing one on whom he had performed this rite of the church in the position in which the prisoner had placed himself'.[8] But having a long-standing fear that mixing Catholic religion and Irish politics would make the Church look seditious, he was also uncomfortably aware O'Farrell's shooting had fuelled anti-Catholic and anti-Irish sentiment, and offered latitude to Parkes: 'what a curse that man is!'.[9]

Archbishop Polding would have promoted the doctrine of purgatory, urging all condemned men to confront their earthly sins to allow a purified soul to go to heaven. He would also have prayed for an O'Farrell confession that all his statements about Irish-Catholic Fenianism and a conspiracy to shoot Alfred and others were not the gospel truth, and so lift the shroud of disloyalty and sedition hanging over the colony's 140,000 Catholics.

Several attempts had been made to persuade O'Farrell to make a full and final statement before his death, and give it to someone respected, such as Sir William Manning or former Colonial Secretary Sir Edward Deas Thomson. But he resisted, not wanting to appear to be seeking an extension to his allotted time to live.

As the scaffold was being prepared in the north-west quadrangle of Darlinghurst Gaol, near the prison workshop and kitchen, the Colonial Secretary was inundated by applicants wanting to witness the historic execution and perhaps hear a dramatic last-minute confession. Parkes deferred all requests to the Sheriff, who decided about 100 people could attend on the morning of Tuesday 21 April, issuing passes to the Mayor of Sydney, the Sheriffs of Victoria and New South Wales, army officers, gaol surgeon Dr Aaron, police Superintendent Orridge, phrenologist Dr Carr and English actor Montgomery.

O'Farrell did not want to make any last-minute statement on the scaffold, but he did want a final word. The day before he would walk the scaffold he asked for some gaol notepaper to write a farewell note to his sister Caroline, and a final statement to his inquisitor Henry Parkes.

Either of his own volition, or abetted by Archbishop Polding and Fr. Dwyer, he wrote his final words and prepared to face what he called 'the great secret'. Would his words reveal final answers to questions about truth, treason and sanity?

On execution-eve, Parkes knew there was little public compunction about the hanging of O'Farrell, but his deeply personal involvement in the so-far unsuccessful efforts to capture any treasonous Fenian co-conspirators was manna for his rivals. Showing his Queensland peer, Sir Arthur Palmer, around Darlinghurst Gaol he received a message that O'Farrell wanted to give him something, but it came with a specific request that it not be opened until after the execution. Parkes was cautious. Perhaps nervous about what O'Farrell might have written, or not confident he could resist opening it until O'Farrell was hanged, he suggested it be handed to a visiting magistrate, William Chatfield, for safe-keeping. Chatfield witnessed O'Farrell's signature and without reading the contents placed it in an envelope which O'Farrell had addressed: 'The Hon. H. Parkes, Colonial Secretary, to be opened to-morrow, April 21, 1868.'[10]

The contents of O'Farrell's statement would be explosive, one way or the other. Parkes knew it, and so did Fr. Dwyer and Archbishop Polding.

As the grandson of the 'Wicklow Chief' in the 1798 Irish uprising, Fr. Dwyer well understood the Irish struggle and the importance of any condemned man's final statement. And he was no fan of Parkes. The Colonial Secretary had angered the chaplain by initially denying him access to O'Farrell, 'for the first time in this colony',[11] because, Parkes told him, he wanted to personally hear O'Farrell 'unburden his mind', and not risk it being 'hermetically sealed' in the chaplain's breast.

Dwyer said when he finally got to see O'Farrell he heard the same story of a Fenian plot to assassinate Alfred and was initially convinced he was dealing with 'a wild enthusiast...a monomaniac'. But a week before the day of execution, 'he became what I may call an altered man'.

> He told me...that he had been long enough playing the fool, that he had now but very little time left to him to lie and he wished to make the best use of it...He pointed out to me the deception that he had been practising, and the object he had in view in making these statements that he had made; and, moreover, he pointed out to me that he had left some papers for the express purpose of their falling into the bands of the police; that he had firmly resolved to take his own life at the same time that he attempted the life of the Prince, and it was for that special reason that he left the document, that it might fall the hands of the police.

His Fenian stories were 'all without foundation…not a particle of truth in it…no man living had the slightest idea of what…he intended to do'.

On his conversations about Fenian conspiracies, O'Farrell said: 'Mr Parkes thinks that he has been drawing me out: but I have been trying to do just the same myself with him'. As Dwyer saw it, O'Farrell was 'stringing' Parkes along.[12]

According to the chaplain, O'Farrell confessed to 'playing the fool' like Brutus with the Colonial Secretary, just as he had written in his notebook. This was just what Archbishop Polding wanted, and what all Irish Catholics would have rejoiced to hear, but he did not trust Parkes. Polding believed Parkes would, if necessary, have 'suppressed, or mutilated or modified O'F's declaration' so they ensured there was a secret copy, 'one officially for Parkes and another to be published in case Parkes did not'.[13]

The Archbishop and chaplain maintained they had no role in the draft, although Dwyer admitted he suggested the omission of one sentence. This was an appeal by O'Farrell to anyone sympathising with him 'not to think of taking revenge on his account', something Dwyer felt would simply put the idea into the heads of 'weak-minded individuals'.[14]

O'Farrell wanted to make a written statement, the chaplain said, as he 'preferred this mode of atonement to a verbal declaration on the scaffold, and I as his spiritual adviser preferred it also, deeming it adviseable that so excitable a nature as his should not be disturbed at the final moment of existence by making a dying speech and declaration'.[15]

The Archbishop even signed a statement verifying O'Farrell's words to be free and voluntary, but he and Dwyer were later accused of doing more than facilitate O'Farrell's final statement. 'Those highest dignitaries of his Church, gentlemen of the most distinguished sanctity, would dare anything for the sake of their religion', one correspondent wrote.[16] The whole transaction, said the

Sydney Morning Herald, was 'most unhappy as connecting in the public mind the Roman Catholic denomination with a transaction for which they ought to have been held entirely irresponsible'.[17]

The Archbishop suggested it was another example of O'Farrell 'amusing himself at the expense of Parkes' right to the end. Having spun the 'perfectly reckless and impenitent' story about a Fenian cell involved in the 'deed of blood', it was now time for O'Farrell, 'about to die and most truly penitent', to tell another story in time for it be on the next mail home to London.[18]

While O'Farrell prepared for his final night, Parkes could only wonder what O'Farrell's statement might reveal. Meanwhile, Fr. Dwyer quietly passed the secret copy to one of O'Farrell's lawyers, William Bede Dalley, who in turn gave it to MP William Macleay, who had achieved fame for a gun battle with Ben Hall's gang of bushrangers, but was now, with John Robertson, former Premier and alleged 'president of the Fenian Society', ready for a possible ambush of Parkes.

Writer W.M. Adams, an ex-fellow of New College, Oxford, told a Catholic meeting that O'Farrell 'like the magicians of old... seems to have determined on giving his persistent questioner one final chance of placing his honesty beyond a doubt, or of sealing his character for ever in the eye of the whole nation'.[19]

That final chance would come when O'Farrell was hanged and his statement could be opened.

The statement done and delivered, O'Farrell went to bed for the last time about 10pm. He reportedly slept soundly until he was roused at 5.15am and at 6am accepted 'a hearty breakfast'. He received a final visit from the Sisters of Charity, who might have reminded O'Farrell of the call of Jesus in Matthew's Gospel: 'I was in prison and you visited me.' He then shook hands with gaol officials and thanked them for their kindness and consideration.

At 8am, officially ratified witnesses waited inside the gaol's large gates. With rumours of a last-minute escape plan—and one letter to the police inspector-general warning a party of 'low blackguard fellows' from Kiama were in Sydney with the intention of 'turning Sydney upside down in case O'Farrell is executed'—the gaol was surrounded by mounted patrols of police and soldiers armed with carbines and fixed bayonets. Some of the guards, ironically, had been seconded from duties at the nearby Lunatic Receiving House.

In Darlinghurst Road, a large crowd gathered for the colony's first hanging for the year and perhaps a glimpse of the most famous criminal they had ever known, wondering if there would be a sensational last-minute statement or confession.

A small bell signalled the hanging party was on its way to the scaffold. In the lead were two warders in uniform, followed by Robert Elliott, a prisoner-turned-hangman described as 'very old white-headed man, dressed in black', and his assistant, a 'thin dilapidated man', known only as 'Bull'. In the rear was the principal gaoler, John Read, Sheriff Harold Mclean, visiting magistrates and other gaol staff.

Amid them all was O'Farrell, dressed in the suit of silver grey tweed he had worn during his trial, with a small black tie and new kid boots. The man who had trained to be a priest had his hands tethered but carried a small crucifix in his right hand, and was accompanied by Fr. Dwyer, dressed in full canonical dress with missal in hand.

'As he emerged, pinioned, from the gateway, (he) cast one inquiring glance upward, and then subsided into perfect nonchalance.'[20]

At the foot of the scaffold, Fr. O'Dwyer and O'Farrell briefly knelt on a mat in a moment of prayer. Psalm 51, the miserere known by the condemned as 'the neck verse', was a plea for God 'to have mercy on me.in your compassion blot out my offence...blot out all my guilt...cleanse me from my sin' and to not scorn a 'humble, contrite heart'. The truly penitent, the condemned were sometimes told, might become a 'trophy of sovereign grace' and be welcomed by 10,000 angels.

O'Farrell shook hands 'affectionately' with Fr. Dwyer, their eyes perhaps silently acknowledging their shared secret, before one of the executioners took his arm to assist him up the steps to the scaffold. But O'Farrell spurned him, appearing to 'regard the touch of the grim functionary as an insult'.[21]

> O'Farrell then moved rapidly, indeed ran sideways up the ladder, and on being placed in position glanced quickly round the crowd, surveyed the scaffold and the rope, and twice repeating his scrutiny, looked up at the fatal beam as if calculating the extent of the fall, apparently desiring to fix himself in a place where no part of his body would touch the framework of the drop-flap.[22]

Behind a temporary barricade, the crowd of witnesses expected, or hoped, to hear a final statement from a condemned man. But his lips remained sealed: his last word would come after his death.

Nor did he offer any emotion, weep or break down as many condemned men did. Perhaps O'Farrell was, at heart, still a true Catholic and comforted that his discovery of the 'great secret' would be one of divine grace. Perhaps he was also drawn to

> the Hope of the Irish Martyr: Oh! these three Irish hearts of love will guard me in the world to come…why should my poor soul today give way to feelings of despair? The Lamb will wash my sins away…with Mary's and my Saviour's love to guard me in the world to come, I've still three Irish friends above – St Patrick, Bridget and Columb.[23]

The hangman's assistant checked the trapdoor mechanism and made the final adjustments on the noose, giving it three tugs to ensure its tightness. This was not a hanging where anyone wanted anything to go wrong, as sometimes happened if the calculations of prisoner body weight and rope length meant the victim suffered agonising strangulation rather than the intended quick neck break. O'Farrell certainly would not want to be part of any botched hanging: 'The cool manner in which he ascended the scaffold, looked up at the drop and assisted the hangman to adjust the rope was the coolest thing I ever witnessed,' the gaoler Read said.[24]

The executioner and condemned both satisfied with the noose, a calico cape was placed over O'Farrell's head. One of the last things visible to him was the top of the steeple of Sacred Heart Church.

As the town's clocks began striking 9am, the crowds outside and inside Darlinghurst Gaol became silent.

O'Farrell continued to remain outwardly calm, as he had been since Clontarf. The *Sydney Morning Herald* reported that:

> Nothing could have been more becoming, in a person situated as O'Farrell was, than the manner in which he has conducted himself ever since his arrest. He has given no trouble to the officers of the gaol or to the government, and he has carefully avoided doing or saying anything that could be construed into an application for commutation of his sentence.

Even on the scaffold he evidenced 'no sign of tremor or trepidation', with 'utmost propriety' and 'entirely self-possessed'. But now it was time. Just 40 days after Clontarf, an event that changed everything, the Sheriff gave his silent signal. The hangman pulled the lever, the trapdoor fell, and O'Farrell dropped 15 feet.

> One sudden jerk and the vital spark was extinct, the only sign of life being a slight contraction of the legs...after a couple of gyratory swings the corpse hung listless...it was perceived that the right jaw of the culprit was broken and there was a slight haemorrhage exuding from his ear.[25]

Dr Aaron pronounced O'Farrell dead, and correspondents began writing their pronouncements. 'Nothing in his chequered life seems to have become him so well as the quitting of it. A less sensational execution is not on record,' said the *Adelaide Observer,* while the

Sydney Morning Herald recorded he had met his fate 'cool, calm and collected'.

Ten minutes after the death pronouncement, the body was cut down and lowered into a coffin and loaded onto a wheelbarrow. Some in the crowd felt moved to touch O'Farrell as the two executioners moved him to the 'dead-house', where the hangmen traditionally had a glass of alcohol. The gaoler ordered some souvenirs be set aside for Henry Parkes: 'I thought you might like to send these articles home, particularly the irons and pads'.[26]

The Death Register recorded 'this wretch who attempted the life of HRH the Duke of Edinburgh at Clontarf on March 12 was executed this day'.[27]

In the 'dead-house' a cast of O'Farrell's face was taken for phrenological study. His body was not taken up by his family, his sisters presumably deciding that they had done enough for their brother and it was time to completely let him go.

But there was still no peace. The burial contractor demanded an extra allowance for the 'additional time and trouble' involved in the 'unusual' handling of O'Farrell's body from the gaol to Newtown railway station under police protection, before he was finally buried, in the dark, in the Catholic section of the new Rookwood cemetery.

Then came rumours the grave had been disturbed and his head removed. Parkes despatched his police chief to investigate and late at night O'Farrell's body was exhumed. It was intact, but Parkes ordered a 24-hour guard for the next week.

And now the final voice of Henry O'Farrell was to be heard from the grave. At 11am the day after the hanging, O'Farrell's final statement, as per his request, was on Parkes' desk, to be opened in the presence of the Inspector-General of Police and the Under-Secretary.

What they read was extraordinary.

> Being now about to appear before my Creator, I feel it my duty to give expression to my heartfelt sorrow for the grievous crime I have committed. From the very bottom of

my heart do I grieve for what I have done. I have hitherto said that I was one of many who were prepared to do the deed, had I not done it. I had not the slightest foundation for such a statement. I was never connected to any man, or body of men, who had for their object the taking of the life of the Duke of Edinburgh.

Never was I in any other than an indirect manner connected with that organisation in Ireland and elsewhere which is known by the name of Fenian organisation.

I wish moreover distinctly to assert that there was not a human being in existence who had the slightest idea of the object I had in view when I meditated on and through the merciful providence of God failed in carrying into effect the death of the Duke of Edinburgh.

I have written to the printers of two Irish periodicals an address to the people of Ireland, and so certain was I of the death of the Duke of Edinburgh that I stated herein that which I believed would be the fact, and I think I have more than implied that I was but one of an organisation to carry the same into effect.

I need but say that the truth of latter portion rests upon slighter foundation than the former, in fact that, unless from mere hearsay, I had no foundation for saying there was a Fenian organisation in New South Wales.

From continually thinking and talking of what I may still be allowed to call 'the wrongs of Ireland', I became excited and filled with enthusiasm on the subject, and it was when under the influence of these feelings that I attempted to perpetrate the deed for which I am now justly called upon to suffer.

H. J. O'Farrell.[28]

But while O'Farrell's execution had 'satisfied the claims of human justice, and sent him to the tribunal of God' according to the *Sydney*

Morning Herald, his final statement raised fresh questions about truth and justice. The statement's existence was a 'smoking gun' in the Legislative Assembly, with speculation about its contents, including rumours it revealed a list of Fenian accomplices. Pro- and anti-Parkes forces were divided on whether the colony's leadership had reacted entirely appropriately after the assassination bid or had needlessly, and opportunistically, created a national crisis.

Parkes' opponent William Macleay asked the Colonial Secretary if he had received a final statement from the condemned man. Parkes confirmed he had, but said it could not be made public because it had not been seen by the Cabinet or Executive Council. As his opponents bayed, Parkes added that O'Farrell's letter 'was opened at the very same time that another statement was opened, of the very highest importance and it would be in the greatest degree detrimental to the public interest for one of these statements to be considered apart from the other.' He urged MPs to not harass his Ministry at such a 'dangerous' time as it grappled with 'a new kind of crime' which would take 'all the power of the government to grapple with' and its hand would be weakened if the contents were made public.[29]

But after giving the government a second chance to produce the document, Macleay quietly rose to his feet and produced from his pocket a copy of O'Farrell's statement and read it out.

Critics and Catholics rejoiced at Parkes' fury. 'O'Farrell knew his man,' the *Freeman's Journal* later declared, 'he had fooled the Colonial Secretary with his stories of bogus conspiracies, and he would baulk him now in death.'

Parkes ordered an immediate investigation into how a 'clandestinely furnished' duplicate was written and had found its way to 'unauthorised' persons. Within a few days Sheriff Harold Mclean reported to Parkes: 'The conclusion I have come to is that the "duplicate" was written in the Sacristy', in the presence of Fr. Dwyer, and was written through, or with his cognisance.[30] Dwyer protested his innocence but was dismissed, leading Archbishop Polding who had verified the authenticity of O'Farrell's statement, to tell friends Parkes was 'angry, vituperative...undignified'.[31]

Whatever the true genesis of the 'confession', Parkes' police chief John McLerie did not think it deserved much credence. 'Dying declarations are not to be relied upon,' he said. He knew many men who in their last moments of life denied facts they knew to be true, and 'as certainly as the sun was shining' O'Farrell's last declaration was inconsistent with what he had written and said about Fenianism. Parkes was of the same view, later telling Parliament. 'I believe the conversations of O'Farrell conveyed the truth...I believe the journal was true, and all the conversations were true, and nothing has occurred which in any way shakes the conclusions which these led to in my mind.'

Others concluded the final statement, made with no prospect of a reprieve and knowing it would be revealed only after his death, meant it was impossible 'for any unprejudiced person to have faith' in O'Farrell's 'Fenian' conversations with Parkes. As a Select Committee argued: 'He was either false in his statements to Mr Parkes or false in his dying statement...if he was capable of deceiving his spiritual adviser, and dying with a lie upon his lips, why should anything said by him which is uncorroborated be accepted for the truth?'[32]

There were questions about whether political obsession and religious zeal was confined to the man lying in Rockwood cemetery, but Parkes still fervently hoped his 'bloodhounds' would produce some rescuing evidence about the Clontarf conspiracy, and the 'new crime' he referenced in Parliament.

Meanhile with O'Farrell despatched into eternity, Alfred safely departed for home and the Mother Country's love and defence 'saved'; New South Wales set aside 28 April as a Day of Thanksgiving, a day for 'an uplifting of the heart' when business and social life would again stop but this time to express thanks to the Almighty for protecting Alfred from an assassin and the colony from abandonment.

> We have seen a great danger turned aside, a general sorrow prevented, and a bitter reproach silenced. That event, which seemed dark as thunder clouds, is now suffused with light, with rainbow hues shedding promise by the contrast between the blackest treason and the old-world affection and loyalty of the Australian people.

The rainbow of relief was more paramount than any doubts about the trial, judgment and execution. As the *Sydney Morning Herald* summarised:

> The life of the Prince was aimed at; the weapon was deadly; the wound was dangerous; the assassin was seized in the act; the object was to subserve a conspiracy claiming assassination as a rightful instrument of war, and contemplating the ruin of an Empire. No one can ask for immunity who accepts such a commission and attempts such a deed. The question of mitigation was one of policy, not of justice. Those who held the balance thought that both demanded life.

The *Herald* said gladness and gratitude would spring from 'every loyal heart'. There was thanksgiving for O'Farrell's bullet being deflected 'just by a metallic substance entwined with an article of dress…the (braces) brass which, deadening the bullet, diverted it from its fatal course' and Alfred's recovery. And also thanksgiving for those who assailed O'Farrell, and that the 'passions of the multitude did not stain the land with the dread crime of murder even of an assassin'.

The latter was especially welcome, as

> the colony would have bent with shame under the infamy of such a deed. All the loyalty of the indignation against the traitor would have been tarnished by the violence of his punishment. Retribution would have been stripped of its dignity, and the assassin and his destroyers would have gone down to posterity defiled by only distinguishable stains.

The newspaper also said that due to the goodness of the Almighty, 'equity' had not been forgotten: 'The assassin had a fair trial and merited punishment…even the confession disperses the last shadow from the colonial name…we are saved from the spectacle of an assassin transformed by the perversity of a faction into patriot, and an execution raised into a martyrdom.'

In conclusion, the *Herald* challenged the British Empire to 'produce a community more indignant at the crime, or more joyful that for the purpose it contemplated it was committed in vain.'

A Thanksgiving Day, but the Church of England stirred the religious divide, declaring O'Farrell sought to slay the Prince merely 'because he was the Queen's son', and urged all church followers to recognise and defend the privileges of Her Majesty's Church 'from the corruptions of the Church of Rome'.[33]

But those not aligned with Parkes and English Protestant loyalty were beginning to make other judgments about 'equity' and 'distinguishable stains'.

The *Freemans Journal* said history was full of instances of

> atrocities and excesses committed by people who fancied themselves assailed by a domestic foe with which the usual machinery of the law was incompetent to deal with. We might seek long and in vain for anything to parallel the blindness and the fatuousness of a multitude of human beings, under the control of strong feelings of love or hatred; a flock of sheep, a mob of wild cattle are reasonable beings compared with men under the influence of a panic of any kind.

Echoing the advice of William Gladstone, it said the only course during a moral panic was to 'wait for the frenzied rush of the public to pass and allow for calmer reflection and argument', but while the law did not recognise a victim's rank the enormity of this crime meant 'the feelings of the people were beyond the control of law'.

'The public thought they were bound to do something more than to let the law take its course and that they were bound to treat O'Farrell something differently from like offenders – they were bound to exhibit their loyalty as well as to vindicate justice.'

An 'amazingly thin varnish of Christianity' then covered the 'barbarism' of some colonial leaders, and those leading the outpouring of indignation were blind to the fact that 'justice was what the country demanded and not vengeance'.

The jury did not have to make a judgment on the facts of the shooting, but on O'Farrell's state of mind, a 'pure question of science' on which it was as unacquainted as most people, with no assistance from others with expertise.

Bitterly, the *Freemans Journal* had only one fault with O'Farrell's execution: 'The office of hangman should…have been put up for public competition – the highest bidder to perform the last offices of the law…we feel certain that some…would pay heavy price for the privilege of playing Jack Ketch.'[34]

The still unanswered question was whether O' Farrell was a 'half sot, half lunatic', or 'completely insane', as the *Adelaide Observer* put it, and deserving, like all of Queen Victoria's would-be assassins, of time in an asylum or in exile.

Beyond the speed and the climate of the trial being grounds for a commutation, a Shoalhaven pioneer, Andrew McKenzie, was one to point out Judge Cheeke made 'a fatal omission' in not impressing on his jury that O'Farrell was entitled to the benefit of some doubt as to his capacity to prove his own lunacy .

While some had 'a blind thirst for vengeance', he said, since the establishment in this colony of responsible government, 'no more egregious error has been committed than the execution of Henry James O'Farrell'.[35]

But the government was unmoved. The Duke of Buckingham advised the Queen that the tendency of the despatches he was receiving from Australia was 'negative entirely the plea of insanity'.

And while the reward of £1000 for any O'Farrell accomplices had yielded nothing, continuing reports of 'seditious meetings having been held'[36] led the government to proclaim an additional reward of £250 for the discovery of 'any treasonable association or place of meeting' to expose attendees.[37]

The conspiracy conviction refused to die with O'Farrell. In London, on the same day as the Thanksgiving celebration, the *Daily Telegraph's* correspondent at the Colonial Office reported that further telegrams had been received intimating 'that the assassination... was...in pursuance of messages sent from conspirators in this country, which ordered the Prince's death'.[38] When this report reached Australia two months later, the *Sydney Morning Herald* said this 'new and painful' development indicated a 'despotic tyranny which literally spans the globe', such that 'leaders of the bloodthirsty brotherhood are served with blind obedience by willing tools at the remotest points of the British Empire' to shoot targets like Prince Alfred in Australia and D'Arcy McGee in Canada.[39]

A few months later, the conspiracy still unproven and rewards still unpaid, Belmore finally expressed some doubts about the whole affair, telling the New Zealand Governor, Sir George Bowen, that despite Parkes' convictions otherwise, on 'the balance of probabilities is in favour of O'Farrell's dying statement that he acted alone'. His judgment was that, regrettably, Parkes had said and done things which were 'irregular', but assured the Colonial Secretary that in despatches to the Secretary of State he had done 'full justice to your zeal in public service and your exertions in doing your duty at a very difficult moment'.[40]

Others began to voice doubts about how the 'difficult moment' had been handled. Melbourne literary magazine The *Australasian* said: 'Whether Fenianism in Australia has any substantial existence, or whether it is a mere phantom, conjured up for political and sectarian purposes by a class or faction, is by no means clear. The balance of testimony inclines in favour of the latter.'[41]

Even the *Sydney Morning Herald,* which had been unambiguously content with the trial and verdict, began conceding some uncertainties around fluctuating and permanent insanity, and whether the effects of delirium tremens on delusion and self-control were such that 'there are…times when the insanity is as real as if it arose from any permanent cause'.

Questions remained about whether O'Farrell was mentally diseased or and morally insane, whether he had confederates or was merely inspired by Fenianism to become a self-appointed lone executioner. Whether his first statements at Clontarf, his notebook and gaol cell interviews were true and sane were debated. Whether his final statement was the truth or 'entirely a concession to religious authority' remained in dispute. 'Opinion on this will be long divided,' the *Herald* acknowledged, 'When history shall record the story it will be told in the language of doubt.'[42]

Marcus Clarke, the 'peripatetic philosopher' columnist who derided Alfred's bad behaviour in Melbourne, now derided royal loyalists. He said the public

> as the public always does, has rushed into extremes and with its usual persistent ignorance has condemned a whole nation…Because the man who shot at the Duke was an Irishman, because he was supposed to be a Fenian, and because some Irishmen are Fenians, forthwith the whole Irish nation is condemned as a nation of assassins.

Public 'morality' had overstepped and politics was 'at a discount', he said.[43]

But Parkes' zeal was not discounted. His posse of 'bloodhounds' and 'spies', the efforts of police in three colonies, generous rewards and a deluge of public reports had not produced anything tangible. Still his reading of the majority public mood was that it was on his side, and there was no diminution in the suspicion that nothing had changed since the colony's first days: Irish Catholics, driven by

Popery and Fenianism, were a security threat, and Australia's safety and security firmly rested on loyalty to the English, protestant and royal loins from which it was born.

Parkes was encouraged by editorials in papers like the *Melbourne Herald* stating the reason Irish Roman Catholics in Australia had been so readily associated with Fenianism and the Clontarf attack was because the Church tolerated Fenian minds, like Gavan Duffy, the editor of *The Advocate*, within its ranks: 'If priests will countenance such a production, and exalt its editor and founder, how can they expect people will pay much regard to their denunciations of Fenianism?'[44]

Henry O'Farrell was dead, but the smoke from his gun was a long way from disappearing.

17

ALFRED SAILS HOME

If there is any disaffection tending to disloyalty amongst any section of this portion of Her Majesty's dominions, it will be the duty of the Government to put it down.
— Prince Alfred

Prince Alfred did not wait for the Executive Council decision on his efforts to stay his assassin's ascension to the scaffold, and he would not want to be on Australian soil for any hanging.

Along with all the souvenirs from the first Royal tour, the *Galatea* was loaded with 800 tons of coal to make haste home to mother and Mother Country, hoping its maximum speed of 13 knots would allow it to arrive as soon as possible after the arrival of the first newspaper accounts of how an immigrant had spilled Royal blood.

Before leaving Alfred had two final duties: to dispense gifts to those who had helped him with various favours, and dispense reassurances to Australians that their loyalty was not seen in disfavour.

He made several more Royal appointments: John Degotardi, as special landscape photographer, for his photographs of Alfred and his crew aboard the *Galatea*; A.W. Sutton as Royal tobacconist and Julius Weisberger as cigar manufacturer for meeting his passion for smoking; and Alfred Anderson for his piano playing. Those who supplied flowers, brushes, combs, perfumes, hosiery, gloves, saddles, calligraphy were all 'appointed' for their favours.

And he would dispense more tangible favours. Two days before departing, he called for William George Vial, who had rushed O'Farrell to prevent a second shot at the Prince. He promised to arrange an annuity of £40 for Vial' s mother in Cornwall and presented him with a gold watch with chain, seal and keys, made by one of London's top jewellers. It was inscribed by a local jeweller: 'To William Vial, in recognition of his services in securing, at great personal risk, the man who made the attempt on my life at Clontarf, March 4, 1868. Alfred.'

To Squadron Commodore Rowley Lambert, a gold diamond and ruby ring, and to his wife a handsome illuminated box, and to Governor Belmore's aide-de-camp, Captain H.M. Beresford, a handsome scarf ring of pearls and emeralds. His coachman, police escorts, and Government House butler and porter received gold pins, chains rings and brooches.

And he found time to sit for an hour at Government House for artist Montagu Scott to do some preparatory drawings and to sit at Scott's George Street studio, with all his decorations, sword, hat and uniform, for a photographic session for what would be a full-length life-sized oil portrait.

On departure eve he mustered his *Galatea* crew to the upper deck to present theatrical friend Walter Montgomery with a sapphire ring in recognition of the 'highly intellectual treats which your several dramatic and most interesting readings and recitals have afforded us' to which Montgomery exhorted all the crew to not let the shooting be 'connected with the generous people of this beautiful land'[1] and presented them with a volume of Shakespeare.

On board Alfred was presented with a carved shield of his crest and coat of arms for the *Galatea* bridge from John Cuthbert's shipyard, which had prepared the ship for its return voyage. Under commission from Alfred, the shipyard also converted one of *Galatea*'s two steam-powered launches, the *Polyphemus*, into a yacht as a gift for Queen Victoria. Those who knew their Greek mythology might have thought it symbolic: a jealous Polyphemus, meaning 'abounding in legend', killed Acis, the lover of sea nymph Galatea.

Alfred also wanted to thank the Nightingale nurses Haldane Turriff and Annie Miller. He invited them onto *Galatea* and in his private cabin entertained them by whistling with one of his parrots, and delighted the women with a handsome gold watch and chain.

The nurses did not know they were then facing Royal scandal and censure in London after Superintendent Lucy Osburn had written privately to her cousins about her experiences in Sydney. She was obviously pleased that she had reached 'the top of the tree' by meeting Lord and Lady Belmore on her arrival, but now 'I have got to a Prince already'. She recounted how 'every evening this week I have sat for about half an hour with HRH'. They were 'quite good friends', and she liked being with him 'alone'.

Osburn's fascinated cousins printed copies of her letter—'to save time and trouble'—to circulate with other relatives and friends, including staff at St Thomas Hospital, where they found their way to Florence Nightingale. She was aghast. Queen Victoria was about to lay a foundation stone at St Thomas. Imagine if she saw comments about Osburn 'liking better to be with him "alone"...not the way for a Matron to speak of a young Officer...much less of a Queen's Son!!'. Not to mention her spending time with him 'in his night shirt or dressing suit', or the suggestion some of her nurses were guilty of 'flirtations' and at risk of damaging 'rumours'.[2]

Nightingale moved quickly, and to her immense relief managed to secure the retrieval of every copy of the letter.

More happily for Osburn, the shooting prompted public appeals for a suitable memorial in Sydney 'in testimony of the heartfelt gratitude of the community at the recovery of HRH'.[3] The Prince authorised his coat of arms to be used at a new Royal Prince Alfred Hospital which opened 14 years later, while Melbourne discussed plans for a Prince Alfred Benevolent Asylum before opening the Alfred Hospital three years later with Haldane Turriff as its founding matron, the first formally trained nurse in the Victorian colony.

The three surgeons who removed the bullet would be rewarded when *Galatea* returned to England, Queen Victoria presenting gold replicas of the bullet they extracted, and the Navy awarding promotions.

Alfred was not short of his own rewards. Onto the *Galatea* went every piece of gold found and gifted in Victoria, 24 gold and silver trowels, a hand-made carriage and a large collection of gifts, including a locally crafted smoking chair, blue morocco leather and silver portmanteau, brush and comb sets, several walking sticks, including one 'mounted with the head of a blackfellow', and large leather-bound albums chronicling his Victorian and NSW visit.

Colonial Secretary Parkes presented the mongoose which Alfred had seen devour snakes at Sydney Museum, two native cats and a 'large and very tame' kangaroo he had reared, one of two given to the Prince, who said that if they survived the trip they would go to his brother Edward to liberate at Sandringham. He was also given numerous parrots, pairs of emus, black swans, black ducks, teal, and a small turtle.

Alfred also had mementoes from his shooting of kangaroos and possums, but the shooting mementoes he most wanted were the pistols which O'Farrell had carried at Clontarf.

Parkes ordered police chief Captain John McLerie to procure the star exhibits and put them in a specially made cedar case for him to present. The inscription plate read:

> The pistols marked Exhibits A and B were exhibits in evidence at the trial of Henry J. O'Farrell, before the Central Criminal Court, Sydney, New South Wales, on the 30th and 31st March 1868, charged with shooting with intent to murder HRH the Duke of Edinburgh, at Clontarf, in that colony on the 12th March 1868. 'A' is the pistol from which the shots were fired, one taking effect in the body of HRH, and the other in the foot of Mr George Thorne, of Sydney. 'B' was found was on the prisoner when apprehended by the police. Office of Inspector-General of Police, Sydney, 2nd April 1868.

The Prince closely studied the pistols, one clearly discharged and the other still with a full chamber, and the bullet which almost killed him, 'considerably indented and flattened at the conical end and showing, beyond all doubt, that it struck a very hard substance'.[4]

Gifts given and received, Monday 6 April was fixed as the end of the first Royal tour. At 8am, under orders from Commodore Lambert, all war vessels in the harbour were dressed, the Royal Standard raised on *Galatea* and *Challenge*r, and royal salutes fired. Just before 1pm Alfred entered the reception room at Government House where 150 invited guests gathered for a farewell luncheon. They included Premier James Martin and Colonial Secretary Parkes and numerous ministers and MPs, Chief Justice Sir Alfred Stephen, foreign consuls, *Sydney Morning Herald* owner John Fairfax and his editor Rev. John West, Royal Navy officers and Alfred's companions Elliot Yorke and Lord Newry.

Also present was Judge Alfred Cheeke, who had sentenced O'Farrell to death, and Butler Aspinall who had been a night-life associate of Alfred in Melbourne before defending his would-be assassin, and who Alfred had generously invited to join him at the Union Club after the lawyer had been blackballed at the Australian club. Tom Pavey, the instructing solicitor on the defence team, later regaled Melburnian dinner companions with 'some humorous accounts of the discomfiture of the Sydney ultra-loyalists when the Duke was seen promenading the streets arm in arm with the barrister they had ostentatiously snubbed'.[5]

Lord Belmore toasted the health of 'Her Most Gracious Majesty the Queen', which received three enormous cheers, and then turned to Prince Alfred:

> The health of the Royal guest of NSW (loud cheers) would, under any circumstances, be received…with the utmost loyalty and enthusiasm, but more especially will it be so now when we have to rejoice at the escape of His Royal Highness from an attempt upon his life both treacherous and deliberate.

He expressed thanksgivings to 'the great Disposer of Events' who had answered weeks of prayers 'from the faithful subjects of the Queen, for the welfare and prosperity of Her Majesty and every member of her family. I give you the health of His Royal Highness the Duke of Edinburgh'.

The enthusiastic cheering meant Alfred was 'so much affected as to be unable to speak for several seconds' and said he wanted to read his words 'as I do not feel equal to the task of speaking extempore. (Encouraging cheers)'.

His final words were to again reassure Australia it would not face Royal denunciation or Empirical distancing. He had previously issued a statement that his confidence in loyalty of 'Her Majesty's faithful subjects in Australia' had not been shaken but just as Australians couldn't stop protesting their unending horror and undying loyalty, so they couldn't get enough Royal reassurance.

In his prepared response, Alfred gave thanks for the 'enthusiastic and hospitable manner' in which he had been received and entertained, and the moved to his main message.

'The universal manifestations of loyalty to the Queen, and attachment to her person and throne, have...been made known to Her Majesty and cannot fail to have given her the liveliest pleasure.'

After the applause subsided, he went on:

> I must...allude to the unfortunate occurrence connected with myself, which marred your festivities and cast a temporary gloom over the community. I sincerely regret... that there should have been any one incident during my sojourn amongst you which should have detracted from the general satisfaction which I believe my visit has given.

Perhaps Alfred was tacitly acknowledging that aspects of the tour, especially in Melbourne, meant satisfaction levels were not universal, but the audience broke into 'loud and prolonged cheering'. Then he gave the people what they were hoping for. 'The meetings and expressions of sentiments which have been called forth by the recent attempt on my life will show their fellow subjects at home, and the world at large, that they not only have loyalty but affection for their Queen and family.'

After more cheering, Alfred gave the loyalists, especially Parkes, the vice-regal imprimatur they were hoping for: 'If there is any disaffection tending to disloyalty amongst any section of this portion of Her Majesty's dominions, it will be the duty of the Government to put it down, and I am certain that it will receive every support from all classes', to which the audience responded with 'prolonged cheering'.[6]

Alfred had underscored to any republican-minded colonists that Australia remained a colony of British subjects, with the implicit continuance of British protection and determination to put down any treasonous 'disaffection' and 'disloyalty'. He would later learn his comments coincided with the first political assassination of the one-year-old Dominion of Canada, where one of its confederation fathers, Thomas D'Arcy McGee, was fatally shot by another alleged Fenian after decrying the violence and secrecy of the Fenian Brotherhood in words which would have resonated in Australia: 'Secret societies are like the farmers in Ireland used to say of scotch grass: the only way to destroy it is to cut it out by the roots and burn it.'[7]

Diplomatically, Alfred made no direct mention of Fenians, Henry O'Farrell or the pending execution decision, and his efforts to have the matter referred to London. He merely said the merciful interposition of Providence meant his injury was not fatal and no further 'evil' consequences were anticipated from his wound but as he was considered 'unequal to any great exertion' for some time, it was advisable to return home immediately. He concluded with his own farewell toast to 'prosperity to the colony of New South Wales, and as this is the last opportunity of addressing an assembly of Australians, I beg to couple with the toast "prosperity to all the Australian colonies"'.

Enthusiastic cheering ringing in his ears, the Prince returned to the harbour where thousands of people and a guard of honour from the 50th Regiment saw him onto a barge to make his way to *Galatea*. The guns at Dawes's Point Battery had announced his imminent departure, but tidal conditions meant it wasn't until 6.30pm that his ship unmoored and began steaming slowly away toward the Heads.

Thousands more on the shore, especially at Mrs Macquarie's Chair and the Botanic Gardens, cheered and waved hats and 'a cloud of white handkerchiefs...showed that the fair sex were not amongst the least demonstrative of Her Majesty's subjects'. The *Times* correspondent wrote 'the ladies are inconsolable. Their Prince is gone...no handsome face looks up to return the fluttering salute of white handkerchiefs or beaming eyes.'[8]

Among an estimated 200 vessels on the harbour, decorated steamers sounded their farewell. The sounds of *Rule Britannia* and *God Save the Queen* were in the air, and the *Challenger*'s band played

Home, Sweet Home, to which the *Galatea*'s musicians responded with *Should Auld Acquaintance be Forgot* and *Homeward Bound.*

Now under a full Australian moon, people 'stood and took a long last look at the noble vessel as she sped through the water on her way back to the dear old country, which so many of us call "home"'.[9]

As he sailed past the near fatal shore of Clontarf, Alfred might have reflected how close the picnic spot had come to being as famous as the Washington Theatre, with him succumbing to the same fate as Abraham Lincoln and Henry O'Farrell as notorious as John Wilkes Booth.

In their *Galatea* diary, John Milner and Oswald Brierley said the feelings of the colony to Alfred could not be better expressed than verses written by District Court Judge Henry Francis, published in the *Sydney Morning Herald*, called 'God Speed the *Galatea*!'. Beyond effusive sentiment and adulation, the Judge said colonists shuddered over the shooting,

> as tho' te assassins guilt were ours; Fenian, or moonstruck miscreant – one or both – What matter? Grant him of that serpent-brood, Pests of the Green Isle, whence St Patrick bann'd The Innocent toads and vipers, what reck we? We bred him not; such reptiles cannot thrive Where ancient feuds are hushed, and loyal blood Renews its glow beneath Australia's sun.[10]

Judge Francis trusted Alfred would 'clasp fond arms around a mother's neck. And sum all mem'ries of Australia's son In one brief record, "Oh! They love us well!"'.

It would be another 10 weeks before Alfred would see how fondly his mother's clasp would be. After arriving at Spithead on 26 June, Alfred first headed to London to dine with his brother, the Prince of Wales, and companions Elliot Yorke and Lieutenant Haig at Marlborough House, before catching a train to Windsor to see Queen Victoria.

The Queen was 'much agitated...very disappointed' when she heard he would not arrive until the next day, before receiving a telegram from him confirming 'he would be coming by the 10 o'clock train tonight'.

'The news of the Prince's return to England very soon spread among the townspeople of the Royal borough, who rapidly decorated their houses and by 4 o'clock the High Street...and other principal thoroughfares were a mass of bunting.' Throngs of people awaited his arrival at the station, and Windsor Castle and church bells were 'pealing merrily'.[11]

Finally, at 10.45pm:

> we heard cheering and in another instant the carriage drove up...in which dear Affie was seated with Louis, Col Liddell and Mr Yorke. In an instant he was out and in my arms, I kissed him repeatedly and he was quite overcome. Took him to my sitting room where we could see how well he was looking. He was full of Australia, how loyal the poor people were and how much they have felt for me, how he would like to return there...after talking with him some little while took him along the corridor to his room and wished him good night.'[12]

His comments about Australia's shame and loyalty moved her to respond to messages of sympathy from the Houses of Parliament: 'The attack on my son's life has, I am sure, only further aroused the loyalty of my Australian subjects, so heartily displayed in his reception.'[13]

Alfred showed her the O'Farrell bullet which she noted was 'quite flattened'[14] but her maternal interest and affection did not last long. While Queen Victoria had hoped a long absence from his 'flatterers' would serve Alfred well, she would be disappointed.

The London newspapers were full of praise. The *Telegraph* said 'the Sailor-Prince may wear with pride the scar which evoked from these young Empire of the Antipodes such intense and loving protestations of loyalty, such touching signs of kindred feelings and anxious sympathies towards Her Majesty and towards Home'.[15] *The Times* said the shooting made the royal visit more of an uncheckered success than otherwise would have been the case.[16]

And the Sailor Prince was happy to be back in the bosom of London, embracing the challenge of renewing acquaintances with 'the fairer sex whom one may have left disconsolate' as he had told diarist Curtis Candler in Melbourne. The day after his return he again joined his brother and Princess of Wales at a Royal Italian opera event at Covent Garden, where he was cheered by the crowd and at Royal party to mark his return and imminent 24th birthday, 30,000 people cheered him and his brother as they watched opera, a fountain display and fireworks, featuring an 80 foot model of *Galatea*.

The Queen's attitude was expressed to her daughter Vicky: 'I am not as proud of Affie as you might think, for he is so conceited himself and at the present time he behaves as if he had done something instead of God's mercy having spared his life.'[17]

Alfred was also spared numerous unpaid bills from his Australian tour. Courtesans, carriage operators, suppliers and artists were among those who found their services were largely gratis. Even the Sydney engraver of the gold watch presented to William Vial for his life-saving efforts tired of trying to have his bill paid and instead fell back on Vial for payment. And the costs of packing and sending all the souvenirs and gifts were 'presented to the Nation' on his return to England.

He was reported to have described his Australian experiences: 'In Adelaide they stole my jewels, at Melbourne my character, and at Sydney they would have taken my life.' Pithy, but said one sceptical newspaper, 'too clever to be fathered to the "royal fancy sailor"'[18]

POSTSCRIPT

For its first 80 years since the First Fleet the colonies were British outposts, its people strongly believing that while they were further from 'home' than anyone else in the Empire, they were 'as thoroughly English as the people of the mother country'[1] with an equal inheritance to everything that had made England 'the great civilising power of the world'.

If distance made the heart grow fonder and more loyal, then this colonial heart could not be fonder or more loyal. But Henry O'Farrell's bullet severely wounded the heart in 1868. For the youngest settlements in the world, whose very life was inexorably tied to the love and support of a distant Mother Country, it was a shot which echoed well beyond Clontarf.

The country was shamed and angered by an assassin bringing ancient and foreign conflict to its distant shores, and in a moral panic the authorities imposed even greater weight to the meaning of loyalty and the sense of 'Englishness'. They abandoned civil liberties and freedoms in the name of a security crisis, disenfranchised republican notions, and instilled political and social divisions that have not yet completely faded.

The original desire of imperial authorities was to utilise Prince Alfred as the public face of a beneficent Empire, reinforcing royalty and loyalty, and repressing the influence of un-English Catholicism and republicanism. Henry O'Farrell's shot ensured a legacy beyond expectations.

For delivering the first taste of intercontinental terror in Australia, Henry O'Farrell paid the extreme price of his personal loyalty and obsession. But Australians also paid the heavy price of their own 'loyalty in convulsion fits'. Long after the worst of sectarianism, bigotry and division began to ease, successive political leaders continued to see Australia through crimson eyes, evincing loyalty to the Mother Country even if it meant the shedding of more blood.

The shame of Clontarf added to the fear of losing the umbilical cord of empirical protection, the fear of any republican threat to Empire or colonies and Britain's dominant influence in identity, foreign policy, trade and law. Australians repeatedly went to war because Britain went to war, often in disproportionately greater numbers and casualties. In a reinforcing cycle of sentiment and sacrifice, New South Wales sent troops to support the British in Sudan in 1885, the colonies competed in 1900 to be the first to land troops in the Boer War: Lord Tennyson, then Governor of South Australia and future Governor-General, told Queen Victoria 'the war has done an infinity of good on this island continent and has welded Australia to the Empire in such a way that the bond of union will, I feel convinced, be henceforth indissoluble'. Those agitating for a separation from Britain, he said, were 'compelled to give up the utterance of their unpatriotic sentiments',[2] or in the words of leading

Victorian barrister-politician Henry Wrixon, could be dismissed as 'a few harmless political lunatics'.[3]

Troops were also sent to help suppress the Boxer Rebellion in China in 1900, and Prime Minister William Cook said in 1914 that all of Australia's resources were for the 'preservation and security of the Empire', and Billy Hughes promoted WWI conscription as a test of loyalty to Britain. Robert Menzies in 1939 declared 'Great Britain has declared war, and as a result Australia is also at war', and John Curtin told Australians after the fall of Singapore in 1942 they were 'the sons and daughters of Britishers'.

O'Farrell's assassination attempt, seen to emanate from a Fenian brotherhood intent on overthrowing imperial authority with bloodshed, severely wounded those yearning for Australia to become fully independent or republican on French, American or Canadian lines. Such ambitions were sacrificed on the altar of royal sentiment and the mutuality of interests with Britain. The shooting provided the 'loyalists' with an even firmer bedrock, ensuring Australia's narrative became more pronounced as a British colony, safe and secure only if it remained loyally wrapped in a Mother Country's arms. Republicanism meant risk, violence, uncertainty and insecurity, epitomised by the blood spilled in the pursuit of freedom in Cromwellian England, Ireland, France and America. And Clontarf.

Henry Lawson wrote in *A Song of the Republic* in 1887 that the 'sons of the south' had to choose between 'the land that belongs to lord and Queen, and the land that belongs to you!' But even with the number of native-born beginning to eclipse the British-born, efforts to overcome inter-colonial rivalry and create a one-Australia continued to be couched in terms of a constitutional monarchy.

Twenty years after Clontarf Australians warmed to a patriotic anthem, *Advance Australia Fair*, which contained more references to the Mother Country than Britain's national anthem. In one verse it saluted the 'true British courage' of Cook, his raising of 'Old England's flag', how 'Britannia rules the wave', and extolled the people 'From England soil and Fatherland, / Scotia and Erin fair, / Let all combine with heart and hand / To advance Australia fair'.

The verse was eventually shelved at Federation in 1901 but the underlying sentiment was not so readily dissolved. *God Save the Queen*, the official national anthem, was replaced by the modified *Advance Australia Fair* in the 1970s but the Fraser Government reinstated it for all royal, vice-regal, defence and loyal toast occasions, and the *Advance Australia* anthem wasn't officially adopted as the national anthem until 1984, with *God Save the Queen* remaining the anthem played at any events attended by the Queen of Australia and any member of the royal family.

And since Prince Alfred's historic visit, every major royal event has been well and truly celebrated. More than 50 royal visits and televised coverage of weddings, births, funerals and anniversaries, have continued to emotionally buttress history and sentiment.

In 1954 some 75 percent of Australia's nine million people were estimated to have turned out to witness the first reigning monarch tour of young Queen Elizabeth, when Prime Minister Robert Menzies, echoing Henry Parkes, said it was a 'a basic truth' that Australians had within them 'sometimes unrealised until the moment of expression, the most profound and passionate feelings of loyalty and devotion' and when they engaged in acts of common allegiance and joy it helped convert individuals into 'a great cohesive nation…the common devotion to the Throne is a part of the very cement of the whole social structure'.[4]

A loyalty epitomised by devotion to royalty and Church of England was also long seen as protection against papal empire ambitions: in 1882 Sir John Pope Hennessy was rejected as Governor of Queensland because he was a Catholic, the first Prime Minister Edmund Barton suffered the ire of the Protestant majority when he met Pope Leo XIII, and when Prime Minister Billy Hughes advocated WWI conscription he questioned Irish loyalties after the 1916 Easter Uprising.

Fear and loathing toward 'disloyal' Irish Catholics gradually dissipated under the weight of substantial contributions by Irish Catholics and even bigger threats. After World War II, Australia's first Immigration Minister, Arthur Calwell recognised the need for a larger Australian population and for 'a society where Irishness and Roman Catholicism would be as acceptable as Englishness and Protestantism'.[5] But prevailing attitudes meant he still had to declare 'the hope for that every foreign migrant there would be ten people from the UK'[6], underscoring a 'white Australia policy'.

It took almost a century after Alfred was first mooted as a King of Australia that the first Australian-born Governor-General was appointed. Even Prime Ministers openly in favour of a republic, particularly Paul Keating and Malcolm Turnbull, have been unable to substantially change the arc of history. John Howard headed the 'no republic' vote in a 1999 referendum, declaring 'I do not believe in changing a constitutional system which works so well and has helped bring such stability to our nation.'[7] He might have been channelling Parkes and Lang when he was reported to have said a republic would come eventually but he just did not want 'this Keating, Catholic, Labor republic'.[8]

With schools long educating that Britain remained the dominant world power, evidenced by a pink-coloured world map in every classroom, the 'Mother Country' ethos continued deep into the twentieth-century and still underpins and influences much of the debate about Australian identity, security, immigration and religion in the twenty-first century.

Fenians were regarded in the nineteenth-century the same way as Al Qaida or ISIS is today, a terrorism movement representing radical beliefs with global ambitions orchestrated from a conspiratorial religious centre. This was brought home less than a decade after O'Farrell when American Fenians committed Australia's first trans-oceanic prison break by snatching six Irish Fenian rebels from Fremantle Prison and sailing them to freedom in the United States.

Even the iconic outlaw Ned Kelly was depicted in a cartoon as an infant sucking on a bottle branded 'Fenianism'. And the term Fenian can sometimes still be heard as a pejorative term for members of the Australian Labor Party who have nationalist views similar to those of the Irish Catholic supporters of Irish independence.

The demonisation of the Irish Catholic 'them' has progressively morphed into successive fears of 'non-whites', communists, Asians, and now Muslims. At the time of the Alfred shooting, migrants, especially Irishmen, were told to abandon their historic feelings and loyalties, even to cease 'wearing of the green', a sentiment similar to calls for Muslims to become 'more Australian' and abandon the burka.

When the then Prime Minister Tony Abbott declared in 2015 'those who come here must be as open and accepting of their adopted country as we are of them'[9] he echoed the *Sydney Morning Herald* of 150 years ago when it said the big lesson of Clontarf was

> the importance of not allowing non-Australian questions to rise to any prominence in Australian affairs'. Australians ought not 'be victimised by the importation of quarrels and hatreds totally foreign to their own affairs…should it not be recognised and enforced as a principle that those who come to settle here shall not disturb the peace and good order of this community by plotting or executing here schemes of vengeance with which Australians have no concern.[10]

The big lesson of Clontarf was that while the 'tyranny of distance' as Geoffrey Blainey famously framed[11], instilled Australia's Britishness and loyalty, it was also no protection. O'Farrell's shot was at least in part a consequence of the birth of world terrorism, as Fenians capitalised on rapid advances in the international movement of people, money, ideology, religion, crime and weapons, a portent of unprecedented challenges being lived today.

The echoes of Clontarf can be heard in today's dealings with international tides of terrorism, nationalism and religion; national issues of security, identity and personal liberty; political challenges of leadership in times of conflict, community fear and distrust; and the community challenges of competing 'truths' and 'correctness'. And especially in the crimes of 'lone wolves' and the challenges of radicalisation and delusion. In 1868 the *Sydney Morning Herald* was convinced that:

> ...the conclusion is inevitable...both...the perpetrators and approvers have been corrupted, their intellect darkened, and their hearts poisoned. They have adopted the fatal error that evil may be done for possible good, that the innocent may be struck down...and that to gain an object said to be political, all the guarantees of social life may be trampled in blood.
>
> It is to a debased literature we owe such crimes. The Government and nation have been cursed in every form of invective, have been threatened with every species of vengeance – the dagger, the brand, the pirate ship – until many minds have been familiarised with the idea of treason and outrage, and have been induced to look upon traitors as patriots, and murderers as martyrs.
>
> The persons who make themselves instruments of such factions are, often like O'Farrell, men of unsound mind, not incapable of reasoning clearly, and responsible for their conclusions, but with the imagination heated, the moral judgment utterly gone, prepared under the inspiration of a prevailing passion to perpetrate, to justify, and to suffer for deeds from which in better days, and under purer influences, they would have recoiled with horror.

The newspaper hoped, ambitiously that O'Farrell would be the last victim of 'popular delusion', and that 'all Australians, of whatever origin, will remember the warning of O'Connell: "He who commits a crime is an enemy to his country"'.[12]

To some the Clontarf 'minute of madness' and subsequent 'reign of terror' when the lives of a Prince and an assassin crossed may seem a past long dead, but much of this past is not dead or even past, and the way ordinary people see their loyalties, and respond to extraordinary threats or challenges remains a story without end.

PRINCE ALFRED's narrow escape from an assassination bid, ensured, as the *Times* said, that if the aim of the visit was to bind the colonies of Australia more closely to the Crown, this was achieved far more completely than would otherwise have been the case.

Alfred laid the inaugural and indelible crimson imprint on Australia, the groundwork for all subsequent Royal tours. His was the most extensive and far-reaching effort to infuse the human face and sentiment of Royalty into the lives of ordinary people in Australia. His 'levees' in Melbourne and Sydney became the now ubiquitous royal walkabouts. His shooting reinforced Victoria's insight—'It is worth being shot at to see how much one is loved'[13]—and that royal legitimacy is inexorably tied to popular sentiment.

The saving of Alfred's life, thanks to his rubber braces and the fortuitous presence of Florence Nightingale nurses, also led to the saving of many other lives through the new hospitals built in his name in Sydney and Melbourne. The Sydney hospital plaque contains a Latin inscription which translates:

> To God all powerful, all merciful—who when Alfred, Duke of Edinburgh in the midst of festivals and rejoicing which the citizens of Sydney welcomed him, was dangerously wounded by a fanatic, preserved him for his Mother, the Queen and for all Britons—the people of New South Wales relieved from the grief and reproach of so terrible an act, dedicated this refuge of the sick and seat of medicine, in the year of human redemption, 1876.

Soon after returning home from Australia, Alfred went to visit his sister Princess Alice in Hesse and took a fancy to her husband's 15-year-old cousin, Maria Alexandrovna, daughter of Tsar Alexander II, but for the next three years he continued on his merry sailor way. This included a return visit to Australia, private but again one where his personal behaviour was questionable. A handbill in Sydney said Alfred received a generous welcome on his 1868 visit and then:

> in consideration of his...misfortune we drew a veil over some things which were not princely and which (his position considered) his youth could not excuse. His second visit has proved to us that twelve months' additional experience, and the chastening hand of Providence, has not made him a wiser and better man. His chosen associates, male and female, were not such as a gentleman (to say nothing of a prince) could be reasonably expected to select.[14]

Officials drew their own veil over a celebrated row with Gov. Belmore, who reportedly told Alfred that if he insisted on inviting two 'vivacious' daughters of an opera singer to a second Government House function it would be 'dishonouring Her Majesty' and he would shut Government House and resign his commission, whereupon Alfred defiantly took the sisters to the theatre instead. He also 'preferred a cosy corner in Redfern where he kept a siren or two'. He went on to make first-ever visits to New Zealand, Japan, India and Hong Kong, during which time he appreciated native Fijian and Maori beauties, took an elephant on board and got himself tattooed.

Back in Europe Alfred finally made the time to renew his acquaintance with Princess Maria. The Tsar and Queen Victoria both resisted the match, with anti-English feeling in Russia following the Crimean War, and the Queen feeling Russia 'unfriendly' towards Britain. Both families tried to find alternate partners, despite their own personal history: a young Prince Alexander fell in love with the distantly related Victoria when they were both in their early 20s, but the Tsar made it clear to his son that being Victoria's prince escort would mean relinquishing the Russian throne, forcing a separation of the two courts for 35 years until Alfred became engaged to Maria.

Alfred, now 29, sent his mother a telegram from Germany: 'Maria and I were engaged this morning. Cannot say how happy I am. Hope your blessing rests in us.' Victoria, who had told Alfred that Maria must be his only love, dutifully sent her congratulations, but noted in her diary that 'there may still be many difficulties, my thoughts and feelings are rather mixed' and told her daughter Vicky 'the murder is out'.

Her concerns were confirmed barely a week after the engagement when she asked the Tsar to bring Maria to Scotland so they could meet. Alexander, who had granted his daughter an extraordinary £100,000 dowry, annual allowance of £32,000 and some of the best Romanov jewels, refused, proposing a meeting in Germany. Victoria declared it 'simply impertinent' that after being on the throne 20 years longer than the Tsar she should bow to Russian wishes, and demanded an Anglican marriage service be held in St Petersburg alongside the Orthodox ceremony.

After Alfred and Maria wed at the Winter Palace in January 1874, the only wedding of her children which Victoria did not attend, the Tsar retained their honeymoon suite at the Alexander Palace for the next 20 years, hoping his beloved daughter would return home. But Maria never returned and Alfred continued his Naval career—eventually becoming Admiral of the Fleet—before the Duchy of Saxe-Coburg and Gotha fell to him in 1893.

Now a German prince, Alfred surrendered his British allowance of £15,000 a year, but retained £10,000 to keep Clarence House as his London residence. His Germanic role was not universally embraced by Englishmen, and in Saxe-Coburg he endured some resistance as a 'foreigner' and later in life told Victoria he 'found it very difficult'.[15]

He and Maria had a son and two daughters, but their marriage became an unhappy one: a silver-wedding function was marred by their son shooting himself, and they would eventually live separate lives.

Alfred also endured money issues. At one point his younger

brother Prince Arthur told his sister Princess Louise that 'Affie is in great monetary difficulties. Mama and Bertie are in an awful state about it.'[16]

Personal and financial issues were compounded by poor health, as he paid the price of being a heavy smoker all his life, and latterly a heavy drinker. After years of breathing and eating difficulties, and finally being fed by tube, Alfred succumbed to throat cancer in July 1900, a week short of his 56th birthday.

Prince Alfred Ernest Albert was the 'dear, gifted and handsome child' Queen Victoria once preferred to be her heir to the British Empire. Now she wrote: 'Oh God! My poor darling Affie gone too… it is heart-rending…he was my own dear child, so full of talent and we had such hopes for him…'[17]. He was buried with German relatives in a mausoleum on a hillside overlooking Coburg. His tombstone, written in German, simply recorded his name, titles, dates and places of birth and death atop a crowned anchor. A simultaneous service was held for Queen Victoria at Osborne Bay, *HMS Australia* fired its guns, the Lord Mayor of London ordered St Paul's bells to toll, and memorial services were held at the cathedral, York Minster, Devonport, Portsmouth and Edinburgh. But the only plaque in England for Alfred was one ordered for the parish church at Sandringham by his brother Edward, who in a few months would take the British throne.

In Australia, his unprincely behaviour took many decades to fade. The *Tocsin* journal said his 'record of immorality has even put in the shade the achievements in the same direction of other members of the Royal Family' and for Royalty to 'cast a glamour over the most degrading forms of sexual excess' meant he was 'about the lowest blackguard who ever soiled Australian shores – convicts included'.[18]

Newspapers headlined 'the Durty Dook – rascally royal renegade' and described him as a 'Royal rascal and roue' who frequented the most notorious night-houses 'in a manner that will not bear description. He was a dirty drunkard, dirtier than a distempered dog. He bilked his paramours and procuresses and pals, and diddled the poor washermen who undertook the unsavoury task of scouring his dirty linen' and 'showed himself to be a disgrace to the name and fame of England.' Alfred's estranged wife Maria finished her days in exile in Switzerland. But her name lives on, thanks to an English bakery which marked their marriage with a small round biscuit stamped with her name. Today it is known as Marie, arguably the most popular biscuit in the world.

In Australia Alfred's name lives on through two hospitals, the foundation stones of Sydney and Melbourne Town Halls, a major college and numerous parks and streets. And through history as the first Royal visitor and first target of a political terrorism.

Henry O'Farrell's fame is that of association with terrorism, whether through conspiracy or madness.

He failed a family destiny to become a priest, but achieved international fame as the 'reverend assassin', as Rev. John Lang branded him, as he was 'a deacon of the Roman Catholic Church… and as the Church…gives an ecclesiastical functionary of this class the title of Reverend, we ought surely to have designated O'Farrell the Reverend assassin.'[19]

O'Farrell was equated to John Wilkes Booth after his assassination of Abraham Lincoln three years earlier. A Royal Navy lieutenant said Clontarf became a place 'of world-wide reputation…the chosen ground of the would-be assassin in his dastardly attempt on the life of the Duke of Edinburgh…the most cowardly tragedy since Wilkes Booth electrified the world in the Washington Theatre'.[20]

His place in history is immortalised on a plaque erected under a huge Norfolk pine at the eastern end of Clontarf Beach which simply records the spot where an attempt was made to assassinate H.R.H. The Duke of Edinburgh (son of Her Majesty Queen Victoria) while he was attending the picnic of the Sailors' Home on March 12, 1868.

On a more contemporary aluminium panel depicting the shooting, an etched panel states:

> Prince Alfred, Duke of Edinburgh (Son of Queen Victoria)...at the Clontarf Picnic Grounds on the 12th March 1868 one Henry O'Farrell attempted to assassinate the then Duke of Edinburgh, Prince Alfred. Prince Alfred miraculously escaped serious injury. The assassin's bullet was impeded by the double thickness of the Duke's trouser braces. The Prince was conveyed to Government House where he was operated on a few days later. The surgeon was assisted in the operation by two nurses trained by Florence Nightingale. The young prince recovered quickly.

Many criminal lawyers and forensic psychiatrists today generally regard O'Farrell's trial and death sentence as its own tragedy, a travesty of justice as the trial was highly prejudicial and crucial evidence, not made known to the jury, was sufficient to show ought to have been put in an asylum or exile rather than a noose. The judgment of eminent legal minds today is that the trial and verdict was 'a legal charade played out so it could be said that the rule of law had been applied', and Henry Parkes' suppression of evidence meant the trial and execution was 'a miscarriage of justice'.[21]

After 150 years the M'Naghten 'knowing right from wrong' insanity defence remains the basis of English and Australian law. The law of the late 19th century was described as 'hopeless confusion' in the *Journal of Mental Sciences*[22] and while there have been some judgments of 'irresistible impulses' allowing more verdicts of 'not guilty on account of unsoundness of mind' there continue to be arguments over reforms to better reflect advances in understanding of mental illness and 'diseases of the mind', fitness to plead criteria, and the efficacy of assessments, verdicts, convictions, punishment and incarceration.

The infamy of the O'Farrell name, and its association with terror and madness, was reinforced when Henry's brother Peter returned to Australia from self-imposed exile in the United States. Still seething over disputes with the Catholic Church, he confronted Archbishop Goold in Brighton in 1882 and, like his brother at Clontarf, shot his target at close range. The first shot of his 'Bulldog' revolver missed, the second hit the Archbishop in the hand. He claimed he only intended to frighten Goold, and the police could not produce the bullets, leading the jury to find him not guilty of wounding with intent to kill, but guilty of unlawful wounding. He was sentenced to two years gaol.

The O'Farrell brothers shot a Prince and an Archbishop for vengeance. In the judgment of the *Freeman's Journal*, it was accepted that Henry O'Farrell 'was mad as a March hare' and that his family were mad too.

Henry Parkes career could have been shot down after Clontarf, after the English press derided his 'political delirium' and a NSW Parliament Select Committee of Inquiry condemned him for secret recording of conversations with the accused; suppression of key evidence from the trial; recruiting and incentivising a released prisoner to secretly hunt for accomplices; pursuing supportive statements from his police chiefs; and misleading of police, public and parliament about government 'intelligence' and alleged affidavits.

The Protestant press remained loyal to Parkes, saying he was to be thanked for underscoring that violence, sedition, Fenianism, and bloodthirsty malignity towards England, was 'a warning to every colonist...that if this country is to be a great country, a country possessing the character of England, possessing the liberty and laws which are the glory of England, it must not be made an Irish country'.[23]

The alternate view was that Parkes had fed discord and dissension by putting class against class and nation against nation in the ambitious pursuit of 'the prizes of the state', only acting 'for avarice and lust for power'.

Critics accused him of engaging in a self-serving 'reign of terror', and leading the country to believe that a secret brotherhood known as Fenianism was a form of Catholic conspiracy and treason. 'It was an outrage on the living and a fraud upon the dead', the *Freeman's Journal* said, and William Dalley, who had been one of O'Farrell's trial lawyers and would become Australia's first Privy councillor, slated Parkes for his 'entire, absolute and unqualified falsehoods' designed to arouse 'bitter sectarian animosities'. Others accused Parkes of engaging in a 'conspiracy against liberty' and a 'treason against truth'.

But Parkes steadfastly rejected the proposition the government had taken 'advantage of this dark crime and tried to make capital of it', steadfastly maintaining O'Farrell was sane and part of a broader conspiracy, and the failure to find any evidence, despite his spies, police, bloodhounds, rewards and *Treason Felony Act*, was merely because the seditious activity had been pushed 'more in concealment' and it was difficult to gain sufficient evidence of secret sedition meetings for prosecution.

His position was clear: 'The peace has been preserved...I think we would have been utterly unworthy of our position of the name of Englishmen if we had not availed ourselves of all the powers and taken all the responsibilities of our position, and met this crisis in the firm and determined manner we did.'

There were no more 'vagabonds offending the British spirit of the people by saying they would refuse to drink the Queen's health' and there were no more 'seditious sentiments flouted'.[24]

While he later publicly insisted 'I don't seek to connect (O'Farrell's) crime with any party or section of the people'[25], he revealingly wrote to Rev. Lang after O'Farrell's hanging: 'The battle which must be fought within a few months – the sooner the better – will be that of Protestantism and Progress against Roman Catholic Usurpation and Retrogression.'[26]

The time would come, Parkes declared, when 'every person in

the country will be perfectly satisfied that the precautions taken by the government of the day were amply justified.'[27]

Twenty years later not every person had yet come to that judgment, so he devoted 12 pages in his book *Fifty Years in the Making of Australian History* to justify himself:

> It seems to me beyond dispute that the attempt of the Duke of Edinburgh's life emanated from a plot. It is impossible that O'Farrell, a young man in the prime of early manhood, without any known vicious propensities, rational in all his conduct and conversation apart from this criminal act, without any individual motive to commit the crime, not goaded on by cruel or desperate feeling, could have deliberately made up his mind alone, unaided and unabetted, to shoot the Prince.[28]

Only once did Parkes even begin to hint he had possibly pursued a madman rather than a sane and treasonous assassin. He told the Select Committee that O'Farrell's notebook, which he had suppressed, was the work of 'the disturbed mind' of a man who was under threat of death if he did not fulfil the task. Nevertheless Parkes continued to assert the notebook was 'true', and 'all the conversations were true, and nothing has occurred which in any way shakes the conclusions which these led to in my mind'.[29]

While Parkes publicly maintained O'Farrell's sanity, the *Freeman's Journal* said it would be charitable to believe 'Sir Henry Parkes is not perfectly sane...'every falsehood he so unblushingly repeats...was disproved long ago, and he perfectly well knows it.'

One truth, which Parkes did acknowledge, was that the affair had 'a thoroughly bad influence on the political life of the country', with rancorous animosities and recriminations, and a series of elections with votes cast 'under the death weight of prejudices contracted from the rancorous animosities of the period...men who were friends before were never friends afterwards'.[30] Parkes made enemies, lost some friends and public face, and resigned as Colonial Secretary in a political dispute six months after the Alfred shooting. He was morally and legally guilty of suppressing evidence and inculcating a grave miscarriage of justice, but as the public put the horror of Clontarf behind them, the irrepressibly ambitious politician was able to rebound and went on to become Premier for the first of five times in 1872. In 1877 he enthusiastically celebrated the Jubilee of Queen Victoria and was appointed KCMG.

Parkes went on to be described by *The Times* as 'the most commanding figure in Australian politics', known as Australia's 'father of federation' after his 'Tenterfield Address' in 1889 in which he asked whether it was time 'for the creation of this Australian continent of an Australian Government and an Australian Parliament', and challenging the colonies that 'surely what the Americans did by war Australians can bring about in peace'. At the Australasian Federation Conference the next year, Alfred Deakin proclaimed that Australians were 'a people one in blood, race, religion and aspiration'.

Parkes advocated the term 'Commonwealth' for its 'common good' meaning, despite its republican overtones dating back to Cromwell's republic in 1649, and an Australian republican pulse evidenced by 15 organisations and 20 newspapers and journals. Queen Victoria also objected to the term, until she was satisfied by Colonial Secretary of State Joseph Chamberlain of the 'common good' rationale and that 'it did not imply anything like a republic, quite the reverse. The Australians merely wished for it, as they did not like having the same name as the Canadians.'[31]

Parkes died of heart failure in 1896, a month after another onset of financial difficulties forced him to auction his library of books and chinaware collection, and before his non-republican model of unity was formalised in 1901 when Australia was federated as a constitutional monarchy, with Queen Victoria still Australia's head of state, although she was to die just three weeks later.

Parkes was present at the historic event, in the form of a bust carried in a car in the federation procession. Australia's colonies had become a 'union under the Crown', just as Parkes desired, formed on the continuing crimson view that republicanism was tantamount to isolation and risk. As Alfred Deakin, who popularised the federation movement and became the second Prime Minister, declared, for many Australians the Mother Country was nearer in thought than their relatives next door.

Parkes may have had 'Napoleonic' ambitions, as his critics complained, and his handling of the assassination aftermath was a moral and legal black mark, but in the wake of Clontarf he reinforced monarchism and branded republicanism with bloodshed and insecurity. He charted an Australia which retained its Britishness, celebrated when Royal heir Prince George retraced his Uncle Alfred's footsteps to reinforce loyalty and royalty at the opening of the first Australian Parliament in 1901.

The bloodshed and terror that changed Australia in the first Royal tour was not mentioned. But it could never be forgotten.

REFERENCES

Amos, Keith, 1988, *The Fenians in Australia 1865-1880,* Kensington: New South Wales University Press.

Annear, Robyn, 2005, *Bearbrass: Imagining Early Melbourne,* Melbourne: Black Inc.

Aronson, Theo, 1972, *Queen Victoria and the Bonapartes,* New York: Bobbs-Merrill.

Benson, Arthur and Esher, Viscount (eds.), 1908, *The Letters of Queen Victoria, Vol 1, A Selection from Her Majesty's Correspondence 1837–1861,* London: John Murray.

Black, Maggie, 2016, *Up Came a Squatter: Niel Ormiston of Glenormiston 1839–1880,* Sydney: New South Publishing.

Blake, Andrew, 1840, *A Practical Essay on Delirium Tremens,* London: Longman and Co.

Blainey, Geoffrey, 1968, *Tyranny of Distance: How Distance Shaped Australia's History,* Melbourne: Macmillan.

Bolitho, Hector (ed.), 1933, *The Prince Consort and His Brother: Two Hundred New Letters,* London: Cobden-Sanderson.

Buckle, George (ed.), 1907, *The Letters of Queen Victoria 1862–69,* London: Murray.

Buckle, George (ed.), 1926, *The Letters of Queen Victoria. Second Series,* London: John Murray.

Buckle, George (ed.), 1932, *The Letters of Queen Victoria, 1886–1901,* London: John Murray.

Bunbury, Turtle, *www.turtlebunbury.com/history*

Callaway, Anita, 2000, *Visual Ephemera: Theatrical Art in Nineteenth-century Australia*, Sydney: University NSW Press.

Candler, Curtis, 1848, *Notes About Melbourne and Diaries*, Melbourne

Clarke, Stephen, 2015, *Dirty Bertie: An English King Made in France,* London: Random House.

Clune, David, & Turner, Ken (eds), 2006, *Premiers of NSW, 1856–1901*, Annandale (NSW): Federation Press.

Condon Brian, (transcr.), 2000, *Diary James Alipius Goold, 1848–1886,* Adelaide: University South Australia. www.library.unisa.edu.au/condon/Goold

Condon, Brian (transcr.), 2000, *Letters and Documents 19th century Australian Catholic History,* Adelaide: University South Australia.

Cowburn, Philip, 1969, *Attempted Association of Duke of Edinburgh, 1868,* Sydney: Journal of Royal Australian Historical Society.

Cozens, Samuel, 1868, *The Attempted Assassination of HRH Prince Alfred,* Launceston: J. S. V. Turner.

Dowd, Christopher, 2008, *Rome in Australia: The Papacy and Conflict in the Australian Catholic Missions, 1834-1884,* Boston, US: Brill.

Esher, Viscount, (ed.) 1912, *The Girlhood of Queen Victoria: A Selection of Her Majesty's Diaries 1832–1840,* London: John Murray.

Fearnaught, Lady Winifred, 1908, *Chronicles of Service Life in Malta,* London: Edwin Arnold.

Finn, Edmund (Garryowen), 1892, *The Cyclorama of Early Melbourne: An Historical Sketch,* Melbourne: Robert Brain, Government Printer.

Finn, Edmund, 1860, *St Patrick's Societies, Their Principles and Purposes,* Melbourne: Walker May and Co.

Frances, Rae, 2007, *Selling Sex: A Hidden History of Australian Prostitution,* Sydney: University NSW.

Fulford, Roger (ed.), 1964, *Dearest Child: Letters Between Queen Victoria and the Princess Royal, 1858–1861*, London: Evans Bros.

Fulford, Roger (ed.), 1968, *Dearest Mama: Letters Between Queen Victoria and the Crown Princess of Prussia, 1861–1864,* London: Evans Bros.

Fulford Roger, (ed.), 1971, *Your Dear Letter: Private Correspondence of Queen Victoria and the Crown Princess of Prussia, 1865–1871,* London: Evans Bros.

Gibbs, Shallard (pub.), 1868, *Complete Report Attempted Assassination of HRH Prince Alfred, Together with a Biography and Portrait of the Assassin O'Farrell,* Sydney: Gibbs, Shallard and Co.

Gilchrist A. (ed.), 1851, *John Dunmore Lang: Chiefly Autobiographical, Vol 2,* Melbourne: Jedgarm.

Gillmor, Don, Turgeon, Pierre, 2002, *Canada: A People's History, Vol 1,* Toronto: McClelland & Stewart.

Godden, Judith, 2006, *Lady Osburn, A Lady Displaced: Florence Nightingale's Envoy to Australia,* Sydney: Sydney University Press.

Haines, G.J., Foster, M.G. & Brophy, F. (eds.), 1962, *The Eye of Faith: The Pastoral Letters of John Bede Polding,* Kilmore (VIC): Lowder.

Hall, Elizabeth, 1991, *Miss Elizabeth R. Hall's Diary*, Milton (NSW): A.C. Skarratt.

Hamilton, George, 1879, *Experiences of a Colonist Forty Years Ago; A Journey from Port Phillip to South Australia in 1839,* Adelaide: Frearson and Brother.

Hawksley, Lucinda, 2014, *The Mystery of Princess Louise: Queen Victoria's Rebellious Daughter,* London: Vintage.

Headon, David & Perkins Elizabeth (eds.*), Our First Republicans*, Sydney: Federation Press, 1998.

Headon, David & Williams, John, 2000, *Makers of Miracles: The Cast of the Federation Story,* Melbourne: Melbourne University Press.

Hibbert, Christopher, 1976, *Edward VII: A Portrait,* London: Allen Lane.

Hibbert, Christopher, 2000, *Queen Victoria: A Personal History*, London: HarperCollins.

Hughes, Robert, 1986, *The Fatal Shore*, New York: Vintage Books.

Hugo, Victor, 1867, *Guide Officiel à l'exposition Universelle de 1867, Paris.*

Jenkins, Brian, 1975, *International Terrorism: A New Mode of Conflict, Los Angeles: Crescent Publications.*

Kiddle, M., 1990, *Caroline Chisholm*, Melbourne: Melbourne University Press.

King, Greg, 2007, *Twilight of Splendour: The Court of Queen Victoria During Her Diamond Jubilee,* Hoboken (US): John Wiley and Sons.

Kiste, John Van der & Jordaan, Bee, 1984, *Dearest Affie: Alfred Duke of Edinburgh, Queen Victoria's Second Son*, Stroud (UK): Alan Sutton Publishing.

Lang, J. D., 1840, *The Moral and Religious Aspect of the Future America of the Southern Hemisphere*, New York: James van Nordern.

Longford, Elizabeth, 1987, *Queen Victoria R.I.*, London: Weidenfeld & Nicolson.

Lyne, Charles. E., 1897, *Life of Sir Henry Parkes, G.C.M.G: Australian Statesman*, London: T. Fisher Uwin.

Magnus, Sir Phillip, 1954, *Gladstone: A Biography*, London: John Murray.

Martin, A. W., 1969, *Parkes: A Biography*, Melbourne: Oxford University Press.

McDonald, D. I., 1970, *Henry James O'Farrell: Fenian, or Moonstruck Miscreant*, Canberra: Canberra and District Historical Society Journal.

McDonald Lynn, (ed.) 2012, *Florence Nightingale and Hospital Reform: Collected works of Florence Nightingale, Vol 16*, Waterloo (Canada): Wilfred Laurier University Press.

McKenna, Mark, 1996, *The Captive Republic: A History of Republicanism in Australia*, Melbourne: Cambridge University Press.

McKinlay, Brian, 1970, *The First Royal Tour, 1867–1868*, Melbourne: Rigby Limited.

Milner, John & Brierley, Oswald Walters, 1869, *Cruise of HMS Galatea, Captain HRH The Duke of Edinburgh K.G. in 1867–1868*, Cambridge: Cambridge University Press.

Moore, J. J. (pub.), 1867, *A Proposal for the Confederation of the Australian Colonies, with Prince Alfred, Duke of Edinburgh, as King of Australia*, Sydney: J. J. Moore.

Moran, Richard, 1981, *Knowing Right From Wrong: The Insanity Defense of Daniel McNaughtan*, New York: The Free Press.

Murphy, Paul Thomas, 2012, *Shooting Victoria: Madness, Mayhem and the Modernisation of the Monarchy*, London: Head of Zeus.

Nairn, Bede, *'Belmore, fourth Earl of (1835–1913)', Australian Dictionary of Biography*, Canberra: National Centre of Biography, Australian National University, Retrieved from *http://adb.anu.edu.au/biography/belmore-fourth-earl-of-2970/text4327*

Neal, Frank, 1990, *Sectarian Violence in the Liverpool Experience, 1819–1914*, Manchester: Manchester University Press.

Newnham-Davis, Nathanial, 1908, *Gourmet's Guide to Europe*, London: Ballantyne, Hanson and Co.

Nightingale, Florence, 1863, *Notes on Hospitals*, London: Longman Green Longman Roberts and Green.

Norrie, Dr Phillip, 2007, *An Analysis of the Causes of Death in Darlinghurst Gaol 1867–1914*, Sydney: University of Sydney.

O'Farrell, P.A.C., 1888, *Priests and their Victims*, Melbourne: William Sinclair.

O'Farrell, Patrick, 1986, *The Irish in Australia*, Kensington (NSW): NSW University Press.

Pakula, Hannah, 1996, *An Uncommon Woman – The Empress Frederick: Daughter of Queen Victoria, Wife of the Crown Prince of Prussia, Mother of Kaiser Wilhelm*, London: Weidenfeld & Nicolson.

Parkes, Henry, 1869, *Irish Immigration Speech of 14 October 1869*, Sydney: Henry Parkes.

Parkes, Sir Henry, 1892, *Fifty Years in the Making of Australian History*, London: Longmans, Green and Co.

Plaidy, Jean, 2008, *Widow of Windsor*, London: Random House.

Rapoport, David, 2004, *The Four Waves of Terrorism*, New York: Taylor and Francis.

Rappaport, Helen, 2001, *Magnificent Obsession: Victoria, Albert and the Death That Changed the British Monarchy,* New York: St Martin's Press.

Richardson, Joanna, 1967, *The Courtesans: The Demi-Monde in 19th Century France*, London: Weidenfield and Nicolson.

Ridley, Jane, 2013, *Bertie: A Life of Edward VII*, London: Vintage.

Rieden, Juliet, 2016, *The Royals in Australia,* Sydney: Pan Macmillan.

Serle, Geoffrey, 1971, *Rush to be Rich: A History of the Colony of Victoria 1883–1889*, Melbourne: Melbourne University Press.

Serville, Paul de, 1980, *Port Phillip Gentlemen and Good Society in Melbourne Before the Gold Rushes,* Melbourne: Oxford University Press.

Serville, Paul de, 1991, *Pounds and Pedigrees*: The *Upper Class in Victoria, 1850–80,* Melbourne: Oxford University Press, Melbourne.

Sullivan, T. D., 1905, *Recollections of Troubled Times in Irish Politics,* Dublin: Sealy, Bryers and Walker.

Summerscale, Kate, 2016, *The Wicked Boy: The Mystery of a Victorian Child Murderer*, London: Bloomsbury Publishing.

Symons, Michael, 1982, *One Continuous Picnic: A History of Eating in Australia*, Adelaide: Duck Press.

Taxil, Leo, 1884, *La Prostitution Contemporaine,* Paris: Librairie Populaire.

Thorne, Emily Nuttall, *'Clontarf', an Account of the Attempted Assassination of Prince Alfred, Duke of Edinburgh, at Clontarf on 12 March 1868,* State Library NSW.

Thorne, Elizabeth, *Reminiscences 1818–1903,* State Library NSW.

Tombs, Isabelle & Tombs, Robert, 2010, *That Sweet Enemy: The British and the French from the Sun King to the Present,* London: Random House.

Travers, Robert, 1986, *Phantom Fenians of New South Wales*, Kenthurst (NSW): Kangaroo Press.

Walker, Nigel, 1968, *Crime and Insanity in England, Vol 1: The Historical Perspective*, Edinburgh: Edinburgh University Press.

Weidenhofer, Margaret (ed.), 1967, *Garryowen's Melbourne: A Selection from the Chronicles of Early Melbourne 1835–1852,* Garryowen (Edmund Finn), Melbourne: Nelson.

Wilson, A.N., 2014, *Victoria: A Life*, London: Atlantic Books, 2014.

Woods, G.D., 2002, *A History of Criminal Law in NSW 1788–1900*, Sydney: Federation Press.

Jerzy Zubrzycki, 1995, *Arthur Calwell and the Origin of Post-War Immigration,* Canberra: Bureau of Immigration, Multicultural and Population Research.

NOTES

CHAPTER 1

SELECTED REFERENCES

Longford, Elizabeth, *Queen Victoria R.I.*, (London: Weidenfeld & Nicolson, 1987), p.67.; *Morning Post*,(8 January 1859, BLN); Plaidy, Jean, Widow of *Windsor*, (London: Random House, 2008), p.268; *The Times*, (8 December 1862, 17 February 1863, 6 May 1864, BLN).

ENDNOTES

1 Viscount Esher (ed.) *The Girlhood of Queen Victoria: A Selection of Her Majesty's Diaries 1832–1840*, (London: John Murray, 1912), pp. 215, 246, 263.

2 Christopher Hibbert, *Queen Victoria: A Personal History*, (London: HarperCollins, 2000), p. 123.

3 John Van der Kiste & Bee Jordaan, *Dearest Affie: Alfred Duke of Edinburgh, Queen Victoria's Second Son*, Stroud (London,: Alan Sutton Publishing, 1984), pp. 16, 45.

4 Jane Ridley, *Bertie, A Life of Edward VII*, (London: Vintage, 2013), p. 15.

5 Helen Rappaport, *Magnificent Obsession: Victoria, Albert and the Death That Changed the British Monarchy*, (New York: St Martin's Press, 2011), p. 29.

6 Ridley, *Bertie*, pp. 16, 26, 79.

7 Roger Fulford (ed.), *Dearest Child: Letters Between Queen Victoria and the Princess Royal*, 1858–1861, (London: Evans Brothers, 1964), p. 267.

8 Ridley, *Bertie*, p. 19.

9 Kiste & Jordaan, *Dearest Affie*, p. 45.

10 Ridley, *Bertie*, p. 23.

11 ibid., pp. 26, 29, 34.

12 Kiste & Jordaan, *Dearest Affie*, p. 17.

13 Ridley, *Bertie*, p. 27.

14 Greg King, *Twilight of Splendour: The Court of Queen Victoria During Her Diamond Jubilee*, (Hoboken, US: John Wiley and Sons, 2007), p. 134.

15 ibid., p. 28.

16 Fulford, *Dearest Child*, pp. 110, 131, 134.

17 Kiste & Jordaan, *Dearest Affie*, pp. 29, 34.

18 Fulford, *Dearest Child*, p. 110.

19 Hibbert, *Queen Victoria*, p. 268.

20 Rappaport, *Magnificent Obsession*, p. 30.

21 Ridley, *Bertie*, p. 48.

22 ibid., pp. 42, 54.

23 Ridley, *Bertie,* p. 58.
24 Rappaport, *Magnificent Obsession,* p. 51.
25 Ridley, *Bertie,* p. 58.
26 Turtle Bunbury, *www.turtlebunbury.com/history*
27 Rappaport, *Magnificent Obsession,* p. 51.
28 Kiste & Jordaan, *Dearest Affie,* p. 42.
29 Roger Fulford (ed.), *Dearest Mama: Letters Between Queen Victoria and the Crown Princess of Prussia, 1861–1864,* (London: Evans Brothers, 1968), p. 53.
30 *Fulford, Dearest Child, p. 295.*
31 Rappaport, *Magnificent Obsession,* pp. 50, 66.
32 Longford, *Queen Victoria,* p. 66.
33 Rappaport, *Magnificent Obsession,* p. 167.
34 Kiste & Jordaan, *Dearest Affie,* p. 31.
35 *The Times,* (30 December 1858, BLN).
36 *Political Examiner,* (15 January 1859, BLN).
37 *www.euryalus.org.uk*
38 *Cork Examiner,* (12 December 1862, BLN).
39 Lady Winifred Fearnaught, *Chronicles of Service Life in Malta,* (London: Edwin Arnold, 1908), p. 104.
40 Longford, *Queen Victoria,* p. 55.
41 Fulford, *Dearest Mama,* pp. 104, 107, 122.
42 Kiste & Jordaan, *Dearest Affie,* p. 85.
43 Fulford, *Dearest Mama,* pp. 108, 121.
44 Rappaport, *Magnificent Obsession,* p. 163.
45 Ridley, *Bertie,* p. 58.
46 Wilson, *Victoria: A Life,* (London: Atlantic Books, 2014.), p. 272.
47 George Earle Buckle (ed.*) Letters of QV 1862–69,* (London: Murray, 1907), p. 48.
48 Fulford, *Dearest Mama,* cited from pp. 51, 211.
49 *QV Journal,* (18 February 1863, NLA).
50 Kiste & Jordaan, *Dearest Affie,* p. 48.
51 Fulford, *Dearest Child,* p. 334.
52 Fulford, *Dearest Mama,* p. 211.
53 ibid., pp. 261, 262, 265, 267, 325, 328, 331.
54 Kiste & Jordaan, *Dearest Affie,* p. 55.
55 George Buckle, *Letters of Queen Victoria,* (London: John Murray, 1926), p. 432.
56 Juliet Rieden, *The Royals in Australia,* (Sydney: Pan Macmillan, 2015), p. 30.
57 Ridley, *Bertie,* p. 98.
58 Curtis Candler, *Notes About Melbourne and Diaries,* (Melbourne, 1848), p. 340.

CHAPTER 2

ENDNOTES

1 Victor Hugo, *Guide officiel à l'exposition universelle de 1867,* (Paris: 1867).
2 Theo Aronson, *Queen Victoria and the Bonapartes,* (New York: Bobbs-Merrill, 1972), p. 67.
3 Rappaport, Magnificent Obsession, p. 194.
4 Longford, *Queen Victoria R. I.,* (London: Weidenfeld & Nicolson, 1987), p. 321.
5 Rappaport, Magnificent Obsession, p. 225.
6 Sir Phillip Magnus, *Gladstone: A Biography,* (London: Murray, 1954), p. 207.
7 ibid.
8 Christopher Hibbert, Edward V11, A Portrait, (London: Allen Lane, 1976), p. 108.
9 ibid.
10 Ridley, *Bertie,* p. 104.
11 *Sydney Morning Herald,* (20 July 1867).
12 *London Illustrated News,* (25 May 1867 BLN).
13 *Sydney Morning Herald,* op cit.
14 Isabelle Tombs & Robert Tombs, *That Sweet Enemy: The British and the French from the Sun King to the Present,* (London: Random House, 2010), p. 375.

15 Joanna Richardson, *The Courtesans: The Demi-Monde in 19th Century France,* (London: Weidenfield and Nicolson, 1967), p. 28.

16 Ridley, *Bertie,* p. 149.

17 Richardson, *The Courtesans,* pp. 28, 31.

18 Nathanial Newnham-Davis, *Gourmet's Guide to Europe,* (London: Ballantyne, Hanson and Co, 1908), p. 6.

19 Stephen Clarke, *Dirty Bertie: An English King made in France,* (London: Random House, 2015), pp. 127, 119.

20 Examiner, (27 April 1867 BLN).

21 Ridley, *Bertie,* p. 105.

22 Hannah Pakula, *An Uncommon Woman - The Empress Frederick: Daughter of Queen Victoria, Wife of the Crown Prince of Prussia, Mother of Kaiser Wilhelm,* (London: Weidenfeld & Nicolson, 1996), p. 253.

23 Ridley, *Bertie,* p. 105.

24 ibid., p. 278

25 ibid., pp. 105,106.

26 Kiste & Jordaan, *Dearest Affie,* p. 68.

27 Robert Travers, *Phantom Fenians of New South Wales,* (Kenthurst, Aust: Kangaroo Press, 1986), p. 11.

CHAPTER 3

SELECTED REFERENCES

The Australasian, (15 February 1842); *Ballarat Star,* (27 March 1868); *Melbourne Daily News,* (13 September 1849); *Port Phillip Patriot,* (30 December 1841)

ENDNOTES

1 *Complete Report Attempted Assassination of HRH Prince Alfred, Together with a Biography and Portrait of the Assassin O'Farrell,* (Sydney: Gibbs, Shallard and Co., 1868), p. 8.

2 Frank Neal, *Sectarian Violence in the Liverpool Experience, 1819–1914,* (Manchester: Manchester University Press, 1990), p. 58.

3 George Buckle, *The Letters of Queen Victoria Second Series,* (London: John Murray, 1926), p. 877.

4 Neal, *Sectarian Violence in the Liverpool Experience,* p. 58.

5 *The Australasian,* (15 February 1842).

6 *Geelong Advertiser,* (24 January 1842).

7 Paul de Serville, *Port Phillip Gentlemen and Good Society in Melbourne Before the Gold Rushes,* (Melbourne: Oxford University Press, 1980), p. 35.

8 Margaret Kiddle, *Caroline Chisholm,* (Melbourne: Melbourne University Press, 1990), p. 195.

9 de Serville, *Port Phillip Gentlemen,* p. 37.

10 Robyn Annear, *Bearbrass: Imagining Early Melbourne,* (Melbourne: Black Inc, 2005), p. 232.

11 de Serville, *Port Phillip Gentlemen,* p. 42.

12 *Edmund Finn, (Garryowen) The Cyclorama of Early Melbourne, an Historical Sketch,*(Melbourne: Robert Brain, Government Printer, 1892), p. 15.

13 *Melbourne Times,* (25 June 1842).

14 *Port Phillip Gazette,* (2 July 1842).

15 *Newcastle Morning Herald and Miners Advocate,* (9 April 1892).

16 *Ballarat Star,* (27 March 1868).

17 *Advocate,* (18 March 1948).

18 Edmund Finn, *Chronicles of Early Melbourne 1835–1852 by 'Garryowen',* (Melbourne: Fergusson and Mitchell 1888), pp. 125.

19 ibid., pp. 647, 652, 650.

20 *Port Phillip Patriot,* (21 September 1846).

21 *Port Phillip Herald,* (24 March 1846).

22 ibid., (18 March 1846).

23 ibid., (19 March 1846).

24 Edmund Finn, *St Patrick's Societies, Their Principles and Purposes,* (Melbourne: Walker May and Co, 1860), p. 4.

25 Finn, *Chronicles of Early Melbourne,* pp. 637, 652.

26 *Port Phillip Herald,* (5 June 1846).

27 *Port Phillip Gazette, (*15 July 1846).

28 Finn, *Chronicles of Early Melbourne* p. 684.

29 *Argus,* (24 July 1846).

30 *Port Phillip Gazette,* (15 July 1846).

31 *Argus,* (24 July 1846).

32 ibid., (14 August 1846).

33 ibid., *(*25 August 1846).

34 Brian Condon (transcr.) *Diary James Alipius Goold,* April 26, May 25 1853, (Adelaide: University South Australia, 2000), www.library.unisa.edu.au/condon/Goold

35 *Argus,* (13 September 1849).

36 *Melbourne Daily News,* (13 September 1849).

37 Condon, *Diary James Goold,* 11 April 1851.

38 *Ballarat Star,* (27 March 1868).

CHAPTER 4

SELECT REFERENCES

Argus, (27 July, 1 August 1854; 3 October 1863; 13, 14, 30 March 1868); *Ballarat Star,* (5 October 1863; 14 March 1868); *Brisbane Courier* (9 December 1865); *Hunter River General Advertiser, (*29 August 1882); *Maitland Mercury,* (2 April 1868; 29 August 1882); *Victorian Government Gazette* (27 October 1863)

ENDNOTES

1. Condon, *Diary James Goold,* March 1852.

2 *Hobarton Guardian,* (1 January 1851).

3 Christopher Dowd, *Rome in Australia: The Papacy and Conflict in the Australian Catholic Missions, 1834–1884,* (Boston: Brill, Lieden, 2008), p. 21.

4 *Advocate,* (26 August 1882).

5 *Argus,* (24 August 1882).

6 *Ballarat Star,* (22 August 1882).

7 *Freemans Journal,* (15 August 1868).

8 *Age,* (16 March 1868).

9 *Ballarat Star,* (19 March 1868).

10 *Sydney Morning Herald,* (19 March 1868).

11 P.A.C. O'Farrell, *Priests and Their Victims,* (Melbourne: William Sinclair, 1888), p. 26.

12 ibid., p. 19.

13 *Ballarat Star,* (27 March 1868).

14 Brian Condon (transcr.) *Letters and Documents: 19th century Australian Catholic History,* (Adelaide: University South Australia), 7 January 1856.

15 *Sydney Morning Herald,* (19 March 1868).

16 *Ballarat Star,* (27 March 1868).

17 ibid., (14, 27 March 1868).

18 *Argus,* (14 March 1868).

19 *Rockhampton Bulletin,* (9 April 1868).

20 *Adelaide Observer,* (4 April 1868).

21 *Ballarat Star,* (27 March 1868).

22 *Freemans Journal,* (21 October 1865).

23 *Empire,* (23 March 1868).

24 *Freemans Journal,* (11 November 1865).

25 Keith Amos, *The Fenians in Australia 1865–1880, (*Kensington: New South Wales University Press, 1988), pp. 3, 7.

26 *Freemans Journal,* (13 January 1866).

27 *Ballarat Star,* (19, 27 March 1868).

28 *A Complete Report Attempted Assassination H.R.H. Prince Alfred,* p. 33.

CHAPTER 5

SELECTED REFERENCES

Adelaide Observer, (9 November 1867); *The Age* (28, 29 November 1867); *Argus* (22 May 1858, 29 November 1867); *Fremantle Herald,* (7 September 1867); Headon, David & Perkins, Elizabeth (eds.*), Our First Republicans,* (Sydney: Federation Press, 1998), pp. 3, 127; *Illustrated Sydney News,* (16 January 1868); *Leicester Chronicle and Leicestershire Mercury United, (*25 May 1867, BLN); *Manchester Times,* (18 January 1868, BLN); *South Australian Register,* (24 February 1863); *Standard,* (14 January 1868, BLN);

Symons, Michael, *One Continuous Picnic, A History of Eating in Australia*, (Adelaide: Duck Press, 1982), pp. 57, 58.

ENDNOTES

1 Brian McKinlay, *The First Royal Tour, 1867–1868*, (Melbourne: Rigby Limited, 1970), p. 9.

2 *QV Journal*, (21 May 1867, NLA).

3 Travers, *Phantom Fenians*, p. 124.

4 Kiste & Jordaan, *Dearest Affie*, p. 55.

5 *Belfast News-Letter*, (16 January 1868, BLN).

6 *The Times*, (14 January 1868, BLN).

7 *The Age* (13 May 1867).

8 Roger Fulford (ed.), *Your Dear Letter: Private Correspondence of Queen Victoria and the Crown Princess of Prussia, 1865–1871*, (London: Evans Bros, 1971), p. 120.

9 Kiste & Jordaan, *Dearest Affie*, p. 58.

10 *The Age*, (10, 11 July 1867).

11 *South Australian Register*, (16 July 1867).

12 *Adelaide Observer*, (20 July 1867).

13 John Milner & Oswald Walters Brierley, *Cruise of HMS Galatea, Captain HRH The Duke of Edinburgh K.G. in 1867–68*, (Cambridge: Cambridge University Press, 1869), p. 130.

14 *Adelaide Observer*, (14 March 1863).

15 *Sydney Morning Herald*, (3 March 1863).

16 de Serville, *Pounds and Pedigrees*, p. 85.

17 *Adelaide Observer*, (14 March 1863).

18 *Empire*, (6 May 1863).

19 *Adelaide Observer*, (24 March 1867).

20 *South Australian Weekly Chronicle*, (9 November 1867).

21 *The Age*, (10 August 1867).

22 *Freemans Journal*, (14 March 1868).

23 *A proposal for the confederation of the Australian colonies, with Prince Alfred, Duke of Edinburgh, as King of Australia*, (Sydney: J.J .Moore, 1867).

24 *Belfast News-Letter*, (16 January 1868, BLN).

25 *Sydney Morning Herald*, (16 August 1853).

26 Lang, J. D., *The Moral and Religious Aspect of the Future America of the Southern Hemisphere*, (New York: James van Nordern, 1840).

27 *The Times*, (14 January 1868, BLN).

28 *Cornwall Chronicle*, (1 February 1868).

29 *The Age*, (14 September 1867).

30 *Empire*, (28 August 1867).

31 *South Australian Register*, (11 July, 10 August, 1 November, 28 November 1867).

32 *The Times*, (14 January 1868, BLN).

33 *South Australia Express and Telegraph*, (1 November 1867).

34 *Southern Argus*, (9 November 1867).

35 *South Australian Register* (28 November 1867).

36 *Empire*, (22 November 1867).

37 McKinlay, *The First Royal Tour*, p. 35.

38 *Argus* (26 November 1867).

39 *Bell's Life in Victoria and Sporting Chronicle*, (30 November 1867).

40 *Argus*, (6 January 1868).

41 *The Times*, (13 January 1868, BLN).

42 *Illustrated Sydney News* (16 December 1867).

43 *The Age*, (27 November 1867).

44 Milner & Brierley, *Cruise of Galatea*, p. 246.

45 *Sydney Mail*, (25 January 1868).

46 Milner & Brierley, *Cruise of Galatea*, p 248.

47 *Ballarat Star*, (24 December 1867).

48 Candler, *Diary*, p. 316.

49 *Ballarat Star* (11 December 1867).

50 Kiste &Jordaan, *Dearest Affie*, p. 176.

51 *Ballarat Star*, (24 December 1867).

52 Milner & Brierley, *Cruise of Galatea*, pp. 254, 257.

53 *Illustrated Sydney News*, (23 January 1868).

54 *Melbourne Punch*, (16 May 1867).

CHAPTER 6

SELECTED REFERENCES

The Age, (10 September 1867); *Spectator*, (23 May 1868); *Sydney Sportsman*, (3 April, 8 May, 19 June 1901); *Truth*, (New Zealand, 11 October 1913); *Truth*, (Sydney, 5 August 1900; 14, 21 September, 5 October 1902).

ENDNOTES

1 *The Age*, (6 January 1868).
2 Candler, *Diary*, p. 98.
3 *Truth*, (Sydney, 5 August 1900).
4 Candler, *Diary*, pp. 60, 98, 99, 292.
5 de Serville, *Pounds and Pedigrees*, p. 60.
6 Candler, *Diary*, pp. 314, 321.
7 *Truth*, (Sydney, 5 August 1900).
8 Candler, *Diary*, pp. 317, 335.
9 *The Era*, (London, 23 February 1868, BLN)
10 Candler, *Diary*, p. 317.
11 *Australasian*, (21 December 1867; 4 January 1868).
12 *Adelaide Observer*, (20 July 1867).
13 Candler, *Diary*, p. 40.
14 *The Age*, (24 December 1867).
15 de Serville, *Pounds and Pedigrees*, pp. 65, 68.
16 Candler, *Diary*, pp. 318, 325, 336.
17 Longford, *Queen Victoria*, p. 66.
18 *The Age*, (6 January 1868).
19 *Truth*, (Sydney, 5 August 1900).
20 *Punch*, (London, 26 January 1868). www.gale.cengage.co.uk/punch-historical-archive.aspx
21 *Australasian*, (11 January 1868).
22 Tocsin (3 February 1898).
23 *Punch*, (23 January, 13 February 1868). www.gale.cengage.co.uk/punch-historical-archive.aspx
24 *Truth*, (Melbourne, 30 October 1915).
25 *Reynold's Newspaper* (5 April 1868 BLN).
26 *Tocsin*, (3 February 1898).
27 *Truth*, (Western Australia, 1 October 1910, 6 November 1915).

CHAPTER 7

ENDNOTES

1 Andrew Blake, *A Practical Essay on Delirium Tremens*, (London: Longman and Co, 1840).
2 *Argus*, (14 March 1868).
3 *Sydney Mail*, (4 April 1868).
4 SR NSW: Colonial Secretary, NRS 906, 4/646, 69/80.
5 *Empire*, (23 March 1868).
6 SR NSW: Colonial Secretary, NRS 906, 4/646, 69/80.
7 *Ballarat Star*, (14 March 1868).
8 *Argus*, (13 March 1868).
9 *Public Records Office Victori*a, Ballarat VA2844.
10 *Argus*, (14 March 1868).
11 *Sydney Mail*, (4 April 1868).
12 *Empire*, (17 March 1868).
13 ibid., (5 February 1867).
14 *Freemans Journal*, (19 January 1867).
15 ibid., (30 March 1867).
16 *Empire*, (23 March 1868).
17 *Ballarat Star*, (17 March 1868).
18 *South Australian Register*, (25 April 1868).
19 *Sydney Morning Herald*, (15 April 1868).
20 *Argus*, (14 March 1868).
21 *Sydney Mail*, (4 April 1868).
22 *Freemans Journal*, (5 October 1867).

CHAPTER 8

ENDNOTES

1 Robert Hughes, *The Fatal Shore*, (New York: Vintage Books, 1986), p. 87.
2 RA VIC/ ADDA20/1045 Diary of Jane Sophia Barker 23 January 1868, p. 2.
3 *Sydney Morning Herald*, (26 January, 14 February, 12 August 1868).

4 *Empire,* (6 May 1863).

5 A. Gilchrist (ed.), *John Dunmore Lang: Chiefly Autobiographical, Vol 2,* (Melbourne: Jedgarm, 1851), p. 474.

6 McKinlay, *First Royal Tour*, p. 136.

7 *Illustrated Sydney News,* (22 February 1868).

8 *Sydney Morning Herald,* (22 July 1868).

9 ibid., (14 July 1868).

10 ibid., (15 February 1868).

11 *Illustrated Sydney News,* (22 February 1868).

12 Milner & Brierley, *Cruise of Galatea*, p.374.

13 *Empire,* (28 March 1868).

14 *Argus,* (19 March 1868).

15 *Empire,* (23 January 1868).

16 ibid., (3 February 1868).

17 ibid., (20 January 1868)

18 RA VIC/ADDA20/1045 Diary of Jane Sophia Barker 23 Jan 1868.

19 *Empire,* (12 March 1868).

20 RA VIC/ADDA20/1046, Rev Creeny to William Buchanan, 18 March 1868.

21 Elizabeth Hall, *Miss Elizabeth R. Hall's Diary,* (Milton (NSW): A.C. Skarratt, 1991), p. 66.

22 *Sydney Sportsman,* (16 March 1904).

23 *Truth,* Melbourne, (30 October 1915).

24 *Queenslander,* (7 March 1868).

25 Symons, *One Continuous Picnic*, p. 58.

26 *Sydney Morning Herald,* (12 March 1868).

27 D. I. McDonald, *Henry James O'Farrell: Fenian, or Moonstruck Miscreant,* (Canberra and District Historical Society Journal, September 1970), p. 2.

28 RA VIC/ADDA20/1046, Rev. Creeny to William Buchanan, 18 March 1868.

29 RA VIC/ADDA20/1280a, Francis Needham, Viscount Newry, to Dr Candler, 14 March 1868.

30 *Freemans Journal* (25 January 1868).

31 ibid., (15 February 1868).

32 *Sydney Morning Herald*, (12 March 1868).

33 *Votes and Proceedings,* p. 329.

34 *Freeman's Journal*, (20 February 1869).

35 *Votes and Proceedings,* pp. 729, 785, 797, 800, 930.

CHAPTER 9

ENDNOTES

1 *Freemans Journal,* (8 February 1868).

2 ibid., (2 March 1867).

3 T.D. Sullivan, *Recollections of Troubled Times in Irish Politics,* (Dublin: Sealy, Bryers and Walker, 1905), p. 103.

4 *Sydney Morning Herald,* (4 March 1865, 12 January 1867).

5 *Empire,* (17 March 1868).

6 *Sydney Morning Herald,* (19 March 1868).

7 *Votes and Proceedings,* pp. 717, 721.

8 *Truth,* (Sydney, 19 September 1897).

9 *Votes and Proceedings* p. 725.

10 *Sydney Morning Herald,* (31 March 1868).

11 *Votes and Proceedings,* pp. 719, 921.

12 *Empire, (*17 March 1868).

13 *Votes and Proceedings,* pp. 718, 727.

14 Travers, *Phantom Fenians,* p. 45.

15 *Sydney Morning Herald,* (31 March 1868).

16 *Votes and Proceedings,* p. 832.

17 *The Times,* (18 May 1868, BLN).

18 *Sydney Morning Herald,* (1 April 1868).

19 RA VIC/ADDA20/1280a, Francis Needham, Viscount Newry to Dr Candler, (14 March 1868).

20 Emily Nuttall Thorne, *'Clontarf', an account of the attempted assassination of Prince Alfred, Duke of Edinburgh, at Clontarf on 12 March 1868,* (mlmss6100. SLNSW), pp. 6, 9, 13.

21 *The Times,* (18 May 1868, BLN).

22 *Votes and Proceedings,* p. 721, 716.

23 *Sydney Morning Herald,* (17 March 1868).

24 *Votes and Proceedings,* p. 720.

25 *Empire,* (27 March 1868).

26 RA VIC/ADDA20/1280a, Francis Needham, Viscount Newry, to Dr Candler, (14 March 1868).

27 Travers, *Phantom Fenians*, p. 22.

28 RA VIC/ ADDA20/1045/ Diary Jane Sophia Barker (23 January 1868), p. 23.

29 *The Times*, (18 May 1868, BLN).

30 RA VIC/ADDA20/1045/Diary Jane Barker (23 January 1868), p. 24.

31 RA VIC/ADDA20/1046, Rev. Creeny to William Buchanan, (18 March 1868).

32 RA VIC/ ADDA20/1045/, Diary Jane Barker 1868, p. 19.

33 Amos, *Fenians in Australia*, p. 52.

34 Samuel Cozens, *The Attempted Assassination of HRH Prince Alfred*, (Launceston: J.S.V. Turner, 1868), p. 10.

35 *The Age*, (18 March 1868).

36 RA VIC/ADDA20/1280a Francis Needham, Viscount Newry, to Dr Candler, (14 March 1868).

37 *Illustrated Home News*, (23 March 1868).

38 *Sydney Morning Herald*, (13 March 1868).

39 *Votes and Proceedings*, p. 742.

40 *Empire*, (27 March 1868, 22 February 1869).

41 *Votes and Proceedings*, pp. 873, 957.

42 Elizabeth Thorne, *Reminiscences 1818–1903*, SLNSW ml doc 1374.

43 RA VIC/ADDA20/1280a Francis Needham, Viscount Newry, to Dr Candler, (14 March 1868).

44 RA VIC/ADDA20/1046, Rev. Creeny to William Buchanan, (18 March 1868).

45 *Sydney Morning Herald*, (17 March 1868).

46 *The Times*, (18 May 1868, BLN).

47 Thorne, *An Account of the Attempted Assassination*, p. 13.

48 RA VIC/ADDA2 0/1046 Rev. Creeny to William Buchanan, (18 March 1868).

49 *Sydney Morning Herald*, (27 March 1868).

CHAPTER 10

SELECTED REFERENCES

The Age, (13 March 1868); *Liverpool Mercury*, (1 May 1868, BLN); *Newcastle Chronicle*, (18 March 1868); *Pall Mall Gazette*, (25 April 1868, BLN); *Sydney Morning Herald*, (14, 16, 20 March 1868); *Sydney Mail*, (21 March 1868).

ENDNOTES

1 *Trewmans Exeter Flying Post*,(July 8, 1868, BLN)

2 RA VIC/ ADDA20/1045/22 Diary Jane Barker 23 January 1868.

3 Florence Nightingale, *Notes on Hospitals*, (London: Longman, Green, Longman, Roberts and Green, 1863), p. iii.

4 *Armidale Express*, (21 March 1868).

5 RA VIC/ADDA20/1280a Francis Needham, Viscount Newry, to Dr Candler, (14 March 1868).

6 RA VIC/ADDA20/1281. HRH Prince Alfred to QV, 27 March 1868.

7 RA VIC/ADDA20/1280a, Needham, op cit.

8 *Sydney Morning Herald*, (31 March 1868).

9 Lynn McDonald (ed.) *Florence Nightingale and Hospital Reform: Collected Works of Florence Nightingale*, vol 16, (Waterloo, Canada: Wilfred Laurier University Press, 2012), p. 737.

10 Judith Godden, *Lady Osburn, A Lady Displaced*, (Sydney: Sydney University Press, 2006), p. 97.

11 RA VIC/ADDA20/1280a, Needham, op cit.

12 *Empire*, (13 March 1868).

13 Philip Cowburn, *Attempted Association of Duke of Edinburgh, 1868*, (Sydney: Journal of Royal Australian Historical Society, 1969), vol.55, p. 31.

14 *Empire*, (14, 23 March 1868).

15 *Sydney Morning Herald*, (15 July 1868).

16 *Argus*, (13 March 1868).

17 RA VIC/ADDA20/129 Earl of Belmore to Secretary of State, Colonial Office.

18 Travers, *Phantom Fenians*, pp. 119, 120.

19 *QV Journal*, (5, 25 April 1868, NLA).

20 Travers, *Phantom Fenians*, pp. 52, 120.

21 *QV Journal*, (18 May 1868, NLA).

22 *Daily News*, (April 27, 1868, BLN).

23 *Nottinghamshire Guardian*, (May 1, 1868, BLN).

24 Kiste & Jordaan, *Dearest Affie*, p. 68.

25 Longford, *Victoria*, p. 446.

26 RA VIC/ADDA20/1280a, Needham, op cit.

27 Hall, *Diary*, p. 151.

28 RA VIC/ADDA20/1281, HRH Prince Alfred to QV, (27 March 1868).

29 RA VIC/ADDA20/1280a, Needham, op cit.

30 *NSW Government Gazette, #71*, (20 March 1868), SLNSW ID 824018.

31 Hall, *Diary*, p. 152.

32 RA VIC/ADDA20/1281, HRH Prince Alfred to QV, (27 March 1868).

33 RA VIC/ADDC24/62 Francis Needham, Viscount Newry, to Delane, (27 March 1868).

34 *QV Journal*, (18, 23 May 1868, NLA).

CHAPTER 11

SELECTED REFERENCES

Advocate, (25 April 1868); *The Age*, (12 March 1868); *Ballarat Star*, (27 March 1868); *Empire*, (25 November 1861; 14, 16, 17, 19 March 1868); *Freemans Journal*, (2 May 1868); *Goulburn Herald*, (20 October 1855); *Newcastle Chronicle*, (18 March 1868); *Spectator*, (26 June 1897 BLN); *Sydney Free Press*, (12 March 1842); *Sydney Morning Herald*, (13, 16, 18 March 1868; 7 February 1890).

ENDNOTES

1 *Sydney Morning Herald*, (13 March 1868).

2 *Armidale Express and New England General Advertiser* (21 March 1868).

3 RA VIC/ ADDA20/1045/19 Diary Jane Barker (23 March 1868).

4 *Brisbane Courier*, (21 March 1868).

5 Travers, *Phantom Fenians*, p. 33.

6 *Sydney Morning Herald*, (16 March 1868).

7 *Sydney Mail*, (21 March 1868).

8 *Examiner*, (19 March 1868).

9 Mark McKenna, *The Captive Republic: A History of Republicanism in Australia*, (Melbourne: Cambridge University Press, 1996), p. 21.

10 *Vote and Proceedings*, p. 896.

11 Sir Henry Parkes, *Fifty Years in the Making of Australian History*, (London, UK: Longmans, Green and Co., 1892), p. 11.

12 Headon & Perkins, *Our First Republicans*, p. 29.

13 *Empire*, (12 February 1851).

14 David Clune & Ken Turner (eds), *Premiers of NSW, 1856–1901*, (Annandale, NSW: Federation Press, 2006), p. 122.

15 *Goulburn Herald*, (20 October 1855).

16 *Sydney Morning Herald*, (12 March 1856).

17 David John Headon & John Matthew Williams, *Makers of Miracles: The Cast of the Federation Story*, (Melbourne: Melbourne University Press, 2000), p. 73.

18 Charles E. Lyne, *Life of Sir Henry Parkes, G.C.M.: Australian Statesman*, (London, UK: T. Fisher Unwin, 1897), p. 20.

19 Headon & Perkins, *Our First Republicans*, p. 138.

20 ibid., p. 167.

21 Travers, *Phantom Fenians*, p. 39.

22 *Votes and Proceedings*, pp. 833, 925.

23 ibid., pp. 718, 723, 724, 733, 942.

24 *Empire*, (14 March 1868).

25 *Argus*, (13 March 1868).

26 *Ballarat Star*, (27 March 1868).

27 *Votes and Proceedings*, p. 727.

28. ibid., pp. 720, 754, 806, 810.
29 Parkes, *Fifty Years*, p. 222.
30 Patrick O'Farrell, *The Irish in Australia*, (Kensington, NSW: New South Wales University Press, 1986), p. 211.
31 *Votes and Proceedings*, pp. 715, 738.
32 *Mercury*, (3 April 1868).
33 *Votes and Proceedings*, pp. 741, 800.
34 ibid., p. 904.
35 ibid., pp. 748, 749, 799, 800.
36 *Sydney Morning Herald*, (10 February 1869).
37 *Votes and Proceedings*, p. 904.
38 A.W. Martin, *Parkes*, (Melbourne, VIC: Oxford University Press, 1969), p. 240.
39 *Freemans Journal*, (2 May 1896).
40 *Kiama Independent and Shoalhaven Advertiser*, (28 October 1869).
41 *Protestant Standard*, (23 April 1870).
42 *Sydney Morning Herald*, (26 March 1868).

CHAPTER 12

SELECTED REFERENCES

Advocate, (18 April 1868); *Argus*, (18, 31 March 1868); *Bendigo Advertiser*, (4 April 1868); *Daily Telegraph*, (27 April, 19 May 1868); *Empire*, (14, 16, 19, 23 March, 30 April 1868); *Express and Telegraph*, (4 August 1868); *Freeman's Journal*, (28 March, 5 December 1868; 13 December 1892); *Gundagai Times*, (28 March 1868); *Leader*, (21 March 1868); *Leeds Mercury*, (10 May 1868, BLN); *Manchester Guardian*, (27 April 1868, BLN); *Morning Post*, (27 April 1868, BLN); *Morning Star*, (27 April 1868, BLN); *Newcastle Daily Chronicle*, (27 April 1868, BLN); *Ovens and Murray Advertiser*, (17, 21 March 1868); *Queanbeyan Age*, (21 March, 11 July 1868); *Queenslander*, (28 March 1868); *Southern Argus*, (15 August 1868); *Standard*, (27, 28 April 1868, BLN); *Sydney Mail*, (28 March, 2 May 1868); *Sydney Morning Herald*, (13, 16, 19, 20, 28, 31 March, 7 December 1868)

ENDNOTES

1 *Bell's Life in Sydney*, (4 April 1868).
2 *Sydney Morning Herald*, (19 March 1868).
3 *Empire*, (22 February 1869).
4 *Spectator*, (23 May 1868). www.archivesspectator.co.uk
5 *Illustrated Sydney News*, (7 August 1868).
6 *Spectator*, (7 November 1868). www.archivesspectator.co.uk
7 *Freemans Journal*, (17 October 1868).
8 *Empire*, (5 August 1868).
9 *Freemans Journal*, (17 October 1868).
10 *Empire*, (5, 6 January 1869).
11 *Sydney Mail*, (21 March 1868).
12 *Freemans Journal*, (2 May 1868).
13 T.D. Sullivan, *Recollections of Troubled Times in Irish* Politics, p. 105.
14 *Australian Town and Country Journal*, (18 July 1895).
15 *The Age*, (24 March 1868).
16 ibid., (17 March 1868).
17 *Advocate*, (28 March 1868).
18 *Freemans Journal*, (14 March 1868).
19 *Empire*, (21 April 1868).
20 *Sydney Morning Herald*, (20 March 1868).
21 *Hamilton Spectator*, (4 April 1868).
22 *Clarence and Richmond Examiner*, (7 April 1868).
23 SRNSW NRS 906 (4/768.1).
24 *Queanbeyan Age*, (21 March 1868).
25 *Votes and Proceedings:* The Sessional papers of 5th Parliament NSW 1868–69, p.743.
26 *Freemans Journal*, (28 March 1868).
27 *Queenslander*, (21 March 1868).
28 *Brisbane Courier*, (21 March 1868).
29 *Freemans Journal*, (21 March 1868).
30 ibid., (27 June 1868).
31 *Tasmanian Times*, (8 April 1868).
32 *Empire*, (30 March 1868).

33 G.J. Haines, M.G. Foster & F. Brophy (eds.), *The Eye of Faith: The Pastoral Letters of John Bede Polding*, (Kilmore: Lowder, 1962), p. 70.

34 *Sydney Morning Herald*, (31 March 1868).

35 *Empire*, (30 March 1868).

36 *Sydney Morning Herald*, (18 April 1868).

37 James Goold, *Diary*, May 1868.

38 *Freemans Journal*, (15 August 1868).

39 *Votes and Proceedings*, p. 882.

40 *Portland Guardian*, (9 April 1868).

41 *Toowoomba Chronicle*, (28 March 1868).

42 *Votes and Proceedings*, pp. 882, 942.

43 *Bath Chronicle and Weekly Gazette*, (6 May 1869).

44 *Freemans Journal*, (1 May 1869).

45 *Sydney Mail*, (28 March 1868)

46 Robert Travers, *Phantom Fenians*, p. 162.

47 Parkes, Henry, *Irish Immigration speech of 14 October 1869*, (Sydney: Henry Parkes), p. 4.

48 Travers, *Phantom Fenians*, p.163.

49 RA VIC/ ADDA20/1045/19, Diary of Jane Barker, (23 March 1868).

50 *Illustrated Sydney News*, (25 March 1868).

51 *Armidale Express and New England General Advertiser*, (21 March 1868).

52 RA F& VISOV/AUS/1867–68. Thanksgiving Sermon, Rev. S.C. Kent, (29 March 1868).

53 *Morning Star*, (27 April 1868).

54 ibid., (28 April 1868).

55 *The Times*, (19 May 1868, BLN).

56 *Reynolds's Newspaper*, (21 June 1868, BLN).

CHAPTER 13

ENDNOTES

1 *Sydney Morning Herald*, (17 March 1868; 7 December 1867).

2 Travers, *Phantom Fenians*, p. 85.

3 Parkes, *Fifty Years in the Making*, p. 131.

4 *Advocate*, (28 March 1868).

5 *Sydney Morning Herald*, (27 March 1868; 20 October 1869; 2 September 1925).

6 McKinlay, *The First Royal Tour 1867–1868*, p. 182.

7 *Sydney Morning Herald*, (27 March 1868).

8 *Sydney Mail* (28 March 1868).

9 *Sydney Morning Herald*, (27, 31 March 1868).

10 ibid., (13 March 1868).

11 *Freemans Journal*, (28 March 1868, 1 August 1868).

12 *Sydney Morning Herald*, (19 March 1868).

13 *Illustrated Sydney News*, (20 April 1868).

14 *Argus*, (14 March 1868).

15 *Sunbury News and Bulla and Melton Advertiser*, (6 January 1894).

16 *Illustrated Sydney News*, (20 April 1868).

17 Richard Moran, *Knowing Right From Wrong: The Insanity Defense of Daniel McNaughtan*, (New York: The Free Press, 1981), p. 70.

18 *Illustrated Sydney News*, (20 April 1868).

19 *Empire*, (1 April 1868).

20 *Votes and Proceedings*, p. 715.

21 *Freemans Journal*, (2 May 1896).

22 *Empire*, (20 March 1868).

23 *Votes and Proceedings*, p. 919–21.

24 M'Naghten is the most commonly used spelling in UK and Australian law texts, although records at the time also recorded it as McNaughten

or McNaughton. More recent research by American criminologist Richard Moran and Scottish bank records suggest the family spelled it McNaghtan.

25 *Empire*, (1 April 1868).

26 *Sydney Morning Herald*, (22 April 1868)

27 *Ballarat Star*, (1 April 1868).

28 *Empire*, (1 April 1868).

29 *Express and Telegraph*, (1 April 1868).

30 *Illustrated Sydney News*, (20 April 1868).

CHAPTER 14

ENDNOTES

1 *Armidale Express*, (21 March 1868).

2 RA VIC/ADDA20/1281. HRH Prince Alfred to QV, (27 March 1868).

3 SRNSW: Colonial Secretary; NRS 905 (4/646), 69/80.

4 *Freemans Journal*, (21 March 1868).

5 *Examiner*, (2 April 1868).

6 SRNSW Colonial Secretary; NRS 905 (4/646) 69/80.

7 RA VIC/ADDC24/62 Francis Needham, Viscount Newry, to Delane, (27 March 1868).

8 *The Times*, (19 May 1868, BLN).

9 SRNSW (4/646) 69/80.

10 *Goulburn Herald and Chronicle*, (1 July 1868).

11 *Express and Telegraph*, (22 April 1868).

12 *Evening News*, (14 April, 1868).

13 *SRNSW NRS 905 (4/625, 4/630, 4/646).*

14 Bede Nairn, *'Belmore, fourth Earl of (1835–1913) Australian Dictionary of Biography, http://adb.anu.edu.au/biography/belmore-fourth-earl-of-2970/text4327*

15 *Empire*, (10, 24 February 1869).

16 *Votes and Proceedings*, p. 933–34.

17 ibid., pp. 831, 832.

18 Paul Thomas Murphy, *Shooting Victoria: Madness, Mayhem and the Modernisation of the Monarchy*, (London: Head of Zeus, 2012), p. 369.

19 Travers, *Phantom Fenians*, p. 97.

20 *Freemans Journal*, (12 June 1869).

21 SRNSW, NRS 905 (4/646) 69/80.

22 *Votes and Proceedings*, pp.744, 745.

23 *Freemans Journal*, (27 February 1869).

24 *Daily Telegraph*, (10 June 1868 BLN).

25 *Maitland Mercury*, (23 April 1868).

26 *Express and Telegraph*, (22 April 1868).

27 *Adelaide Observer*, (25 April 1868).

28 *Empire*, (27 March 1868).

29 Nigel Walker, *Crime and Insanity in England, Vol 1, The Historical Perspective*, (Edinburgh: Edinburgh University Press, 1968), p. 188.

30 *The Times*, (27 April 1868, BLN).

31 *Empire*, (19 May 1868).

32 *Sydney Morning Herald*, (6 April 1868).

33 *Daily Telegraph*, (19 May 1868, BLN)

34 *Sydney Morning Herald*, (22 April 1868).

35 *Portland Guardian*, (23 April 1868).

CHAPTER 15

ENDNOTES

1 *Sydney Morning Herald*, (6 April 1868).

2 *Freemans Journal*, (12 June 1869).

3 *Votes and Proceedings*, pp. 717, 719, 727.

4 *Sydney Morning Herald*, (19 February 1869).

5 *Adelaide Observer* (13 February 1869).

6 *Freemans Journal*, (19 December 1868).

7 *Empire*, (22 April 1868).

8 *Sydney Morning Herald*, (24 April 1868).

9 *Empire*, (22 April 1868).

10 *Votes and Proceedings*, p. 715.

11 *Sydney Morning Herald*, (18 February 1869).

12 *Votes and Proceedings*, p. 715.

13 *Adelaide Observer*, (13 February 1869).

14 *Votes and Proceedings*, pp. 715, 716–17, 718, 719, 720–21, 722, 723, 724, 725, 733, 957.

15 *Empire*, (20 March 1868).

16 *Votes and Proceedings*, pp. 717, 719, 724.

17 *Adelaide Observer* (13 February 1869).

CHAPTER 16

SELECTED REFERENCES

Adelaide Observer, (4, 25 April 1868); *Empire*, (22 April 1868; 13 February 1869); *Sydney Morning Herald*, (18 January 1866; 22 April 1868; 15 January 1871)

ENDNOTES

1 *Sydney Morning Herald*, (18 April 1868).

2 This appeared in both *The Age* (2 April 1868), *Sydney Morning Herald*, (8 April 1868).

3 *Votes and Proceedings*, pp. 717, 719, 720, 722.

4 *Sydney Empire*, (22 April 1868).

5 *Leader*, (28 March 1868).

6 *Sydney Empire*, (22 April 1868).

7 *Votes and Proceedings* pp. 722, 821, 937.

8 *Sydney Morning Herald*, (22 April 1868).

9 Travers, *Phantom Fenians*, p. 106.

10 *Sydney Morning Herald*, (22 April 1868).

11 *Freemans Journal*, (13 February 1868).

12 *Votes and Proceedings*, pp. 866, 867, 868, 869.

13 Travers, *Phantom Fenians*, p. 106.

14 *Votes and Proceedings*, p. 868.

15 *Sydney Morning Herald*, (19 October 1868).

16 *Armidale Express and New England Advertiser*, (9 May 1868).

17 *Sydney Morning Herald*, (2 January 1869).

18 Travers, *Phantom Fenians*, p. 106.

19 *Freemans Journal*, (9 May 1868).

20 *Sydney Empire* (22 April 1868).

21 *Sydney Morning Herald*, (22 April 1868).

22 *Freemans Journal*, (25 April 1868).

23 ibid., (23 March 1867).

24 *Votes and Proceedings*, p. 822

25 *Armidale Express and New England General Advertiser*, (25 April 1868).

26 Amos, *Fenians in Australia*, p. 73.

27 Dr Phillip Norrie, *An Analysis of the Causes of Death in Darlinghurst Gaol 1867–1914*, (Sydney: University of Sydney 2007), p. 101.

28 *Freemans Journal*, (25 April 1868).

29 *Sydney Morning Herald*, (22 April 1868).

30 *Freemans Journal*, (2 May 1896).

31 Travers, *Phantom Fenians*, p. 106.

32 *Votes and Proceedings*, pp. 729, 786, 803, 843.

33 *Sydney Morning Herald*, (22, 28, 29 April 1868).

34 *Freemans Journal*, (25 April 1868).

35 ibid., (16 May 1868).

36 RA VIC/MAIN/S/27/43 Duke Buckingham to QV, (14 June 1868).

37 *Empire*, (22 April 1868).

38 *Daily Telegraph*, (29 April 1868, BLN)

39 *Sydney Morning Herald*, (30 June 1868).

40. Bede Nairn, *Belmore, fourth Earl of* (1835–1913), http://adb.anu.edu.au/biography/belmore-fourth-earl-of-2970/text4327

41 *Australasian*, (28 March 1868).

42 *Sydney Morning Herald*, (19 December 1868).

43 *Australasian*, (21 March 1868).

44 *Examiner*, (21 March 1868).

CHAPTER 17

ENDNOTES

1 *Empire*, (7, 8 April 1868).
2 Osburn, *A Lady Displaced*, pp. 119, 120.
3 *Empire*, (21 March 1868).
4 *Sydney Morning Herald*, (8, 13, 22 April 1868).
5 *Table Talk*, (17 June 1892).
6 *Sydney Morning Herald*, (7 April 1868).
7 Don Gillmor & Pierre Turgeon, *Canada: A People's History, Vol 1*, (Toronto, Canada: McClelland & Stewart, 2002), p. 278.
8 *The Times*, (15 June 1868, BLN).
9 *Sydney Morning Herald*, (7 April 1868).
10 Milner & Brierley, *Cruise of Galatea*, p. 446.
11 *The Times*, (27 June 1868).
12 *QV Journal*, (26 June 1868, NLA).
13 *Sydney Morning Herald*, (15 July 1868).
14 *QV Journal*, (2 July 1868, NLA).
15 *Daily Telegraph*, (19 May 1868 BLN)
16 *The Times*, (19 May 1868, BLN)
17 Lucinda Hawksley, *The Mystery of Princess Louise: Queen Victoria's Rebellious Daughter*, (London: Vintage, 2014), p. 95.
18 *Reynolds's Newspaper*, (21 June 1868, BLN).

POSTSCRIPT

SELECTED REFERENCES

Freemans Journal, (9 May 1868; 10, 17, 31 December 1892); *Portland Guardian*, (20 May 1869); *Sydney Morning Herald*, (4 May. 22 October 1869; 21 May 1872); *The Times*, (11 February 1890, BLN); *Truth*, Sydney, (5 August 1900); *Truth*, Western Australia, (1 October 1910; 6 November 1915); *Western Australian Sunday Times*, (18, 19 August 1900)

ENDNOTES

1 Martin, *Henry Parkes*, p. 194.
2 Buckle, *Letters of Queen Victoria*, p. 457.
3 Geoffrey Serle, *Rush to be Rich*, (Melbourne: Melbourne University Press, 1971), p. 197.
4 *Sydney Morning Herald*, (4 February 1954).
5 Jerzy Zubrzycki, *Arthur Calwell and the Origin of Post-War Immigration*, (Canberra: Bureau of Immigration, Multicultural and Population Research, 1995), p. 3.
6 *Canberra Times*, (23 November 1946).
7 PM Statement, 27 October 1999.
8 *The Australian*, (10–11 September 2016).
9 *Australian* (24 February 2015).
10 *Sydney Morning Herald*, (16 March 1868).
11 Blainey, Geoffrey, *Tyranny of Distance: How Distance Shaped Australia's History*, (Melbourne: Macmillan, 1968).
12 *Sydney Morning Herald*, (22 April 1868).
13 Paul Thomas Murphy, *Shooting Victoria*, (London: Head of Zeus, 2012), p. 458.
14 *Cornwall Chronicle*, (17 May 1869).
15 Buckle, *Letters of Queen Victoria*, p. 347.
16 Hawksley, *Mystery of Princess Louise*, p. 274.
17 *George Buckle (ed.), Letters of Queen Victoria, 1886–1901*, (London: John Murray, 1932), p. 579, 581.
18 *Tocsin*, (3 February 1898).
19 *Empire*, (22 February 1869).
20 James Bruce, *Cruise Around the World, 1869–70*, (London: J. D. Potter, 1871), p. 121.
21 Woods, G.D., *A History of Criminal Law in NSW 1788-1900*, (Sydney: Federation Press, 2002), p. 240.
22 Kate Summerscale, *The Wicked Boy: The Mystery of a Victorian Child Murderer*, (London: Bloomsbury Publishing, 2016), p. 167.

23 *Protestant Standard,* (30 October 1869).

24 *Sydney Morning Herald,* (26 June 1868).

25 *Freemans Journal,* (10 December 1892).

26 A.W. Martin, *Journal of Religious History,* (Malden (USA): 1976), p. 85.

27 *Sydney Morning Herald,* (26 June 1868).

28 Parkes, *Fifty Years in the Making of Australian History,* p. 201.

29 Votes and Proceedings, p. 843.

30 Parkes, op cit., p. 201.

31 Buckle, *Diary of Queen Victoria,* p. 566.

ABBREVIATIONS USED

BLN British Library of Newspapers

NLA National Library of Australia

QV Journal Queen Victoria Journal

RA Royal Archives

SLNSW State Library of New South Wales

SRNSW State Records New South Wales, from Colonial Secretary; NRS 905, Letters Received, [4/625,4/630,4/646] and Colonial Secretary; NRS 906, Special Bundles- Alleged Fenian conspiracy re attempted assassination of Duke Edinburgh,1867–68, [4/768.1]

Votes and Proceedings The Sessional papers of 5th Parliament NSW 1868–69 (www.parliament.nsw.gov.au/hansard) contain the proceedings, transcripts of evidence and documents, and findings of a Select Committee of Inquiry into the 'alleged conspiracy for purposes of treason and assassination'.

The resources in Selected References denote that a small portion of quoted words were used but not enough to warrant their own endnotes.

INDEX

N

O

P

ACKNOWLEDGEMENTS

The story of Alfred's visit was first told by Brian McKinlay in *The First Royal Tour 1867–1868,* and referenced in historical journal articles and books on Fenians, in the 1970s and 1980s.

With memory and knowledge fading with each generation, and more archival material now available, my ambition was to weave a more complete story of what happened 150 years ago when the very different lives of a Prince and a would-be priest came to intersect on Sydney Harbour and how a young nation and its leaders responded to the most significant event since settlement.

And to appreciate how that history is, in an achingly familiar way, still being played out today, underscoring William Faulkner's observation: 'The past is never dead. It's not even past'.

In my efforts to bring this story to life, I have needed the expertise, assistance, encouragement and plain good sense from many. They range from the vice-regal to very regular people.

I gratefully acknowledge the permission of Her Majesty Queen Elizabeth II to quote from materials in the Royal Archives, and the valuable assistance of her staff at Windsor Castle, particularly during the tenure of Senior Archivist Miss Pam Clark, and the various staff and volunteers at Windsor, led by Volunteers Manager

Miss Allison Derrett, who facilitated access to original documents and verifications.

On royal matters, I am also grateful for the interest, encouragement and helpful suggestions received from Jane Ridley, Professor of History at Buckingham University and author of the best-selling *Bertie: A Life of Edward VII* and Helen Rappaport, a specialist in Victorian history and author of *A Magnificent Obsession: Victoria, Albert and the Death that Changed the British Monarchy.* I also acknowledge the value of earlier research by John van der Kiste and Bee Jordaan, authors of *Dearest Affie: Alfred, Duke of Edinburgh*, one of the few books on the life of Prince Alfred. The Records Office of NSW were most helpful in helping locate and provide access to colonial material at the Western Sydney Records Centre, and I particularly acknowledge the support of Gail Davis, Senior Archivist Research and Publications. The staff of the State Library of Victoria were also most helpful in locating rare books and historical records, as were the staff of the National Library in Canberra.

In addition to the books cited in the bibliography, I acknowledge the assistance and advice of numerous others, especially on colonial justice and terrorism history, particularly Professor Mark Finnane, director of Griffith University's Prosecution Project on criminal justice history in the Griffith Criminology Institute; Dr Gregory Woods, QC, former NSW District Court judge and author of *History of Criminal Law NSW 1788–1900*; Professor Sean Brawley, of the Department of Modern History and International relations at Macquarie University and head of a project surveying politically motivated violence in Australia; Professor Greg Barton, of Deakin University, a scholar of terrorism and countering violent extremism.

Of many individuals who provided valuable input and guidance I particularly acknowledge: Mr Roy Jinks, Historian of the Smith & Wesson company in Massachusetts; Dr Phillip Norrie on Darlinghurst Gaol; Professor Geoffrey Blainey, on Australian history; James Sherwood, archivist at Henry Poole & Co (Savile Row) Ltd, tailor to Prince Alfred; Edward Said of the Sliema Heritage Society, and historian and Judge Giovanni Bonello, on Malta; Dr Anita Callaway of the University of Sydney on Alfred ephemera; Dr Martyn Jolly, of the Australian National University School of Art on Alfred photography; Jennifer Burrell of the Ballarat & District Genealogical Society on early Ballarat medical records; Dr Patrick Morgan on early Irish Catholic history in Melbourne; John MacRitchie, Local Studies Librarian at Northern Beaches Council, on Clontarf; Dr Richard Reid, curator and historian, on Irish Australian history; Leila Elmoos, historian at City of Sydney, and Nerida Campbell, of Sydney Living Museums, on Sydney history.

I acknowledge the mostly anonymous newspaper writers who wrote the first drafts of Australian history and the anonymous volunteers who now help the National Library give those drafts a digital life through its Trove database. No library, archives, museum or historical centre can provide what they do without the supporting efforts of volunteers, and I salute them.

And I thank my family and those friends who hold a special place in my life for being with me in my story.

Finally, I thank publisher David Tenenbaum and his team at Melbourne Books, especially Mei Yen Chua for her editing, for their enthusiastic support for untold or under-told stories about ourselves.

THE AUTHOR

Steve Harris is a former newspaper editor, editor-in-chief and publisher at *The Age, Sunday Age,* and *Herald Sun*. He is a life member of the Melbourne Press Club and a John S. Knight Fellow at Stanford University. His first book, *Solomon's Noose*, the true story of a young convict who chose to become Queen Victoria's longest serving hangman, was published in 2015.